DATE DUE

OC 29 '96			
AP 30 '97			
OC 21 '97			
AP 30 '98			
MY 27 '99			
OC 1 1 '99			
OC 1 0 '00			
OC _ 6 '05			
NO _ 1 '05			
NO 2 9 '05			

DEMCO 38-296

JAZZ PANORAMA

A Da Capo Press Reprint Series

THE ROOTS OF JAZZ

JAZZ PANORAMA

From the Pages of *The Jazz Review*

EDITED BY

MARTIN T. WILLIAMS

DA CAPO PRESS • NEW YORK • 1979

Library of Congress Cataloging in Publication Data

Jazz review.
    Jazz panorama.

    (The Roots of jazz)
    Reprint of the 1962 ed. published by
Crowell-Collier Press, New York.
    1. Jazz music—Addresses, essays, lectures.
I. Williams, Martin T. II. Title.
ML3561.J3J33 1979   785.4′2   79-16173
ISBN 0-306-79574-4

This Da Capo Press edition of *Jazz Panorama*
is an unabridged republication of the
first edition published in New York in 1962
by The Crowell-Collier Press. It is reprinted
by arrangement with Macmillan Publishing Co., Inc.

Published by Da Capo Press, Inc.
A Subsidiary of Plenum Publishing Corporation
227 West 17th Street, New York, N.Y. 10011

JAZZ PANORAMA

JAZZ PANORAMA

From the Pages of *The Jazz Review*

EDITED BY

MARTIN T. WILLIAMS

THE CROWELL-COLLIER PRESS

CONTENTS

ILLUSTRATIONS

Introduction

WE BEGAN *The Jazz Review* to supplement what already existed. We were convinced there were areas of jazz history and biography that needed to be set down. We also felt that there were kinds of interviewing and kinds of analysis and criticism that needed to be tried. For the former especially, certain British and continental jazz magazines were something of a challenge to us, but for all the kinds of essays and reviews that we wanted to publish the main challenge was that we knew such history and criticism was being thought about and, in some cases, actually being written, but was not being published.

We also felt there was a large audience for jazz which was not being reached, which jazz needed for its own growth—and which needed to know jazz.

At first we used to get a few letters from readers which said, in effect, you can't talk about jazz that way. Since we were publishing almost every conceivable kind of interview, biography, history, impressionism, and exact analysis, we wondered what "way" the letter writers had in mind. We also wondered why we couldn't discuss jazz "that way," since we obviously *were* discussing jazz all those ways. But basically what we were trying to do, of course, was to discuss jazz as if it were a music, an important music with an important heritage, and discuss jazz musicians as if they were creative people rather than public celebrities or colorful old characters.

For the record, the "we" who began *The Jazz Review* were, first Martin Williams and Nat Hentoff as editors, Israel Young and Leonard Feldman as publishers. Our art editor, beginning with the second issue, was Hsio Wen Shih, who

later became publisher and brought in Bob Cato to design
the magazine. We had meanwhile asked Gunther Schuller to
become contributing editor.

We have not followed the usual manner of putting antholo-
gies together—that is, with major articles up front and reviews in back. If you consult the Table of Contents you will
notice that we begin in the twenties and end in the sixties,
but we begin with Jelly Roll Morton, who is a far more sophisticated musician than blues singer Lightnin' Hopkins, with
whom we end. It seemed logical to follow Danny Barker's
reminiscences on Morton and Dr. Souchon's memoir of King
Oliver with discussions of their music, but Nat Hentoff's
"Afternoon with Miles Davis" involved Davis's comments on
music from all periods, and it's difficult to know where such
an essay belongs if one is using the history of jazz as his
standard. What Davis's comments do represent, we believe,
is that jazz has a continuing evolution and that the jazz musician is a part of what an academician might call an "historical process," and he knows it and takes his place in it as an
individual. Davis's comments on Louis Armstrong tell us much
about both men. Following them, pianist Dick Katz's comments on Miles Davis are the comments of a musician turned
(for the occasion) excellent critic.

Basically we have followed a kind of historical perspective
in putting these pieces together. But, for example, in one form
or another the so-called Dixieland style is a continuing fact
in jazz music. And Dick Hadlock's piece on the subject, since
it covers everything from Bunk Johnson through Bix Beiderbecke to the current situation at Eddie Condon's, might belong almost anywhere—but is still a part of the contemporary
scene.

We have also tried to make this a representative collection,
and our selection has thereby become somewhat arbitrary.
Thus we have regretfully omitted the analytical pieces on
Erroll Garner and Duke Ellington which Mimi Clar contributed, those on John Coltrane and Art Blakey from Zita
Carno, George Russell's careful reviews, and others, for fear
of an overemphasis on analysis.

We wish there might also have been room for Henry Woodfin's appreciation of Kenny Dorham, Harvey Pekar's on Lennie Tristano, Mait Edey's on Art Tatum, and Bruce King's on Baby Dodds. We have also deliberately been a bit jingoistic with American contributors, although many reviews by English critics have graced our pages, particularly by Max Harrison (for example, on Dizzy Gillespie and the other early modernists), by Michael James (on Jackie McLean), by Ronald Atkins, and by our blues commentators, Englishman Paul Oliver and Belgian Yannick Bruynoghe. . . . Perhaps we are saying that we would like to think that one volume is not enough. But, then, there can always be another.

We have mentioned too few names here, to be sure, and it is perhaps to all our voluntary contributors—writers, musicians, photographers—and to our investors, that we should dedicate this anthology. But we think they all would agree that any dedication really belongs to the musicians who play jazz.

MARTIN WILLIAMS

JAZZ PANORAMA

Jelly Roll Morton in New York

by Danny Barker

*Guitarist Danny Barker is from New Orleans and like most
musicians from that city is a fine storyteller. Perhaps his most
famous job as a musician was with Cab Calloway when he
played with Dizzy Gillespie, Chu Berry, Jonah Jones, Cozy
Cole, et al. He is currently at work on two kinds of writing:
a factual and theoretical account of New Orleans music and
its players, and a fictionalized account of the many "characters" with whom he grew up in that city.*

*Barker's final remarks on changes of style (and mere changes
of fashion) perhaps best set the stage for our anthology.*

WHEN I ARRIVED in New York City, in 1930, my uncle Paul
Barbarin and Henry "Red" Allen, my old friend, took me
to the Rhythm Club which was known for its famous jam
sessions and cutting contests.

The club was owned and operated by Bert Hall, a trombone
player, politician and gambler who had left Chicago for New
York. Bert introduced many reforms in Local 802 that were
for the protection of its Negro members who, lots of times
after working in clubs owned by racketeers, were doubtful of
getting paid until the money was in their hands. (Before the
coming of Bert there was The Bandbox, another club owned
by a trumpet player named Major.)

The afternoon I walked into the Rhythm Club, the corner
and street was crowded with musicians with their instruments
and horns. I was introduced and shook hands with a lot of
fellows on the outside. Then we entered the inside which was
crowded. What I saw and heard, I will never forget. A wild

cutting contest was in progress and sitting and standing around the piano were twenty or thirty musicians, all with their instruments out waiting for a signal to play choruses of Gershwin's *Liza*.

It was a Monday afternoon and the musicians gathered at the club to get their pay for weekend jobs and to gossip and chew the fat. But this Monday the news had spread that the famous McKinney's Cotton Pickers, from the Graystone Ballroom in Detroit, were in town to record for Victor and start an eastern tour. At that time the Cotton Pickers, Fletcher Henderson, and the Casa Loma orchestra were considered the best bands in the land.

This day, at the Rhythm Club, most of the famous leaders, stars and sidemen were there; the big names I'd heard and read about: Benny Carter, Don Redman, Horace Henderson, Fess Williams, Claude Hopkins, Sonny Greer, John Kirby, Johnny Hodges, Freddie Jenkins, Bobby Stark, Chick Webb, Big Green and Charlie Johnson.

Around the piano sat three banjo players: Bernard Addison, Ikie Robinson, and Teddy Bunn with his guitar.

Paul tells me, "See those three fellows, they are the best banjo players in New York City and that guy standing behind them is Seminole—you watch him." Which I did.

After each of the banjo players played dozens of choruses, the crowd yelled, "Seminole! Cut them cats!" And after much applause and persuasion Seminole, who was left-handed, reached for a banjo that was tuned to be played right-handed, and to my amazement he started wailing on the banjo, playing it upside down; that is, playing everything backwards. I later learned that, being left-handed, Seminole did not bother to change the strings; he just taught himself.

After his solos the banjos were quiet—they just played rhythm. Then in rushed a comical little fat young fellow carrying some drums which he hurriedly set up. Paul said, "That's Randolf, he plays with the Tramp Band—a vaudeville act." Randolf played eccentric and trick novelty drums; he was very clever with all sorts of rhythm and clever beats. Then the crowd yelled for Chick Webb, who washed Randolf away.

Paul says, "Watch this." Then it was a trumpet battle—
Bobby Stark, Rex Stewart and Cuba Bennett. Cuba Bennett
was the most highly respected trumpet player at that time in
New York City. He is a cousin of Benny Carter, and the great
band leader boasted with authority that he could play more
beautiful and complex solos than anyone in the whole world.
When he played, everybody in the street and on the sidewalks
rushed in. He was terrific. I'll never forget that, as I had never
heard a trumpet like that. He was everything they claimed he
was. While I was listening someone said, "That cat is only
pressing on the second and third valve." I never saw much of
him after that, as he went to Camden, New Jersey, to live.
But any time trumpet players were discussed, Cuba Bennett
was spoken of with reverence. I must have heard this about
a hundred times from different musicians who had passed
through Camden, New Jersey, on tours:

"We passed through Camden, so we stopped at that gin
joint where Cuba hangs out at. He still plays great. He's got
a family and you couldn't pull him out of Camden for a million dollars."

At this session, John Kirby, who had just bought a new
bass, was playing and like an amateur was searching for the
positions on the fingerboard of the bass. I asked Paul who
was that cat trying to play that bass.

Paul said, "That's John Kirby. He's the best tuba player in
New York City. He works with Fletcher Henderson." I was
amazed at his playing because I had heard the greatest bass
players: Chester Zardis, Al Morgan, Albert Glenny, Jimmy
Johnson, Ransom Knolling, Simon Marrero and dozens of fine
bass players in New Orleans.

The crowd called for Pops Foster. Kirby handed him the
bass and then stood by with all the other bass tuba players
and watched Pops with popeyed interest as he slapped a dozen
choruses on *Liza*.

In 1930 Pops Foster and Wellman Braud were the only two
string bass players in New York City, other than a few Cuban
and Puerto Rican bass players. The most renowned was Tizol,
who is an uncle of Juan Tizol of Duke Ellington fame who

wrote *Caravan*. The band leaders in New York City were finally convinced that the bass fiddle belonged and sounded better in the band than the tuba. So there was a mad change-over to the bass fiddle, and Pops Foster had hundreds of students and imitators.

I am watching the jam session with interest when Paul says, "Come over here and meet Jelly Roll and King Oliver."

In the meantime, here's that Seminole seating himself at the piano and playing *Liza* like as if he had written it, as the crowd screams their praise.

In the next few years I learned that Seminole was a wizard at playing the banjo, piano and xylophone. But, like Cuba Bennett, he went to Atlantic City, N. J. and became a legend of the past.

Paul leads me through the crowd to where King and Jelly are standing. I had noticed Fletcher Henderson was playing pool and seemed unconcerned about who was playing in the jam session, or who was there. And whenever I saw him at the Club he was always playing pool seriously, never saying anything to anyone, just watching his opponent's shots and solemnly keeping score. All the other musicians watched the game and whispered comments because he was the world's greatest band leader.

Paul tells King and Jelly, "Here's my nephew, he just came from New Orleans."

King Oliver says, "How you doing, Gizzard Mouf?" I laughed, and Jelly says, "How you Home Town?"

I said, "Fine," and from then on he always called me "Home Town."

Jelly, who was a fine pool and billiard player, had been watching and commenting to Oliver on Fletcher's pool shots. King could play a fair game also.

Jelly says (and he doesn't whisper), "That Fletcher plays pool just like he plays piano—assbackwards. Just like a craw-fish," and Oliver laughs and laughs until he starts coughing.

The session goes on and on, and I notice that nothing, the ovations, comments, solos, or anybody or anything, moves Henderson in the least.

That evening I went with King Oliver to his rehearsal. He did not play much as he was having trouble with his teeth.

Jelly Roll spent most of the afternoon and evenings at the Rhythm Club and every time I saw him he was lecturing to the musicians about organizing. Most of the name and star musicians paid him no attention because he was always preaching, in loud terms, that none of the famous New York bands had a beat. He would continuously warn me: "Home Town, don't be simple and ignorant like these fools in the big country towns." I would always listen seriously because most of the things he said made plenty of sense to me.

Jelly was constantly preaching that if he could get a band to rehearse his music and listen to him he could keep a band working. He would get one-nighters out of town and would have to beg musicians to work with him. Most of the time the musicians would arrive at the last moment, or send a substitute in their place. I learned later that they were angry with him because he was always boasting about how great New Orleans musicians were. At that time most working musicians were arrangement-conscious following the pattern of Henderson, Redman, Carter and Chick Webb. Jelly's music was considered corny and dated. I played quite a few of these one-nighters with Jelly and on one of these dates I learned that Jelly could back up most of the things he boasted of.

The band met at the Rhythm Club and left from there in Jelly Roll's two Lincoln cars about three in the afternoon to play in Hightstown, New Jersey, at a playground that booked all the famous bands at that time.

On the way we came upon a scene of much excitement. A farmer in a jalopy had driven off a country road right in the path of a speeding trailer truck. The big truck pushed the jalopy about a hundred feet, right into a diner. The diner was full of people who were having dinner. The impact turned the diner over and the hot coffee percolator scalded the waitresses and customers. Nobody was badly hurt but they were shocked and scared and screaming and yelling.

We pulled up and rushed out to help the victims who were frantic. Jelly yelled loudly and calmed the folks down. He

took complete charge of the situation. Jelly crawled into the
overturned diner and called the state police and hospitals.
They sent help in a very short time. Then he consoled the
farmer, who was jammed in his jalopy and couldn't be pulled
out. His jalopy was crushed like an accordion against the diner
by the big trailer. The farmer was so scared he couldn't talk
and when the emergency wrecker finally pulled his jalopy free
and opened the door and lifted him out, I noticed that he
was barefooted. I remarked to Jelly that the farmer was barefooted. Jelly told me that happens in a wreck. The concus-
sion and force cause a person's nerves to constrict and their
shoes jump off.

Jelly talked to all the officials at the scene and they thanked
him for his calls and calmness in an emergency. We got back
in the cars and drove off.

As we rode, Jelly spoke on and on of how white folks are
scared to die. I rode in the car with Jelly and I can't recall
who it was, but it was either Tommy Benford or Ward Pinkett
who kept on disagreeing with everything Jelly said, which was
the usual procedure whenever he had an audience around the
Rhythm Club.

We passed some men who were hunting in a field. They
were shooting at some game that were flying overhead.

Jelly said, "Them bums can shoot. When I was with Wild
West shows I could shoot with the best marksmen and sharp-
shooters in the world."

Either Benford or Pinkett said, "Why don't you stop all
that bullshit?" and that argument went on and on.

When we arrived at Hightstown and drove into the entrance of the playground and got out of the cars, I noticed
a shooting gallery. So I said to Jelly, "Say Jelly, there's a
shooting gallery."

Jelly's eyes lit up and he hollered, "Come here all you
cockroaches! I'm going to give you a shooting exhibition!"

We all gathered around the shooting gallery and Jelly told
the owner, "Rube, load up all of your guns!"; and the man
did.

Jelly then shot all the targets down and did not miss any.

The man set them up again and Jelly repeated his performance again.

Then he said, "Now cockroaches, can I shoot?" Everybody
applauded. Jelly gave me the prizes, as the man shook his
hand. Then he and Jelly talked about great marksmen of the
past as his hecklers looked on with respect.

As he and I walked to the dance hall, I asked Jelly how
did he know the man's name was Rube.

Jelly said, "Home Town, on circuses, carnivals, medicine
shows, all concession owners are called 'Rube' and when anybody connected with the show gets in trouble with someone
or people from the town, he hollers, 'Rube!' and the show
people rush to his defense and rescue. Show folks stick together."

From then on I had a sympathetic respect for Jelly. I also
noticed that his hecklers did not dispute him in a vicious
way like the cats on the corners in New Orleans did.

As I look back on past scenes, situations, and the whys and
reasons for many great musicians falling by the wayside, to be
forgotten by the public, that first Rhythm Club visit comes
to my mind. The musicians played spontaneous, creative solos
under critical eyes in competition with the world's finest jazz
musicians, and many an unknown joined these sessions and
earned an international reputation.

Then I think of Fletcher Henderson's indifference to the
activity there. He was the acknowledged King; his band was
the greatest in the world. He knew it because he was being
copied by everybody. His sidemen were the best and he paid
the highest salaries. Every colored musician knew and read
about his famous sidemen: Hawkins, Rex, Walter Johnson,
Buster Bailey, Russell Smith, John Kirby, Jimmy Harrison,
and those before these—Don Redman, Benny Carter, Big
Green, Louis Armstrong, Joe Smith, Tommy Ladnier.
Fletcher had hired and fired the greatest jazz names in
America. . . . Then Jelly and Oliver watching his pool game.

It was a new era. They had become famous with bands
which were smaller and which gave the sidemen freedom to
express themselves. But the sound that Fletcher presented to

the jazz scene was streamlined, big, powerful, and arranged especially to bring out the best in the instrumentalists of his band. The songs, scores and arrangements were copied and imitated by all the big jazz bands (exceptions were Guy Lombardo and Ted Lewis). And as time marched on Jelly and Oliver stood on the sidelines with their plans and music, as the fickle public hurriedly paraded by.

Ten years later, Fletcher Henderson, still cool and indifferent, stood on the sidelines as *his* fickle public hurriedly passed him by, rushing to hear Jimmie Lunceford and his youthful bunch of excellent soloists, novel arrangements, continuous music (intermission once a night). Lunceford gave his audience their fill of beautiful music. His band played; his sidemen did not wander off as was the problem of leaders in the past. He popped the whip. In the past the leaders had around them famous soloists and sidemen and gave them publicity and billing on marquees and posters. But Lunceford's band was billed as the "Lunceford Special." No name but his.

Then came the great musical revolution. The new generation rebelled against the old system of being buried in a section, and blowing tonal and rhythm patterns, while the so-called stars, pets and musicians—the friends of bookers, agents, jive critics and magazine writers got all the credit. Youth wanted to express themselves and they did—right back to the old system in New Orleans.

"You play your part and I play mine, so we'll both express ourselves. You don't tell me what you want and I don't tell you. We will all variate on the theme."

King Oliver: A Very Personal Memoir

by Edmond Souchon, M.D.

Dr. Souchon was born and raised in New Orleans in, as he puts it below, "the citadel of white caste privileges." In 1901, at four, he was captivated by the music, soon to be called jazz, that he heard in the city streets. His reminiscences of one man who played that music are probably unique in jazz writing, for they not only tell us about Joe Oliver, they give us insight into how it felt then, and how it feels now after over fifty years for a man so born, so raised and still living in the city of his birth, to have been so captivated.

THIS IS A memoir about a great musician, Joe Oliver. It begins in the molten period of a magnificent American art before Oliver's star had begun its ascent. It is written by a surgeon who, by the fortunes of birth, came to life within the citadel of southern white caste privileges and who has reached middle age following the main course of the wonderfully proud, prejudiced and all too human oligarchs (the books have called them so) who were his forebearers. But it also springs from a turbulence of honest feelings from the heart and mind of one who, regardless of birth, luck, privileges, place or time, was fortunate enough to hear the great Joe Oliver blasting the heavens and shaking the blackberry leaves in funeral parades through the fringes of his neighborhood.

A rather pampered and sheltered child I was, arrayed in the ridiculous trappings of that Little Lord Fauntleroy era of "southern aristocracy" which now seems unbelievable. So I was dressed—in about 1901-2 at the age of four or five— when my Negro nurse first took me walking into the dense

Negro neighborhood to hear Joe Oliver play. The impact of this experience—the power and beauty of that music—has never left me. I followed the career of this New Orleans artist with a fidelity at least as great as that which I gave to medical faculties or to the gentle pomp and circumstances of my privileged world.

Surrounded by my corduroy breeches, knee-high leather leggings, stiff starched Lord Fauntleroy collar with soft flowing tie, I suddenly found myself relegated to the care of Armotine. All that was missing from my picture was a foreign governess who spoke several languages. In her stead was Armotine, Tine to me. Thank God she was colored, or this story could never have been.

Tine was many-faceted. She was my boss, my instructor, and my protector. She was also the most interesting person to cross my life up to that point. Undoubtedly, she was one of the finest cooks in the city of New Orleans. When starting to prepare the evening meal, she would keep her eye on my play in the side yard beneath her kitchen window. The ritual of a spicy *fine herb* sauce or the preparation of a *roux* for *grillarde* was accompanied by hours of never ending song. Her deep contralto was clear and soft, with a rhythm that often made me stop playing to listen and pat my foot. Her songs were an admixture of Creole folk songs, church hymns, and up-to-date hits of the late '90s or early 1900's. One refrain she repeated so often that I remember the words perfectly. It went:

> Ain't that man got a funny walk,
>   Doin' the 'Ping-Pong' 'round Southern park.
> Nigger man, white man, take him away,
>   I thought I heard them say.

There were innumerable verses to this song. Tine would shush me if I started to sing any of the less refined ones along with her. And there was another song which she seemed to like almost as well as the first. I always sang it for people if I was certain they would not go tell my mother; I knew I could always get a laugh, although I hadn't the slightest idea of its meaning.

I have learned many verses to this song since then, but I still like the one Tine taught me the best:

> I'm Alabamy bound, I'm Alabamy bound,
> I'm Alabamy bound,
> And if you want my cabbage patch,
> You gotta hoe the ground.

Every afternoon, Tine would take me for a walk, either up or down St. Charles Avenue, seldom on the side streets. Occasionally, when she fancied she needed something very special for preparing dinner, Mom would grant me permission to accompany Tine to Terrell's Grocery on First and Dryades. By coincidence (or was it?) a thrilling thing happened every time we went to Terrell's Grocery; Tine's intuition, or the grapevine, passed the word along. Invariably, the most exciting parade went by. And always Tine and I marched along with a long black wagon, accompanied by men in tinseled uniforms, plumed hats and sabers. A hundred kids my age skipped along. There were plenty of grownups too, following on the sidewalks and in the streets. I never got tired, even when I missed my afternoon nap.

Someone mentioned that the heavy man playing that short, stubby instrument at the head of the band was working for a family a few houses down the street from ours. He was their butler-yardman, and only played music on his time off. I did not understand all this at all. Everybody seemed to love this man. Somehow I thought that possibly I did too. That man was Joe Oliver.

By 1907, I had grown to the point where I was taking street cars all by myself and making my way around the city, and a few months before Tine's death, I heard one of her friends tell her that "Joe Oliver was playing at a cabaret down in the district." My heart beat fast. I had not heard him in a long time, and I missed his music. I knew that the "district" was spoken of vaguely and in whispers. It was a place where no "nice people" went. Maybe I heard mention of it because my mother's sister had married an alderman who had passed the law restricting a "certain element" (the prostitutes) to this area.

I learned that kids were never allowed in that section of the city, but that newsboys were an exception, tolerated "along the fringe" but not in the main streets. Afraid to venture on my escapade alone, I prevailed on one of my more venturesome pals to accompany me. We dug up the oldest clothes we could find, tore them in many places, and rubbed them in the dirt; a half dozen copies of *The Daily States* or the *New Orleans Item* under our arms, and the disguise was complete.

The "Big 25" where Oliver was playing was just one block from Basin Street, and about three quarters of a block from Canal. The time was just after dusk. Our objective was reached without so much as a side glance of suspicion from the grownups along the way. The streets were practically deserted. But our hearts were in our throats! When we arrived, not one sound was issuing forth. We were crestfallen: the music started at 9:00 P.M.

A couple of Friday nights later we were at it again, this time after dark. Except for faint red lights that shone through half-drawn shutters and the sputtering carbon lights on the corner, there was not much illumination. We could see strange figures peering out through half-open doorways. A new cop on the beat immediately tried to chase us, but the peeping female figures behind the blinds came to our rescue. They hurled invective of such vehemence—"Let them poor newsboys make a livin', you — — —" that he let us go. We told him we were only going as far as Joe Oliver's saloon to bring him his paper. It seemed to satisfy him.

We could now hear that music from half a block away; it probably would have taken more than one policeman to stop us. The place was twice as long as it was wide. It was a one-story wooden frame building at sidewalk level, lengthwise parallel to the street. There was a bar at the Iberville end, and a sort of dance hall to the rear, nearer Canal Street. Quick glances through the swinging doors showed us that the inside was fairly well lighted. But outside the building there were many deep shadows, and the sputtering carbon arc-light on the corner was out more than on. Gutters three feet wide and almost as deep ran alongside the sidewalk. A tall telegraph pole stood just in front of the dance hall, across the gutter. In its shadow we sought refuge until someone discovered us and told us to move on. After listening to the music for almost an hour and a half, with reluctance we turned homeward. That trip was just the beginning. We came there many Friday nights. They got to know us and hardly noticed that we were there. We sat on the gutter's edge, our feet dangling, and drank in that sound.

Sometimes Oliver would come outside for a breather. We wondered how we might approach him to get him to say a few words to us. Finally, I ventured, "Mr. Oliver, here is the paper you ordered." I'll never forget how big and tough he looked! His brown derby was tilted low over one eye, his shirt collar was open at the neck, and a bright red undershirt peeked out at the V. Wide suspenders held up an expanse of trousers of unbelievable width. He looked at us and said, "You know damn well, white boy, I never ordered no paper." We thought the end of the world had come. Suddenly, we realized that he had not spoken loud enough for anyone to hear us! Then he went on, much more friendly, "I been knowin' you kids were hanging around here to listen to my music. Do you think I'm going to chase you away for that? This is a rough neighborhood, kids, and I don't want you to get into trouble. Keep out of sight and go home at a decent time." We were *in!* We had really made it!

But gradually, the city law agencies and police began to adopt a tougher policy in the district. We thought it best that we quit. But we tapered off; we couldn't stop all of a sudden.

Ten fast years went by. Then came Tulane University from 1913 to 1917. None of us had forgotten Oliver and the memory of his music. We were invited to the regular Saturday night "script" dances at the Tulane gymnasium. For one dollar, you got yourself and your best girl in from eight to twelve. On the bandstand, surrounded by his entire band, was Joe Oliver! My bunch, jazz lovers all, scarcely missed a Saturday night for the next four years. There were seven of us who hardly danced at all but surrounded the bandstand the whole evening. In retrospect, its hard to believe that we were so lucky. Gradually, we learned the players' names, and they learned ours. We got special kicks out of listening to the little drummer who quietly sang risqué parodies on the tunes the band was playing. A bunch of white boys in the deep South, second lining with utter rapture to a Negro band! In those narrow times, such a thing was unheard of!

We were so imbued with the music that as soon as the dance was over, and we had absorbed all we could, we'd go over to somebody's house and attempt to imitate on string instruments what Oliver's band had been doing on brass and woodwind. The fact that fifty years later, four of that same group still play together many of the old tunes which Oliver featured is evidence, I think, of how deeply the experience imbedded itself. It is also proof—to ourselves and to others— that we were actually there; it was no figment of our imaginations.

Then World War I. The district was closed by order of the Secretary of the Navy, and all the good musicians moved away. For us, France, back to America, and, for me, medical school. On graduation, I was in Chicago to finish a two-year internship. It was late 1924, I believe, that my passing all final exams called for special celebration. A party began to shape up. Someone heard us bragging about the great bands to which we had danced in New Orleans and informed us that in a black-and-tan joint on the South Side the greatest jazz band of all times was currently playing. There was no further discussion.

Prohibition was at its maudlin height. The place was far from inviting from the outside, dingy and needing several coats of paint. Ancient paper decorations and faded flowers hung dejectedly from unpainted walls and peeling columns. A long, winding ill-lit hallway seemed to take us back of some large hotel or building. The place smelled of last week's beer. But the closer we got to the dance hall, the more excited we became. No one had mentioned the name of the band playing there, but it was only necessary for a few musical strains to meet us for us to realize that something familiar was greeting us.

A rather pretentious floor show was in progress as we made our way to our table. A brilliant spotlight followed the performers on the dance floor, but gloom made the faces of the musicians undistinguishable. The bandstand supported about ten chairs, and the musicians were decked out in tuxedos or dress suits (I am not sure which) with much tinsel and fancy braid. A heavy man was their leader, and he was following the cues of the dancers and singers. The floor-show star that night was Frankie "Halfpint" Jackson.

Suddenly we realized we were looking at someone on the bandstand who greatly resembled Joe Oliver. We could hardly wait for the floor show to stop, so the lights would go up for dancing.

It was Oliver all right. But his was a much more impressive figure now. The transition from the red undershirt and suspenders of Storyville's "Big 25" to the clean white shirt at the Tulane gymnasium to the formidable figure he now presented, was almost too much to believe! He was now "King," the most important personage in the jazz world, surrounded by his own hand-picked galaxy of sidemen. His cordial welcome to two old New Orleans friends almost made us ashamed of the lumps in our throats—the same lump I had had when, in newsboys' clothes, we offered him a newspaper. His affability that night equaled his kindness to us youngsters who had braved the terrors of Storyville to hear him play.

The turmoil and excitement which was going on around us in that speak-easy was nothing compared to what was going on within our hearts. The realization of the very privilege which had been ours over these thirty years suddenly burst on us. Joe Oliver is long dead. His body lies in an almost unmarked grave. I have all the records he ever made. These are brittle and fragile. The "Big 25" has been torn down. I've taken pictures of that, but these too are perishable. What remains for me is the *sound* of Joe Oliver. Perhaps auditory memory is better than visual. It is easy for me to recall many,

many tunes which the Oliver band played in the very early days at "Big 25." Maybe when our first venturesome escapades into Storyville were going on, we were too excited—perhaps not interested—we do not recall one name at "Big 25" other than Joe Oliver. But the tunes, yes!

At Tulane, it was different. Every man in the band was known to every one of us. Names such as Johnny Dodds, Sidney Bechet, Johnny St. Cyr, Kid Ory, Baby Dodds, Pops Foster, Tilman Braud, Armand J. Piron, Clarence Williams, Steve Lewis. There were many others, too, in Joe's Tulane groups, for personnels varied from week to week. But the sound of the band remained just as thrilling with each group. And Joe Oliver was always there, or the band wouldn't have been hired. And the tunes they played were always the same.

I believe without fear of memory-tricks that by the time Oliver was playing at Tulane gymnasium, he had acquired a technique that was much more smooth, and that his band was adapting itself to the white dances more and more. At "Big 25" it was hard-hitting, rough and ready, full of fire and drive. He subdued this to please the different patrons at the gym dances. It is easy to recall this when I recall a transition which one of jazz's most popular tunes underwent. Sometimes, when Joe would be playing for a private party at a home or a ball, a midnight supper would be served to the guests. In order to get the couples into line and stop the dancing, Oliver was requested to play a march to which no one could dance. He would use *High Society*. It was played at a very slow marching tempo, the same tempo his band used in marching funerals and processions. It was a shuffle, easy to walk to. And the first part seemed interminable, before he broke into the chorus which has immortalized Alphonse Picou. You couldn't even do a "slow drag" to it, as it was played then. Gradually, the tempo of this tune was quickened, and it was converted into a dance tune, almost the same as we know today; the transition probably took three or four years!

Historians have often said that the early New Orleans bands played an ensemble style almost entirely, with few if any solos. I am afraid that I must disagree. However, the manner in

which solos began finding their way into such bands as Joe
Oliver's was without plan from the leaders or of the sidemen.
Early New Orleans groups *were* trained to play ensemble almost entirely, with occasional breaks for a particular instrument. But during parades and at dances the cornet or trumpet
might get tired and without warning simply drop out. Or maybe he had blown a few bad ones, so he simply stopped playing
and blew saliva out of his horn. Immediately, as he stopped,
either the clarinet or the trombone took the lead—sometimes
both instruments did this, playing unison lead. When the
trumpet man decided his lip was rested, he resumed playing
at any time and at any place in the piece. It was not those
Chicago musicians, or the New Yorkers who first started passing it around; New Orleans did it, long ago.

The Chicago Oliver group was a magnificently drilled band.
Each member was a star, intent on making the over-all sound
of the band good. Each, too, was a fine soloist in his own
right. But Joe Oliver saw to it that nobody outshone him. The
sidemen's solos were few and shorter than those Oliver ap-
propriated to himself. It was without doubt the very best
music in Chicago at that time, and they still had that beat.

The records which I have, made during the Chicago stage
and afterwards, seem to be collector's items, a yardstick by
which the neophyte judges other bands, and which many attempt to copy. I disagree sadly that these are representative
of Oliver at his greatest. By the time Oliver had reached Chicago and the peak of his popularity, his sound was not the
same. It was a different band, a different and more polished
Oliver, an Oliver who had completely lost his New Orleans
sound.

Regressing in our discussion, and trying after fifty years to
conjure up as fairly as a sexagenarian can do, I had these
thoughts:

In Chicago Joe Oliver was at his most popular and polished, but he was already on the way out. Instead of realizing
the treasure that was his in playing New Orleans music, he
was trying to sound like a big white band!

Even at Tulane Oliver's style was beginning to change. It

was still very great music, but something in the inner feeling of the band was shaking itself loose from the roots from which it had sprung. Perhaps playing together too often is the reason, for who can dispute that head arrangements, repeated night after night with the same musicians, can become just as deadly as the written score can? Perhaps it was a desire to "improve" (let's not use the word "progress").

There are no bands playing today whose sound faintly resembles that of Oliver's band at "Big 25." Jazz histories have many times told me whom I had been listening to in that bistro and possibly I now call up the sound of these men by suggestion; I doubt my own memory. We kids were not interested in who was playing in the band, as long as it was Joe Oliver's band. Even if I readily admit I knew the name only of Joe Oliver, I still have my complete and honest belief that this first Oliver I heard was the most thrilling. It was rough, rugged, and contained many bad chords. There were many fluffed notes, too. But the drive, the rhythm, the wonderfully joyous New Orleans sound was there in all its beauty. This is what the recordings made in Chicago missed. Those records even miss conveying the way that Oliver was playing in Chicago when I heard him.

Jelly Roll Morton

by Guy Waterman

In 1939, Jelly Roll Morton recorded an album called NEW
ORLEANS MEMORIES *and it has been in print almost continuously since then. On its most recent appearance on LP, Guy
Waterman took occasion to write a review in which he related Morton's music to the ragtime playing that had preceded him.*

Jelly Roll Morton: NEW ORLEANS MEMORIES, Commodore FL 30000.
Jelly Roll Morton, *piano* and *vocals.*
*Mamie's Blues; Michigan Water Blues; Buddy Bolden's Blues;
Winin' Boy Blues; Don't You Leave Me Here; Original Rags; The
Naked Dance; The Crave; Mister Joe; King Porter Stomp.*

SIDE 1 HERE consists of the five classic blues. For traditional
jazz it would have been difficult to select a more representative yet moving five: the two twelve-bar numbers, *Mamie's
Blues* and Tony Jackson's *Michigan Water Blues,* are combined
with *Don't You Leave Me Here, Buddy Bolden's Blues,* and
the incomparable *Winin' Boy.* Perhaps it is wise to refrain
from comment on these blues numbers on the grounds that so
much of the qualities which so urgently appeal to the listener
are direct in nature and almost personal.

Side 2 is susceptible to the more usual approach. For example, take the fascinating lead number, the transformation
of Scott Joplin's *Original Rags* from ragtime into Jelly's jazz.
(Incidentally, the LP label erroneously identifies *Original Rags*
as a collaboration between Scott and Joplin; either that or the
hyphen is a misprint.)

The most obvious indications of Jelly's jazz approach stem,

in the right hand, from the improvisation and, in the left hand, from the anticipated downbeats and the octave runs of four sixteenth-notes, Jelly's trade-mark. Actually, however, these devices do not explain the full transformation which Jelly brings about. The gulf which separates ragtime, as the early rag composers understood it, from jazz as Jelly epitomized it—this gulf has to do more with the type of beat which the two develop and the nature of the momentum which builds up. The difference is reflected in the entire organization of the tune.

The whole approach to *Original Rags* reflects Jelly's break from ragtime. Joplin, in the original writing of the tune, plainly states the standard, vigorous opening theme. He then gives the second strain a lighter, floating quality, an effect heightened by altogether omitting the left hand in bar 1. Then in the third theme, Joplin comes down to classic ragtime with the typical right-hand phrases of the idiom. (musical Ex. 1.) All three themes are repeated. Then, after a return to the first strain, Joplin moves quickly to two unrepeated final strains.

Ex. I

The handling of Jelly, the jazz pianist, is quite different. Dispensing with half the introduction, he establishes his momentum very quickly and moves forward. He rides over Joplin's crude attempts to set up some kind of variety of approach to the three different strains. Jelly forces all of the first three themes to be identical in spirit, fused together to build up his new jazz-type momentum. He gets the beat swinging lightly, experimenting with sixths in the left hand, a resource which ragtime never tolerated but which become more and more frequently used in jazz—as in Hines especially, or the Lion (see, for example, *Willie's Blues* on the Dot LP) or Art Tatum.

Nothing could more clearly indicate the nature of Jelly's

transformation than bars 4 and 12 of the C strain. Recall that
in Joplin's original, this is a full typical ragtime strain. In bars
4 and 5, the phrase could scarcely be more characteristic (the
right hand only is significant for the contrast here), Ex. 2.

Ex.2

Bar 12 reflects the crudeness of early ragtime's harmonic
changes. The progression is from tonic to submediant, the
change which all of jazz made so rich and so varied. It is the
change which "makes" such tunes as *Salty Dog, A Good Man
Is Hard to Find, Ballin' The Jack, Jada,* and countless others.
But the change was not exploited in ragtime. Later rags did
somewhat better, thanks largely to the musicianship of James
Scott and Joplin's own late-developing interest in harmony
and even tonality. But this is an 1899 rag, and Joplin can
come up with nothing better than the figure shown in Ex. 3.

Ex.3

In Joplin, of course, this strain is repeated verbatim (at least
in these two bars).

Now note Jelly's right hand in bar 4. The phrase departs
from the Joplin original in the slightest and yet most important
respect. See Ex. 4, as compared with Ex. 2.

Ex. 4

Now note bar 12. The first time through, the right hand merely "jazzes up" what is really the same phrase as in the original Joplin version. But the left hand departs considerably, with one of those marvelous progressions from tonic to sub-mediant which abound in jazz. Incidentally, the particular series of sixths, used in the left hand, is selected so as to fit well harmonically both with Joplin's right hand (Ex. 3) and even more with Jelly's slight modification of it. See Ex. 5.

Ex. 5

Now the second time through, the left hand contains basi-cally the same thoughts, simplified somewhat in order to avoid dissonance with the new right-hand phrase. The right-hand phrase is wholly different now and clearly pursues the ideas contained in the first eleven bars, a possibility which had evi-dently escaped Joplin. Note for example that the last five notes are now identical (or almost—I'm not at all sure I've notated this exactly as it is played, since the last note of the phrase may be G rather than C) to the equivalent five notes in bar 4. The progression to submediant (instead of the dominant found in bar 5) is made quite clear in the left hand in the first beat of bar 13. (musical Ex. 6.)

This is the kind of thing which Joplin delighted in during later years (within the ragtime framework, of course). His missing it is the kind of missed opportunity which is natural enough to find in this maiden flight in ragtime composing.

Just one further thing on Jelly's handling of bar 12, again in contrast to Joplin's: note how in *both* choruses the phrase

Ex. 6

established in bar 12 is used for the whole last four bars. And, since the second time through the phrase of bar 12 is tied to the first eleven bars as well, this means that Jelly has succeeded in tying the whole chorus together. Then by his handling of the D strain (discussed below), he further prolongs the momentum which is what he is striving for, as distinguished from the stop-and-go techniques of ragtime. Jelly's momentum, built up as it is without a deep breath all the way from the beginning of C—five choruses all told—makes his abrupt final ending (also discussed below) all the more effective.

This creation of bars 13 through 16 on the basis of the single phrase of bar 12 is not to be glossed over lightly. This way of tying together a piece, by having the phrasing overlap the bounds of the four-square structure is a splendid artistic achievement. I believe I am correct in saying, for example, that this is the basic resource of Charlie Parker's musical genius. I know it is what elevates J. S. Bach to his high place. In fact, it is found wherever great not simply good musicians are found.[1]

Moving on past the first three strains—*without* recapitulating strain A—Jelly revises the D strain wholesale, making it a kind of bridge rather than a separate theme of its own. He even ends it with a semicadence propelling the motion into E.

---

[1] Actually it would be more accurate to say that it is found wherever great musical moments are found since some rather mediocre musicians seem to stumble on the things very occasionally.

This is definitely *not* in Joplin's original; in fact, note the decided stop in bar 16 of Joplin's strain D.

The E strain, which is played only once in the Joplin original is repeated in Jelly's version, suggesting (but it is only a suggestion) the "jamming out" of a jazz tune.

But note how in one respect Jelly does follow Joplin's pattern. Despite the fact that both right hand and left hand have departed far from the original in the details, the pattern remains of holding off the final return to home tonic until the third beat of the last measure, rather than the first beat as was Jelly's usual practice.

In ragtime, ending as late as the third beat of the last measure is feasible because of various permissible ways of closing the whole thing off (or going to the next strain) in the short space of two beats. Jelly and jazz generally were not used to these confinements. In the blues, for example, the performer has two full measures to finish something off. At the end of a jazz tune, he frequently can do without the final fourth beat entirely—he normally does in the blues and much other jazz. It is almost correct to say that jazz choruses are not typically sixteen whole bars but rather an upbeat plus fifteen whole bars plus three beats of the sixteenth. The home tonic is usually reached by bar 15, the first beat of bar 16 at the very latest.

Jazz is not used to facing this problem of not reaching the home tonic until the third beat of the last bar and having to shut up shop in two beats. Nowhere else in the ten tunes on this LP does Jelly encounter the problem. Any jazz musician who has tried to end *Save It Pretty Mama* or *You Can Be Kissed* in any but an unorthodox manner knows what the problem is. So it is interesting to note how Jelly does manage to pull out. He solves the identical problem in identical fashion on The Red Hot Peppers' number, *Cannonball Blues* (there, of course, the problem was self-imposed). The device he uses is so simple yet gets the job done with striking effectiveness. It is worth noting.

None of this is to say that the "transformation" of *Original Rags* is all net gain. While Jelly's wandering left-hand sixths are most interesting, they must substitute for some very pretty

little left-hand lines in the Joplin original, especially the endings of the first and last strains. These are shown in Ex. 7 and
8, respectively (omitting the chords which go with them, of
course).

Ex. 7

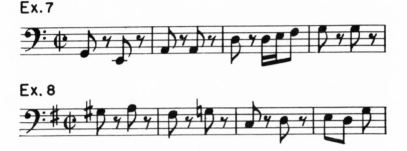

Ex. 8

The rest of side 2 includes *The Crave,* a Spanish-tinge number; *The Naked Dance;* and *Mister Joe* and *King Porter,* the
two tours de force.

The Naked Dance is hardly a first-class Jelly number but
one or more points are worth digging. For example, the poetic phrasing in the third chorus (the first in E flat) is just delightful musical logic.

In the sixth chorus, which is the second B strain, listen for
the left hand. In J. Lawrence Cook's transcription he indicates merely a repeat of the fifth chorus. Nothing could be
further from the truth. The left hand actually takes off in a
fine melody of its own, as shown in Ex. 9. This is not a
melody suitable for right-hand handling, but it is decidedly
the line which Jelly has his attention on. The right hand is
merely accompaniment at this point. In Jelly one must always
be careful to know where the lead is. In trio recordings, for
example, he frequently took piano choruses while the clarinet
was going full blown. And in much of the Red Hot Pepper
material, the lead is in some obscure place (for example, Pop
Foster's bass in the banjo chorus in *Black Bottom Stomp*).

Also note that consistently in the À flat choruses in *The
Naked Dance,* Jelly hits the seventh (a third inversion, if you
will) of the dominant, when the ear would expect (and J.

Ex. 9

Lawrence Cook notates) the root of the chord. In Ex. 9, the
first appearance of this unexpected D flat is shown in bars 13
and 14. In the five choruses which follow this, all in A flat,
the note constantly substitutes for E flat. I know of no explanation of this in terms of the musical effect it creates. More
likely it was just something Jelly had in his fingers, that he
happened to go a note too low every time, but, since the D
flat *is* in the chord, he felt no great compulsion to correct the
error. At least this is my guess.

King Oliver

by *Larry Gushee*

Larry Gushee's tribute to King Oliver in the form of an extended record review is, in a sense, the result of over forty years of praise for Oliver's 1923 recordings. It is also a result of Gushee's new and individual perception of this music and great love and respect for its players.

Louis Armstrong 1923: WITH KING OLIVER'S CREOLE JAZZ BAND, Riverside RLP 12-122. Joe (King) Oliver, Louis Armstrong, *cornets;* Honore Dutray, *trombone;* Johnny Dodds, *clarinet;* Lil Hardin Armstrong, *piano;* Bill Johnson, *banjo;* Baby Dodds, *drums.*
Chimes Blues; Just Gone; Canal Street Blues; Mandy Lee Blues; Weather Bird Rag; Dippermouth Blues; Froggie Moore; Snake Rag.
Add Stomp Evans, *saxophone:*
Mabel's Dream; Southern Stomps; Riverside Blues.

THE TITLE OF this album may be commercial good sense; musically, however, it is simply nonsense. There have been blessed few bands that have ever played together like Joe Oliver's, and Louis' presence is but one of many elements responsible. And his contribution is, in a sense, a negative one, for he is rarely heard in the role in which he found real greatness, that of genial, poignant, triumphant soloist, set off by subordinate, if not run-of-the-mill, musicians. Here and there we hear a phrase, sometimes only a single tone, played with the warm, slightly irregular vibrato so different from Joe Oliver's. We know it is Louis and are thankful for that knowledge.

If a band can be said to have a clearly recognizable and highly original sound, it must consist of something more than the arithmetic sum of a certain number of individual styles. I suspect that the *sine qua non* is discipline, which chiefly finds expression as consistency and limitation. Individual talent and skill do not even come into question here, at least as they are generally thought of, for one of the paradoxes of style is that poor musicians can create a fine sound (Unconscious Poetry of the People Dept.). Begin with a group of musicians out of the common run, and who are guided by some dominant principle or personality, and the resultant sound will be truly unique, pleasing to the ears because it is musical, to the soul because it is integral. This is what makes the first records of Charlie Parker and Dizzy Gillespie, the Mulligan Quartet, the Original Dixieland Jazz Band, stylistically great as well as musically pleasing.

And so these recordings, in their way, are a norm, and object lessons of what a jazz band needs to be to be great. Unfortunately, it is not quite possible to say to the infidel, "Listen and believe," for so much of the music escaped the acoustical recording technique. Happily, the imagination will gradually supply much of what the ear cannot perceive, much as it can fill in (indeed, is expected to fill in) the gaps in a figure, incompletely sketched.

Our idea of how this band *really* sounded, however, will always contain one element of uncertainty, barring the discovery of time travel, since the recorded sound of the Creole Band depended to so great an extent on the company that recorded it. On this reissue the sides made for Gennett (all except 3 on side 2) must have been cut in marshmallow—with Johnny Dodds crouched inside the recording horn. It seems to me that the Paramounts (the above-mentioned exceptions) must sound more like actuality: clarinet is toned down, cornets are strong, with the second part actually being heard, the piano chording does not run together in an amorphous droning, and the bass line is generally clearer, the more so since it is reinforced by Stump Evans' bass sax.

Still, the Gennetts are in the majority here, and assisted by Riverside's remastering, they sound fine. Chiefly they sound fine because Oliver, like Jelly Roll in his happiest days, knew the sound he wanted, and had the brass and the guts and the prestige to run a band his way. Whether the tempos, so often felicitous, were Joe Oliver's independent choice, or determined by prevailing dance style I cannot know. The fact remains that the Creole Band (and the New Orleans Rhythm Kings) played a good deal slower than bands like the Wolverines and the Bucktown 5, which recorded only a year later. The tempos they chose never exceeded their technical limitations, while, for instance, the Wolverines and, especially, the later Chicagoans often played too fast for comfort (theirs and ours). I am sure that this accounts for much of the superb swing of the Creole Band.

But even more important is the manner in which the separate beats of the measure are accented. Here we tread on thin ice, the subjective conditions of hearing being difficult to verify objectively. Different people must hear the relative amplitudes of the beats differently—how else to account for the fact that many contemporary emulators of this style seem, to my ears, to accentuate the secondary beats far too much, rather than playing a truly flat four-four as did Oliver's rhythm section? You see, though, that I already beg the question. On the other hand, some of the so-called revival bands manage to reproduce the effect of the Creole Band's rhythm, while failing in other respects. The trouble is, I suspect, that the horns sound as if they are working too hard, and any suggestion of laboriousness immediately sets a band apart from the relaxed assurance and ease of the older group.

The truly phenomenal rhythmic momentum generated by Oliver is just as much dependent on *continuity* of rhythmic pulse—only reinforced by uniformity of accentuation in the rhythm section and relaxed playing. One never hears the vertiginous excitement of Bix, or Tesch; one never feels that, with a little less control, a break or an entire chorus would fall into irrationality or musical *bizarrerie*. Oliver's swing is exciting after a different fashion: it is predictable, positive, and consistent. Only rarely is the total effect *manqué,* as in *Froggie Moore,* where the stop-and-go character of the tune makes consistency more difficult to achieve.

Its consistency is, as I have said, largely the result of Oliver's personal conception of a band sound. How much he molded the musicians to fit the ideal pattern of his own imagination, or how much he chose them with the knowledge that they would fit in, without trying to change their personal styles, is something we can't determine since we lack recordings by New Orleans bands before 1923. We have no record of how Louis sounded before he came to Chicago—we know he is full of the spirit of King Joe, although their ideas of instrumental tone were divergent. Dodd's rare gift of phrasing, his ability to bridge the gap between trumpet phrases (generally those of the tune itself) and to place the final note of his own phrase on the beginning of a trumpet phrase, we know from many other records, but none of them antedate these sides. And the rhythmic approach, too, is initiated by the Creole Band, with due note taken of Ory's 1921 *Sunshine* date; we hear it again but infrequently, perhaps a bit in NORK, certainly in the Tuxedo Band, in Sam Morgan's Band, and in many of Bunk's records, and other more recent ones in that tradition.

The impression of consistency is made all the stronger by the refusal of the musicians to permit themselves too much freedom. In successive choruses of a tune Oliver's sidemen often play the same part note for note, or with only slight variation—notice Dutray in *Froggie Moore,* especially; Dodds in the same tune and in *Snake Rag.* The ODJB did this too, but there is always an undertone (overtone to some) of the ludicrous—visions of tiny mechanical men playing chorus after chorus identically come to us, and one wonders how or why they go on. . . . Dutray, to be sure, often plays a pretty strict harmony part, as if from an orchestration, but there is a good deal more besides, and his mannerisms, his agility and grace, are strictly his own and not from the public domain.

A riff produces somewhat the same kind of excitement as does Oliver's "consistency," stemming ultimately from the irritation born of sameness, and expectation of change unfulfilled by the riff itself, but heard in a superimposed solo. The excitement of riffs, however, is bought too cheap, and works best in the immediacy of ecstatic suspension of our normal listening habits, most effective in the physical presence of a band. The Creole Band's way is less obvious, more complex, and, in the long run, makes a *record* that remains satisfying for year after year.

All these words will never convince someone against his will, and perhaps some will never feel or know why the Creole Jazz Band is so great and sets the standard (possibly, who knows, only because of an historical accident) for all kinds of jazz that do not base their excellence on individual expressiveness, but on form and *shape* achieved through control and balance.

My panegyric tone admits of modification in some instances. The Paramount *Mabel's Dream* is too slow—in fact, the tempo is an exception in the group of tunes on this record, neither as slow as the *andante Southern Stomps* and *Riverside,* nor as fast the rather relaxed *Chimes Blues.* The latter is too relaxed for its own good, the tricky chimes effects are dated and special, and Louis solos better elsewhere (*Riverside* and *Froggie Moore*).

But all of this is trivial. I love this band and its myth, the perfection it stands for and almost is, its affirmation and integrity, the somber stride of *Riverside Blues,* the steady roll of *Southern Stomps,* the rock of *Canal St. Blues,* the headlong sprint of *Weather Bird;* I love the musicians in this band, too, although my affection is tinged with sadness to think that, with the exception of young Louis, already himself but not yet complete, none of them ever again realized himself so well within a band. This is no reproach to them; it is only the result of the paradoxical fact that this band, recorded only a generation ago and marking the beginning of consistent recording of jazz, was one of the very best that jazz has ever known.

Conversation with James P. Johnson

by Tom Davin

In the early 1930's the late Tom Davin worked as publicity man for several Harlem night clubs. He later became an editor of magazines and books, but never lost his love for jazz and particularly the Harlem "stride" school. He did his interviewing of James P. Johnson on successive Saturdays at the latter's Jamaica, Long Island, home.

Pianist Dick Wellstood wrote in a record review:

One of the most famous quotes of 1957 was the remark made by Thelonious Monk while he was listening to the playback of one of his solos: "That sounds like James P. Johnson." Strangely enough, Monk does sound like James P. from time to time, and so do Fats, Basie, Tatum, and Duke (as well as Willie Gant and Q. Roscoe Snowden). Since James P. has had such a strong influence on so many well-known pianists, it is amazing that . . . the average fan confuses him with Pete Johnson ("Do you really like boogie woogie?") and the average musician thinks of him affectionately, if dimly, as an early teacher of Fats Waller.

James P. was not Pete Johnson, nor a mere "teacher" of Fats Waller. He was a much more interesting musician than Waller. His bass lines are better constructed, his right hand is freer and less repetitive, his rhythm is more accurate, and his playing is not so relentlessly two-beat as that of Fats. Although he lacked the smooth technique of Tatum (and of Fats) and the striking harmonic imagination of Ellington, he nonetheless carved out a style which was rich enough in general musical resources to have re-created at least fragments of itself in the playing of such unlike musicians as Monk and John Lewis.

Unfortunately, James P.'s recording career was a bit too long. He was playing his best in the thirties, but he is currently represented on record either by recordings of his old piano rolls, which sound exactly like piano rolls, or by records from the forties, which were made after his health had begun to fail.

Davin's own introduction to the series of conversations went this way:

His show music includes: Plantation Days, Runnin' Wild, Keep Shufflin, Sugar Hill, Meet Miss Jones *and* De Organizer, *a one-act opera with libretto by Langston Hughes.*

In the symphonic field, his orchestral compositions embrace the Harlem Symphony, Symphony in Brown, Suite in Sonata Form on the St. Louis Blues for Piano and Orchestra, Drums *(African themes and rhythms arranged for orchestra),* Carolina Balmoral *arranged for symphony orchestra, as well as many others.*

This is quite a range of achievement for an informally taught, honky-tonk piano player. Who has topped it?

In The Story of Jazz, *Marshall Stearns writes: "In the early fifties, James P. Johnson, old and sick, often wondered what could have happened to his beloved ragtime. For a brief moment, it seemed that the large compositions on which he had been working were about to be accepted and played, along with the time-honored classics of Mozart and Beethoven. Johnson's concertos were quite as complex and, in a sense, twice as difficult to play as Mozart's. Perhaps his Afro-American folk origins betrayed him, for the average classical musician is utterly incapable of the rhythmic sensitivity that is necessary to play Johnson's pieces. Only an orchestra composed of Smiths (Willie the Lion), Wallers, and Johnsons could have done it."*

Two years before he died, in 1955, I was fortunate to be able to interview him extensively about the early New York jazz scene, the people and music which influenced his style. From the notes on his career, these conversations emerge.

We have included here excerpts from two of the conversations which we published—the two which caused most comment, as a matter of fact. The entire series plus Davin's other manuscripts will form the basis of a posthumous book, now in progress, on Harlem jazz and James P. Johnson's career.

Q. James P., how did you get launched as a professional pianist?

A. I told you before how I was impressed by my older brothers' friends. They were real ticklers—cabaret and sporting-house players. They were my heroes and led what I felt was a glamorous life—welcome everywhere because of their talent.

In the years before World War I, there was a piano in almost every home, colored or white. The piano makers had a slogan: "What Is Home Without A Piano?" It was like having a radio or a TV today. Phonographs were feeble and scratchy.

Most people who had pianos couldn't play them, so a piano player was important socially. There were so many of them visiting and socializing that some people would have their pianos going day and night all week long.

If you could play piano good, you went from one party to another and everybody made a fuss about you and fed you ice cream, cake, food and drinks. In fact, some of the biggest men in the profession were known as the biggest eaters we had. At an all-night party, you started at 1:00 A.M., had another meal at 4:00 A.M. and sat down again at 6:00 A.M. Many of us suffered later because of eating and drinking habits started in our younger socializing days.

But that was the life for me when I was seventeen.

In the summer of 1912, during high-school vacation, I went out to Far Rockaway, a beach resort near Coney Island, and got a chance to play at a place run by a fellow named Charlie Ett. It was just a couple of rooms knocked together to make a cabaret. They had beer and liquor, and out in the back yard there was a crib house for fast turnover.

It was a rough place, but I got nine dollars and tips, or about eighteen dollars a week over-all. That was so much money that I didn't want to go back to high school. I never got but quarters when I played before.

Q. Oh, you *did* play professionally before?

A. Yes, but it didn't count. When I was about eight in Jersey City, I was walking down the block, and a woman came out of a doorway and asked me if I wanted to make a quarter. She knew I could play a little, from neighbors, so she took me into her parlor where there were about three or four couples drinking beer, set me down on the piano stool and said: "Go ahead and play and don't turn your head."

I played my *Little Brown Jug* tune and a couple of other hymns and nursery-rhyme arrangements for a couple of hours. I never looked around.

She gave me a quarter, and I went on my way. I guess she was running some kind of sporting house. They were all around the neighborhood.

Q. Excuse my interruption. Tell me more about Far Rockaway.

A. There was another place there called "The Cool Off," located down near the station. Some Clef Club members played there, and they used to come over after hours to hear me play dirty. Kid Sneeze was among them, and Dude Finley, a pianist who played a rag in D minor that had the same trio that was later used in *Shake It, Break It, Throw It Out The Window; Catch It Before It Falls.*

That fall, instead of going back to school, I went to Jersey City and got a job in a cabaret run by Freddie Doyle. He gave me a two-dollar raise.

In a couple of months, Doyle's folded up, and I came back to Manhattan and played in a sporting house on 27th Street between 8th and 9th Avenues, which was the Tenderloin then. It was run by a fellow named Dan Williams, and he had two girl entertainers that I used to accompany.

Q. What type of music were you playing in 1912?

A. Oh, generally popular stuff. I played *That Barbershop Chord* . . . *Lazy Moon* . . . Berlin's *Alexander's Ragtime Band.* Some rags, too, my own and others . . . Joplin's *Maple Leaf Rag* (everybody knew that by then) . . . his *Sunflower Slow Drag* . . . *Maori*, by Will Thiers . . . *The Peculiar Rag* and *The Dream,* by Jack the Bear.

Then there were "instrumentals"; piano arrangements of medleys of Herbert and Friml, popular novelties and music-hall hits—many by Negro composers.

Indian songs were popular then, and the girls at Dan Williams' used to sing *Hiawatha* . . . *Red Wing* . . . *Big Chief Battleaxe* . . . *Come With Me To My Big Teepee* . . . *Pony Boy*—all popular in the music halls then.

Blues had not come into popularity at that time—they weren't known or sung by New York entertainers.

Q. Had you done any composing by that time?

A. No, but I was working out a number of rags of my own that they wanted to publish at Gotham & Attucks, a Negro music publishing firm whose offices were at 37th Street, off Broadway. I couldn't write them down and I didn't know anybody who would do them for me.

Cecil Mack was president of Gotham & Attucks. All the great colored musicians had gathered around the firm—Bert Williams, George Walker, Scott Joplin, Will Marion Cook, Joe Jordan, Tim Brymm.

They had a lot of hit songs . . . *Just a Word Of Consolation* . . . *Red, Red Rose* . . . *Down Among the Sugar Cane* . . . *Good Morning, Carrie*. Gussie L. Davis, who wrote white-style ballads for them, was the composer of *The Baggage Coach Ahead*, the greatest tear-jerker of the time.

Q. Were you long at Dan Williams' place?

A. No, only a couple of months. I had a number of jobs in the winter of 1912-13. One was playing movie piano at the Nickelette at 8th Avenue and 37th Street. They had movies and short acts for short money. Many vaudeville acts broke in there. Florence Mills first sang there I recall.

In the spring of 1913, I really got started up in The Jungles. This was the Negro section of Hell's Kitchen and ran from 60th to 63rd Street, west of 9th Avenue. It was the toughest part of New York. There were two to three killings a night. Fights broke out over love affairs, gambling, or arguments in general. There were race fights with the white gangs on 66th and 67th Street. It was just as tough in the white section of Hell's Kitchen.

Q. Where did you play there?

A. In 1910 and 1911, I used to drop in at Jim Allan's place at 61st Street and 10th Avenue, where I'd wear my knickers long so they wouldn't notice that I was a short-pants punk. After they heard me play, they would let me come when I wanted.

So, in the spring of 1913, I went uptown and got a job playing at Jim Allan's. It was a remodeled cellar, and since it operated after hours, it had an iron-plated door—like the speak-easies had later. There was a bar upstairs, but downstairs there was a rathskeller, and in the back of the cellar there was a gambling joint.

When the cops raided us now and then, they always had to go back to the station house for axes and sledge hammers, so we usually made a clean getaway.

My NEW YORK JAZZ album [on Asch] tried to show some types of music played in The Jungles at that time . . . Joplin's *Euphonic Sounds* . . . *The Dream* . . . Handy's *Hesitation Blues*.

One night a week, I played piano for Drake's Dancing Class on 62nd Street, which we called "The Jungles Casino." It was officially a dancing school, since it was very hard for Negroes to get a dance-hall license. But you could get a license to open a dancing school very cheap.

The Jungles Casino was just a cellar, too, without fixings. The furnace, coal, and ashes were still there behind a partition. The coal bin was handy for guests to stash their liquor in case the cops dropped in.

There were dancing classes all right, but there were no teachers. The "pupils" danced sets, two-steps, waltzes, schottisches, and "The Metropolitan Glide," a new step.

I played for these regulation dances, but instead of playing straight, I'd break into a rag in certain places. The older ones didn't care too much for this, but the younger ones would scream when I got good to them with a bit of rag in the dance music now and then.

The floor of the dancing class was plain cement like any cellar, and it was hard on the dancers' shoes. I saw many actually wear right through a pair of shoes in one night. They danced hard.

When it rained, the water would run down the walls from the street so we all had to stop and mop up the floor.

The people who came to The Jungles Casino were mostly from around Charleston, South Carolina, and other places in the South. Most of them worked for the Ward Line as longshoremen or on ships that called at southern coast ports. There were even some Gullahs among them.

They picked their partners with care to show off their best steps and put sets, cotillions and cakewalks that would give them a chance to get off.

The Charleston, which became a popular dance step on its own, was just a regulation cotillion step without a name. It had many variations—all danced to the rhythm that everybody knows now. One regular at the Casino, named Dan White, was the best dancer in the crowd and he introduced the Charleston step as we know it. But there were dozens of other steps used, too.

It was while playing for these southern dancers that I composed a number of Charlestons—eight in all—all with the same rhythm. One of these later became my famous *Charleston* when it hit Broadway.

My *Carolina Shout* was another type of ragtime arrangement of a set dance of this period. In fact, a lot of famous jazz compositions grew out of cotillion music—such as *The Wildcat Blues*. Jelly Roll Morton told me that his *King Porter Stomp* and *High Society* were taken from cotillion music.

The dances they did at The Jungles Casino were wild and comical—the more pose and the more breaks, the better. These Charleston people and the other Southerners had just come to New York. They were country people and they felt homesick. When they got tired of two-steps and schottisches (which they danced with a lot of spieling), they'd yell: "Let's go back home!" . . . "Let's do a set!" . . . or, "Now, put us in the alley!" I did my *Mule Walk* or *Gut Stomp* for these country dances.

Breakdown music was the best for such sets, the more solid and groovy the better. They'd dance, hollering and screaming until they were cooked. The dances ran from fifteen to thirty minutes, but they kept up all night long or until their shoes wore out—most of them after a heavy day's work on the docks.

Q. Who were some of the other ticklers in The Jungles at that time?

A. Well, there was Bob Gordon, the March King, who played at Allan's before me, He wrote *Oh, You Drummer!* which was popular because it had a lot of breaks for drums.

Then there was Freddie Singleton who used to relieve me at The Jungles Casino now and then. When I would lay off at Allan's, I would play at Georgie Lee's near by, which was laid out the same as Allan's, except that it had a cabaret in the back room, instead of gambling.

About this time, I played my first "Pigfoot Hop" at Phil Watkin's place on 61st Street. He was a very clever entertainer and he paid me $1.50 for a night's playing with all the gin and chitterlings that I could get down.

This was my first "Chitterlin' Strut" or parlor social, but later in the depression I became famous at "Gumbo Suppers," "Fish Fries," "Egg Nog Parties," and "Rent Parties." I loved them all. You met people.

When I was at Allan's, I met Luckey Roberts at a party.

Q. What was Luckey like in those days of his prime?

A. Luckey Roberts was the outstanding pianist in New York in 1913—and for years before and after. He had composed *The Elks March . . . Spanish Venus . . . Palm Beach Rag . . . The Junkman's Rag.*

Luckey had massive hands that could stretch a fourteenth on the keyboard, and he played tenths as easy as others played octaves. His tremolo was terrific, and he could drum on one note with two or three fingers in either hand. His style in making breaks was like a drummer's: he'd flail his hands in and out, lifting them high. A very spectacular pianist.

He was playing at Barron Wilkins' place in Harlem then, and when I could get away I went uptown and studied him (I was working at Allan's from 9:00 P.M. to 7:00 A.M.). Later we became good friends, and he invited me to his home. Afterwards, I played at Barron Wilkins', too, as did my friend Ernest Green, who first introduced me to Luckey. Ernest was a good classical pianist. Luckey used to ask him to play the *William Tell Overture* and the *White Cavalry Overture*. These were considered tops in "classical" music amongst us.

Ernest Green's mother was studying then with a piano and
singing teacher named Bruto Gianinni. She did house cleaning
in return for lessons—several Negro singers got their training
that way. Mrs. Green told me: "James, you have too much
talent to remain ignorant of musical principles." She inspired
me to study seriously. So I began to take lessons from Gianinni, but I got tired of the dull exercises. However, he taught
me a lot of concert effects.

I was starting to develop a good technique. I was born with
absolute pitch and could catch a key that a player was using
and copy it, even Luckey's. I played rags very accurately and
brilliantly—running chromatic octaves and glissandos up and
down with both hands. It made a terrific effect.

I did double glissandos straight and backhand, glissandos in
sixths and double tremolos. These would run other ticklers out
of the place at cutting sessions. They wouldn't play after me.
I would put these tricks in on the breaks and I could think of
a trick a minute. I was playing a lot of piano then, traveling
around and listening to every good player I could. I'd steal
their breaks and style and practice them until I had them perfect.

From listening to classical piano records and concerts, from
friends of Ernest Green such as Mme. Garret, who was a fine
classical pianist, I would learn concert effects and build them
into blues and rags.

Sometimes I would play basses a little lighter than the melody and change harmonies. When playing a heavy stomp, I'd
soften it right down—then, I'd make an abrupt change like I
heard Beethoven do in a sonata.

Some people thought it was cheap, but it was effective and
dramatic. With a solid bass like a metronome, I'd use chords
with half and quarter changes. Once I used Liszt's *Rigoletto
Concert Paraphrase* as an introduction to a stomp. Another
time, I'd use pianissimo effects in the groove and let the dancers' feet be heard scraping on the floor. It was used by dance
bands later.

In practicing technique, I would play in the dark to get completely familiar with the keyboard. To develop clear touch and

the feel of the piano, I'd put a bed sheet over the keyboard and play difficult pieces through it.

I had gotten power and was building a serious orchestral piano. I did rag variations on the *William Tell Overture,* Grieg's *Peer Gynt Suite* and even a *Russian Rag* based on Rachmaninoff's *Prelude in C Sharp Minor,* which was just getting popular then.

In my *Imitators' Rag* the last strain had *Dixie* in the right hand and *The Star Spangled Banner* in the left. (It wasn't the national anthem then.) Another version had *Home, Sweet Home* in the left hand and *Dixie* in the right.

When President Wilson's "Preparedness" campaign came on, I wrote a march fantasia called *Liberty.*

From 1914 to 1916, I played at Allan's, Lee's, The Jungles Casino, occasionally uptown at Barron Wilkins', Leroy's and Wood's (run then by Edmund Johnson). I went around copping piano prize contests and I was considered one of the best in New York—if not the best. I was slim and dapper, and they called me "Jimmie" then.

Q. Had you done any composing yet?

A. I had started to compose my first rag about this time (1914), but nothing was done with it, and I threw it away. I also wrote and threw away a number of songs, although some people seemed to like them.

Entertainers used to sing blues to me, homemade blues, and I'd arrange them for piano, either to accompany them or play as solos. One of these homemade blues, *All Night Long,* was made into a song by Shelton Brooks who also wrote *The Darktown Strutters' Ball.*

Then I met Will Farrell, a Negro song writer, and he showed me how to set my pieces down in writing. He also wrote lyrics for them. With him, I set down my first composition to be published, *Mamma's and Pappa's Blues.*

There had been a piece around at the time called *Left Her On The Railroad Track* or *Baby, Get That Towel Wet.* All pianists knew it and could play variations on it. It was a sporting-house favorite. I took one opening strain and did a paraphrase from this and used it in *Mamma's and Pappa's Blues.* It was also developed later into *Crazy Blues,* by Perry Bradford.

I had composed *Carolina Shout* before that. It wasn't written down, but was picked up by other pianists. My *Steeplechase Rag* and *Daintiness Rag* had spread all over the country, too, although they hadn't been published.

With Farrell, I also wrote *Stop It, Joe!* at this time. I sold it, along with *Mamma's and Pappa's Blues* for twenty-five dollars apiece to get enough money for a deposit on a grand piano.

In the summer of 1914, I went for a visit to Atlantic City and heard Eubie Blake (who composed *Shuffle Along* later), one of the foremost pianists of all time. He was playing at The Belmont, and Charles Johnson was playing at The Boat House, both all-night joints.

Eubie was a marvelous song player. He also had a couple of rags. One, *Troublesome Ivories,* was very good. I caught it.

I saw how Eubie, like Willie Smith and Luckey Roberts, could play songs in all keys, so as to be ready for any singer— or if one of them started on a wrong note. So I practiced that, too. I also prepared symphonic vamps—gutty, but not very full.

While in New Jersey that summer, I won a piano contest in Egg Harbor; playing my *Twilight Rag* (which had a chimes effect in syncopation), *Steeplechase Rag,* and *Nighttime in Dixieland.*

There was a pianist there who played quadrilles, sets, rags, etc. From him, I first heard the walking Texas or boogie-woogie bass. The boogie woogie was a cotillion step for which a lot of music was composed. I never got his name, but he played the *Kitchen Tom Rag* which was the signal for a "Jazz" dance.

When I came back to New York, I met the famous Abba Labba in the Chelsea district. To this day, I can't remember his right name, either. He was a friend and pupil of Luckey Roberts'.

Abba Labba was the working girls' Jelly Roll. His specialty

was to play a lot of piano for girls who were laundresses and cooks. They would supply him with stylish clothes from their customers' laundry and make him elaborate rosettes for his sleeve guards. The cooks furnished him with wonderful meals, since they had fine cold kina (keena) then. Cold kina was leftover food from a white family's dinner that the cook was entitled to. This was an old southern cooks' custom: they fed their own family with these leftovers and they were sure to see that there was plenty of good food left. That's why old southern home cooking was so famous—the cook shared it.

Most of the full-time hustlers used to cultivate a working girl like that, so they could have good meals and fancy laundry.

Abba Labba had a beautiful left hand and did wonderful bass work. He played with half-tone and quarter-tone changes that were new ideas then. He would run octaves in chords, and one of his tricks was to play *Good Night, Beloved, Good Night* in schottische, waltz and ragtime.

I fell on his style and copied a lot of it.

Q. Were there other pianists you learned tricks from at this time?

A. Oh, yes. I was getting around town and hearing everybody. If they had anything I didn't have, I listened and stole it.

Sam Gordon played at The Elks Café at 137th and 138th Streets and Lenox Avenue. He was a great technician who played an arabesque style that Art Tatum made famous later. He played swift runs in sixths and thirds, broken chords, one-note tremolandos and had a good left hand. He had been a classical pianist and had studied in Germany. He picked up syncopation here.

Fred Bryant from Brooklyn was a good all-around pianist. He played classical music and had a velvet touch. The piano keys seemed to be extensions of his fingers. Incidentally, as far as I know, he invented the backward tenth. I used it and passed it on to Fats Waller later. It was the keynote of our style.

Down in Chelsea, there was a player named Fats Harris,

who looked like Waller did later. He had a rag in D called
Fats Harris's Rag, a great stomp tune.

Then in the fall of 1914, I went over to Newark, New Jersey, and first met Willie (The Lion) Smith and Dickie Huff
who were playing on "The Coast," a tough section around
Arlington and Augusta Streets. I played at Kinney Hall and
Lewis', which was located in an old church.

Both were great players. I don't have to tell you about Willie,
he's still playing great. He's the last of the real old-time ticklers
—along with Luckey.

Q. What was Willie (The Lion) Smith like in his young days?

A. Willie Smith was one of the sharpest ticklers I ever met—
and I met most of them. When we first met in Newark, he
wasn't called Willie The Lion—he got that nickname after his
terrific fighting record overseas during World War I. He was
a fine dresser, very careful about the cut of his clothes and a
fine dancer, too, in addition to his great playing. All of us
used to be proud of our dancing—Louis Armstrong, for instance, was considered the finest dancer among the musicians.
It made for attitude and stance when you walked into a place,
and made you strong with the gals. When Willie Smith walked
into a place, his every move was a picture.

Q. You mean he would make a studied entrance, like a theatrical star?

A. Yes, every move we made was studied, practiced, and developed just like it was a complicated piano piece.

Q. What would such an entrance be like?

A. When a real smart tickler would enter a place, say in winter,
he'd leave his overcoat on and keep his hat on, too. We used
to wear military overcoats or what was called a Peddock
Coat, like a coachman's; a blue double-breasted, fitted to the
waist and with long skirts. We'd wear a light pearl-gray Fulton
or Homburg hat with three buttons or eyelets on the side, set
at a rakish angle over on the side of the head. Then a white
silk muffler and a white silk handkerchief in the overcoat's
breast pocket. Some carried a gold-headed cane, or if they

were wearing a cutaway, a silver-headed cane. A couple of fellows used to wear Inverness capes, which were in style in white society then.

Many fellows had their overcoats lined with the same material as the outside—they even had their suits made that way. Pawnbrokers, special ones, would give you twenty or twenty-five dollars on such a suit or overcoat. They knew what it was made of. A fellow belittling another would be able to say: "G'wan, the inside of my coat would make you a suit."

But to go back . . . when you came into a place you had a three-way play. You never took your overcoat or hat off until you were at the piano. First you laid your cane on the music rack. Then you took off your overcoat, folded it and put it on the piano, with the lining showing.

You then took off your hat before the audience. Each tickler had his own gesture for removing his hat with a little flourish; that was part of his attitude, too. You took out your silk handkerchief, shook it out and dusted off the piano stool.

Now, with your coat off, the audience could admire your full-back or box-back suit, cut with very square shoulders. The pants had about fourteen-inch cuffs and broidered clocks.

Full-back coats were always single-breasted, to show your gold watch fob and chain. Some ticklers wore a horseshoe tie-pin in a strong single-colored tie and a gray shirt with black pencil stripes.

We all wore French, Shriner & Urner or Hanan straight or French last shoes with very pointed toes, or patent-leather turnup toes, in very narrow sizes. For instance, if you had a size 7 foot, you'd wear an 8½ shoe on a very narrow last. They cost from twelve to eighteen dollars a pair.

If you had an expensive suit made, you'd have the tailor take a piece of cloth and give it to you, so that you could have either spats or button cloth-tops for your shoes to match the suit.

Some sharp men would have a suit and overcoat made of the same bolt of cloth. Then they'd take another piece of the same goods and have a three-button Homburg made out of it.

This was only done with solid-color cloth—tweeds or plaids were not in good taste for formal hats.

There was a tailor named Bromberger down on Carmine Street, near Sheridan Square in the old 15th Ward, who made all the hustlers' clothes. That was a Negro section around 1912. He charged twenty-five to forty dollars a suit.

Another tailoring firm, Clemens & Ostreicher, at 40th Street and 6th Avenue, would make you a sharp custom suit for $11.75—with broadlap seams (¾ in.), a finger-tip coat, shirred in at the waist with flared skirts, patch pockets, five-button cuffs and broad lapels.

Up on 153rd Street there was a former barber named Hart who had invented a hair preparation named Kink-No-More, called "Conk" for short. His preparation was used by all musicians—the whole Clef Club used him. You'd get your hair washed, dyed and straightened; then trimmed. It would last about a month.

Of course each tickler had his own style of appearance. I used to study them carefully and copy those attitudes that appealed to me.

There was a fellow named Fred Tunstall, whom I mentioned before. He was a real dandy. I remember he had a Norfolk coat with eighty-two pleats in the back. When he sat down to the piano, he'd slump a little in a half hunch, and those pleats would fan out real pretty. That coat was long and flared at the waist. It had a very short belt sewn on the back. His pants were very tight.

He had a long neck, so he wore a high, stiff collar that came up under his chin with a purple tie. A silk handkerchief was always draped very carefully in his breast pocket. His side view was very striking.

Tunstall was very careful about his hair, which was ordinary, but he used lots of pomade. His favorite shoes were patent-leather turnups.

His playing was fair, but he had the reputation of being one of our most elegant dressers. He had thirty-five suits of clothes —blacks, grays, brown pin stripes, oxfords, pepper and salts. Some men would wear a big diamond ring on their pinky, the right-hand one, which would flash in the treble passages. Gold teeth were in style, and a real sharp effect was to have a diamond set on one tooth. One fellow went further and had diamonds set in the teeth of his toy Boston bulldog. There was a gal named Diamond Floss, a big sporting-house woman, a hot clipper and a high-powered broad, who had diamonds in all her front teeth. She had a place in Chelsea, the West 30's, in the Tenderloin days.

Q. Where did these styles come from, the South?

A. No, we saw them right here in New York City. They were all copied from the styles of the rich whites. Most of the society folks had colored valets and some of them would give their old clothes to their valets and household help.

Then we'd see rich people at society gigs in the big hotels where they had Clef Club bands for their dances. So we wanted to dress good, copied them and made improvements.

Q. Please tell me more about the great ticklers' styles.

A. As I was saying, when I was a young fellow, I was very much impressed with such manners. I didn't know much about style, but I wanted to learn. I didn't want to be a punk all my life.

In the sporting world of gamblers, hustlers and ticklers, the lowest rank is called a punk. He's nothing. He doesn't have any sense; he doesn't know anything about life or the school of the smart world. He doesn't even know how to act in public. You had to have an attitude, a style of behaving that was your personal, professional trade-mark.

The older Clef Club musicians were artists at this kind of acting. The club was a place to go to study these glamorous characters. I got a lot of my style from ticklers like Floyd Keppard, who I knew in Jersey City, Dan Avery, Bob Hawkins, Lester Wilson, Freddie Tunstall, Kid Sneeze, Abba Labba, Willie Smith and many others.

I've seen Jelly Roll Morton, who had a great attitude, approach a piano. He would take his overcoat off. It had a special lining that would catch everybody's eye. So he would turn it inside out and, instead of folding it, he would lay it length-wise along the top of the upright piano. He would do this very slowly, very carefully and very solemnly as if the coat was worth a fortune and had to be handled very tenderly.

Then he'd take a big silk handkerchief, shake it out to show it off properly, and dust off the stool. He'd sit down then, hit his special chord (every tickler had his special trade-mark chord, like a signal) and he'd be gone! The first rag he'd play was always a spirited one to astound the audience.

Other players would start off by sitting down, wait for the audience to quiet down and then strike their chord, holding it with the pedal to make it ring.

Then they'd do a run up and down the piano—a scale or arpeggios—or if they were real good they might play a set of modulations, very offhand, as if there was nothing to it. They'd look around idly to see if they knew any chicks near the piano. If they saw somebody, they'd start a light conversation about the theater, the races or social doings—light chat. At this time, they'd drift into a rag, any kind of pretty stuff, but without tempo, particularly without tempo. Some ticklers would sit sideways to the piano, cross their legs and go on chatting with friends near by. It took a lot of practice to play this way, while talking and with your head and body turned.

Then, without stopping the smart talk or turning back to the piano, he'd *attack* without any warning, smashing right into the regular beat of the piece. That would knock them dead.

A big-timer would, of course, have a diamond ring he would want to show off to some gal near by that he wanted to make. So he would adjust his hand so that the diamond would catch her eye and blind her. She'd know he was a big shot right off.

A lot of this was taught to me by old-timers, when they would be sitting around when I was a kid and only playing social dance music. I wasn't a very good-looking fellow, but I dressed nice and natty. I learned all their stuff and practiced it carefully.

In the old days, these effects were studied to attract the

young gals who hung around such places. Ed Avery, whose style I copied, was a great actor and a hell of a ladies' man. He used to run big harems of all kinds of women.

After your opening piece to astound the audience, it would depend on the gal you were playing for or the mood of the place for what you would play next. It might be sentimental, moody, stompy or funky. The good player had to know just what the mood of the audience was.

At the end of his set, he'd always finish up with a hot rag and then stand up quickly, so that everybody in the place would be able to see who knocked it out.

Every tickler kept these attitudes even when he was social- izing at parties or just visiting. They were his professional per- sonality and prepared the audience for the artistic perform- ance to come. I've watched high-powered actors today, and they all have that professional approach. In the old days they really worked at it. It was designed to show a personality that women would admire. With the music he played, the tickler's manners would put the question in the ladies' minds: "Can he do it like he can play it?"

Q. The high-style clothes you described seem to have disap- peared in recent years. How did it happen?

A. Well, full-back clothes became almost a trade-mark for pimps and sharps. Church socials and dancing classes discrim- inated against all who wore full-back clothes. They would have a man at the door to keep them out. So, in self-defense, the hustlers had to change to English drape styles, which were rumored to be worn only by pansies and punks.

Q. Don't tell me that those sharp hustlers frequented church socials?

A. Oh, yes. Some of the toughest guys would even attend Sunday school classes regularly, just to get next to the younger and better-class gals there. They wore the square style of pinch-back coats and peg-top pants and would even learn hymns to impress a chick they had their eye on. They were very versatile cats.

Fats Waller

by Martin Williams

The last of the more famous Harlem "stride" players was Fats Waller, and, although he was decidedly a world unto himself, Art Tatum was directly influenced by the school. From Waller the mantle passed to Count Basie, and then to Thelonious Monk, but the style has been thoroughly transmuted by both of these players.

Martin Williams' comments on Fats Waller's Numb Fumblin' *was the first entry in the department which we called "Reconsiderations"—a place where recordings from the past could be reviewed whether or not they were currently available on an LP. Primarily, we believed the performances repaid careful listening and should not be forgotten; secondarily, we hoped to alert younger musicians to ideas which they might find fruitful in their own playing and composing.*

FATS WALLER'S (1929) *Numb Fumblin'* is a twelve-bar blues in form, but like most of the blues that come from the Northeast, it does not have that quality of deep sadness or joy that one hears in southern and southwestern blues, but one of pensive introspection, in this case modified by Waller's natural extroversion. It may have been a preset piece to some extent, but if it were entirely improvised, Waller's innate compositional gifts might well account for its structure. There are six choruses, and the basic structural principle consists of alternating predominantly almost "low-down" rhythmic statements (choruses 3, 5) with sparkling, predominantly short-noted (almost virtuoso) lyric melodies (choruses 2, 4, 6). As the performance proceeds, the motifs in the rhythmic choruses become increasingly complex and, in parallel, the lines in the melodic choruses do the same. Furthermore, the four-bar introduction suggests the lyric choruses but is simple enough melodically to suggest the rhythmic ones at the same time, and the first chorus which has some interesting substitute harmonies, is, similarly, strongly but simply rhythmic, a blues *melody* of a pronounced rhythmic quality. The transition into chorus 2 is interesting because the first four bars of 2 are based on a rather ordinary *rhythmic* figure of implied triplets but the following eight develop an original *melodic* line.

The details of developments within the melodic choruses are also interesting. The fourth begins with a continuous six-bar phrase, the sixth with a lovely shimmering line of cleanly played thirty-second notes unbroken for almost eight bars and with a striking metric organization.

The details of the rhythmic choruses are also important: in the third the treble carries rather simple figures against the left hand's timekeeping; in the fifth, the bass line carries a simple, almost boogie-woogie-like riff and the treble makes a counterrhythm above it.

The performance is made continuous not only by the fact that, as I say, there is a paralleling of the increasing complexity as Waller alternately takes up each of the motifs, the rhythmic and the melodic, but by his use of an over-all dynamic building. Thus, the last two choruses, although contrasting, are both still not only relatively complex but played at an equivalent dynamic level. Furthermore, Waller ends each chorus with the same two-bar device—a very common practice, of course, in much blues piano.

There is a great deal of rather ordinary material in this performance. The second chorus begins with a hoary Waller cliché and, if isolated, the third would be almost an empty stall-for-time. And that motif which he used to end each chorus is very ordinary. But as parts of a total structure, these things have an ingenious *raison d'être* and appropriateness. And if one did isolate choruses 4 and 6, he would have playing excitingly original in itself.

If Waller was just "playing the blues" on this record, such a structure would be extraordinary. But even if the main outlines were preset, an organization of no little subtlety is there.

Art Tatum

by Dick Katz

Although Dick Katz clearly wanted to discuss Tatum, the task of getting him to sit down and write the review which follows was almost laborious. When he did write it, he came up with a definitive essay.

THE ART TATUM–BEN WEBSTER QUARTET, Verve MGV 8220. Art Tatum, *piano;* Ben Webster, *tenor saxophone;* Red Callender, *bass;* Bill Douglass, *drums.*
All the Things You Are; My One And Only Love; My Ideal; Gone With the Wind; Have You Met Miss Jones; Night and Day; Where or When.

THE ART TATUM–BUDDY DE FRANCO QUARTET, Verve MGV 8229. Art Tatum, *piano;* Buddy DeFranco, *clarinet;* Red Callender, *bass;* Bill Douglass, *drums.*
Deep Night; This Can't Be Love; Memories of You; Once In a While; A Foggy Day; Makin' Whoopee; You're Mine You; Lover Man.

TATUM-CARTER-BELLSON TRIO MAKIN' WHOOPEE, Verve MGV 8227. Art Tatum, *piano;* Benny Carter, *trumpet* and *saxophone;* Louis Bellson, *drums.*
Blues in C; A Foggy Day; You're Mine You; Undecided; Under a Blanket of Blue; Makin' Whoopee.

THE IDEA OF combining artists of the stature of Art Tatum and Ben Webster is not a new one but, in this instance, it creates unique problems—and solutions.

Those who are familiar with the nature of Tatum's unique gifts probably feel, as I do, that his kind of talent seemed to preclude his being an accompanist or group player. He was first and foremost a soloist. He enjoyed being the orchestra and soloists and rhythm section—all the time. For him to share any of these functions with other instrumentalists often appeared to the listener to be a major concession.

Through the years, Tatum devised a fantastic vocabulary of pianistic devices such as an endless variety of ascending and descending arpeggios, runs, octave slides, "dragged thumb" double thirds, etc. Many a pianist was carried away trying to master this phase of Tatum, but the passing years have taught us that these were probably the least of his artistic accomplishments. There was a certain fascination in watching his musical sonar and radar guide those dazzling runs right to the target, but it is a tribute to his greatness to note that he avoided the obvious horrors which many virtuosos confuse with music.

It is my opinion that Tatum's uniqueness was expressed not so much in the blinding, supersonic piano technique, but in a sublime harmonic and rhythmic imagination. He was not essentially an inventor of melodies like Teddy Wilson or Lester Young. However, his mastery of diatonic, chromatic, and impressionist harmony has yet to be equaled in jazz with the exception of Charlie Parker. His deft and imaginative voice-leading and handling of sudden key-shifts, modulation, etc. gave him a kind of freedom that often conveyed a feeling of "any key, no key, or all keys." He was a complete musical entity and his harmonic language has not yet been assimilated. Rhythmically, he could be unbelievably subtle. Many a so-called ad lib passage was really in strict tempo! He was also a master of rubato and cross-rhythm. Over, under, and around all this he would superimpose his carefully disciplined array of pianistic tricks and arpeggios. But this was merely the icing —and it is often necessary to tune it out in order to appreciate the substance.

Now, this complete musical independence and predilection for extravagance on Tatum's part has often made the prospect of others playing with him a dubious venture. In fact, this series of albums has a kind of "throw them to the lions" quality—the lions being Tatum's ten fingers. Most of Tatum's early recorded performances with horns had an almost comic quality, as if Art were completely unaware of their presence. (A notable exception was the Esquire All-Star session on Commodore.) His trio performances, however, while not quite so artistic as his solo ones, were nevertheless a remarkable achievement. Moreover, they spawned the King Cole and, later, the Oscar Peterson trios and a whole generation of similar-sounding units. (Although the brilliant but short-lived Clarence Profit trio would figure prominently in any evaluation of the piano-bass-guitar combination.)

Of the three albums discussed here, the one with Ben Webster is vastly superior to the other two. It is the least self-conscious and the most creative and artistic.

Tatum's and Webster's respective conceptions complement each other beautifully. Both are masters at paraphrasing a melody, and both lean heavily on the "variations on a theme" technique, rather than the "running the changes" style (Coleman Hawkins, for example). Besides, Tatum's style, stripped to essentials, reveals an ingenious kind of inner thematic development. Ben Webster is a truly functional player. He makes every note important and has that marvelous sense of drama, space, and note placement shared by other great jazz artists such as Louis Armstrong, Lester Young, Miles, and Monk.

This record is blessed with a feeling of complete assurance, security, and authority. Tatum and Webster reveal their very strong sense of identity throughout. Ben Webster, happily, is obviously familiar with the eccentricities of Art's style and, very intelligently, allows him complete freedom to stretch out. (This is one place where "stretch out" means just that.) Ben, in effect, plays an obbligato or accompaniment to Art in many places in the album.

All the Things You Are, taken much slower than usual, opens, as many Tatum solos do, with a Liszt-like ad lib chorus. (This sort of thing probably caused many a pianist to reconsider.) Webster enters like an Othello and plays with such definition that Tatum's busy, lacy accompaniment sets up a kind of rhythmic counterpoint which actually is more like a continuation of his solo. The effect is somewhat like a thousand satellites whirling around a slower-moving planet; or, to put it another way, Webster, because of his uncluttered style, is like the central design in a complex mosaic. Also, there is a very satisfying kind of relaxation and poise that pervades all these performances.

My One and Only Love continues the reflective mood set by the preceding track. However, Tatum's insistence on playing the melody along with Webster is a little like an accompanist expecting the singer to forget the melody—certainly superfluous when Ben Webster is doing the "singing."

My Ideal is played slightly faster than the other two ballads and displays a more sensitive Tatum. He plays some fantastic things with Ben, and occasionally has an almost Erroll Garner-like feeling, but much more refined. Red Callender's bass and Bill Douglass' brushes accomplish the nearly impossible task of blending with Tatum and Webster while never hindering them.

Side 2 opens with a delicious version of *Gone With the Wind* played at a walking ballad tempo. Art's two opening choruses are extremely absorbing, featuring some interplay between left and right hands that far outdistances anything I've heard before or since in jazz piano. Ben Webster's dramatic entrance is like a beautiful surprise—what a sound—and what time!

Have You Met Miss Jones is quite different from any of the overjazzy versions I've heard others do. It is played as a ballad, much slower than usual. This allows Tatum and Webster to savor and make full use of the lovely chord changes in this Rodgers and Hart classic. When played too fast, it often takes on the quality of a musical obstacle course. Art makes it sound as if his way is the only way. Ben's role on this track is confined to one gorgeous statement of the melody.

Night and Day is Ben Webster's. Tatum opens the piece with a diffuse and overbusy chorus that is rhythmically a bit tense and stylistically stiff. Ben steps in and straightens everybody up by preaching his statements with a relaxed and elegant sense of time. *Night and Day* becomes almost like a loping blues (yet never becomes overfunky) due to Ben's blues-tinged line. Also drummer Bill Douglass uses sticks behind Ben and comes very close to sounding like a Sid Catlett or a Kenny Clarke, a tailor-made sound for Ben. The contrast (no sticks anywhere else in the album) is stunning. Art, however, sounds almost mechanical in his solos on this tune.

Art Tatum and Ben Webster represent to me a kind of romanticism in jazz which has now itself become classic. Theirs is an artistry rarely matched in any era of jazz. The kind of maturity and depth of their expression is much too scarce today.

The Art Tatum–Buddy DeFranco Quartet is another matter entirely. The only thing that DeFranco seems to have in common with Tatum (on this record, at least) is that he can play the clarinet almost as fast as Tatum can play the piano. Musically, this fact proves nearly fatal. Whereas Ben Webster and Tatum provided each other with a kind of rhythmic counterpoint (slow line against a fast line), DeFranco and Tatum get to sounding like a runaway alarm clock. Admittedly, *what* and even, *how* to play in the face of a musical avalanche like Tatum is no small problem, but technical competition is not the answer. DeFranco seems trapped by Tatum's virtuosity, and Tatum is affected by DeFranco's. What results is some brilliant technical improvising—but little melodic or rhythmic development. It's a little like watching two magicians expose all their tricks in public. And rabbits are coming out of hats on every tune.

The album opens with *Deep Night* and is quite pleasant until DeFranco and Tatum start practicing exercises together. Note Art's Garner-like left hand behind DeFranco.

On *This Can't Be Love,* the rhythm is not together, and there is a slight pull between Callender and Douglass. Good DeFranco—but his jazzy bop clichés don't fit too well in this context. The fours exchanged by clarinet and piano have a certain fascination, like watching a juggling act and waiting for someone to drop something—but of course no one ever does.

Memories of You is very stiff with innumerable clarinet and piano arpeggios and few melodies—none of which are memorable except the tune itself.

Once in a While is undistinguished except for some fairly settled Tatum statements and deft harmonic shifts. Side 2 opens with a nervous, foggy *Foggy Day* which does have some beautiful Tatum. The clarinet and piano on this track reminds me of an old Decca 78 called *With Plenty of Money and You* which sported some pretty funny Marshall Royal clarinet and a fantastic spontaneous descending run in double thirds by Royal and Tatum. Of course, Art washed the whole band away on that one.

Makin' Whoopee is about the best collaboration on the album. It has a worked-out figure on the melody (a descending chromatic chord thing) that comes off very well. Also, De Franco plays more straightforwardly here and is less mechanical. And Tatum ate up the fast-moving changes on this piece.

You're Mine You is a relaxed but innocuous-sounding performance with a Muzak-like feel. Both Tatum and DeFranco concentrate on technical matters and communicate little. *Lover Man* is much better. DeFranco plays his most arresting solo on the album—it is almost entirely in the lower register and seems to blend better with the piano. Although his ideas are mostly "chord conscious," he plays with considerable feeling, and Tatum actually settles into some beautifully spaced accompaniment, proving he *could* subordinate himself when he felt like it. Art's solo following Buddy's is masterful. This album, however, is useful mainly as a display of impeccable instrumental technique and craftsmanship—which is, in itself, a kind of artistry.

The Tatum-Carter-Bellson trio is still another matter. The sound or timbre of alto sax, piano, and drums is difficult for me to enjoy no matter how good the players. In this case, I find Benny Carter's sound rather objectionable. I have been a long-time admirer of his imaginative and tasteful playing and writing, but on this record he creates a kind of romanticism that is not convincing. He brings to mind Johnny Hodges who, however, is so completely rhapsodic a player that he creates his own point of reference. But Carter has obviously been deeply affected by Charlie Parker, and thereby has added an eclectic quality to his own work. Specifically, his lush sound doesn't seem to match his sometimes sardonic melodic ideas. Hodges, however, remains beautifully intact—a true unabashed dramatic romantic—the "Lily Pons" (to quote Bird) of the alto. I have always preferred Carter's trumpet playing to his alto.

Blues in C: Four magnificent choruses by Tatum start what promises to be a great record. Tatum proves here how masterful and towering a blues player he was, and reveals a lyricism and melodic gift that was too often buried under his barrage of technique. After Tatum's choruses, Bellson and Carter could have gone home because any further comment would have been redundant. Unfortunately, Carter breaks the spell with some very pale blues playing. Bellson switches from impeccable brushes to sticks which sound very plodding and metallic, due mostly to the absence of bass which, despite Tatum's all-time champion left hand, tends to make the drums sound isolated and noisy. The brushes, however, are effective throughout the album. Tatum saves Carter and Bellson from banality by returning with more great blues to finish a side that runs the gamut from mediocrity to greatness.

A Foggy Day doesn't compare with the DeFranco version but has good Carter and scintillating Tatum. *You're Mine You* is just too too sweet for me, and Carter's alto fairly drips with the nectar of something. Tatum's piano solo is different from the one with DeFranco—both are fine. Side 2 opens with an exciting *Undecided*. The first few choruses remind me of someone in a canoe fighting the rapids while being carried downstream to the falls—Carter is in the canoe and Tatum is the rapids. However, it sounds good and the interplay between the two is one of the high spots in the album. *Under a Blanket of Blue,* however, almost falls under a blanket of corn.

The album closes with *Makin' Whoopee*—great Tatum, but the alto-drums sound has worn me down to closing this review.

This series is an important one, though it is very inconsistent, and for recording Webster and Tatum together (to say nothing of the fantastic eleven LPs of solo Tatum) Norman Granz deserves our gratitude.

Norman Granz is to be congratulated for putting Art Tatum's name on all the album sleeves. It's always nice to know who the piano player is.

Jazz in the Twenties:
Garvin Bushell

by Nat Hentoff

Probably no better evidence of the impact of the New Orleans jazz—at least the New Orleans jazz of King Oliver and Louis Armstrong—has ever been put on paper than that which Garvin Bushell gave in the course of his reminiscences. His words also put a great deal of jazz history into perspective.

Bushell is now—very actively—a professional musician and teacher in New York. He has been bassoonist with the Radio City Music Hall Orchestra and Chicago Civic Orchestra. In jazz, he replaced clarinetist Omer Simeon in the Wilbur De Paris band upon the former's death in 1959.

GARVIN BUSHELL WAS born in Springfield, Ohio, September 25, 1902. Both his mother and father were singers and voice teachers. An uncle played clarinet in a circus band. Bushell grew up in Springfield until 1919 when he settled in New York.

One of the early Springfield bands he remembers was the Willis and Wormack unit which included tenor saxophonist Milton Senior. "He was about the first tenor saxophone anyone in that area had heard. He eventually joined the McKinney Cotton Pickers. When I got to New York, I was told about Nappy Lee, who was said to have been the first saxophonist there, about 1910.

"We didn't call the music jazz when I was growing up," Bushell says, "except for the final tag of a number. After the cadence was closed, there'd be a one-bar break and the second bar was the tag—5, 6, 5, 1. Sol, la, sol, do. Da da—da DUM!

That was called the jazz. The first time I saw the word was on Earl Fuller's record of *Oh Miss Liza Jane,* around 1916. The label said Earl Fuller's Jass band. Around the same year I also heard a song that was called *The Jazz Dance.*

"Ragtime piano was the major influence in that section of the country. Everybody tried to emulate Scott Joplin. The change began to come around 1912 to 1915 when the four-string banjo and saxophone came in. The players began to elaborate on the melodic lines; the harmony and rhythm remained the same. The parade music in Springfield was played by strictly march bands, but there was instrumental ragtime—and improvisation—in the dance halls.

"I started on piano when I was six and continued for four years. I took up the clarinet at thirteen. Another uncle was a pianist, a devotee of Scott Joplin, and *Maple Leaf Rag* was one of the first things I heard. People then were also playing the fast western, what later came to be called boogie woogie. It meant a fast bass, and it was said to have come out of Texas.

"We first heard instrumental ragtime in the circus bands which usually had about fourteen men—brass, clarinets and rhythm. They were Negro bands; the players improvised; and they played blues. They traveled all over the country, but the men in the band were mostly from Florida, Georgia, Tennessee, Louisiana. I don't know how my uncle got in there. I don't know when they started, but in 1912 my uncle was in his thirties and he'd been playing in circus bands nearly all his life."

Bushell started to go to Wilberforce University and during the summer vacation he played in tents and theaters as part of the band for *Ol' Kentuck'.* "In the shows, we played and improvised on pop tunes and all of Scott Joplin. Everybody played Scott differently. The main theme would be stated, but then everybody did little things of his own."

Leaving Wilberforce, Bushell went to New York in 1919 to stay. "The Negro dance bands I heard were often from thirty to fifty pieces. They played dance music at places like the New Star Casino on 107th Street and Lexington and at the

Manhattan Casino, now Rockland Palace. There were sometimes twenty men playing bandolins, a combination of the
banjo and violin that was plucked. Among the leading con-
ductors were John C. Smith, Allie Ross (who later conducted
Blackbirds), Happy Rhone, and Ford Dabney who had been
in it from the beginning and was much bigger than Jim
Europe.

"They played pop and show tunes. The saxophone was not
very prominent as a solo instrument, but the trumpet, clarinet
and trombone were. The soloists, especially the trumpet players, improvised, and those trumpet players used a whole series
of buckets and cuspidors for effects. The bands played fox-trot
rhythm and still adhered to the two-beat rhythmic feel. The
jazz bands, however, that I'd heard in Springfield, or had
heard about, played in four. The Creole Band with Freddie
Keppard and Sidney Bechet had come to New York around
1915, and I was told they played in four. In fact, Tony Spargo
with the Original Dixieland Jazz Band was about the only jazz
player I heard doing it in two. I remember I went to hear
that band at Reisenweber's. I had to stand at the back door
with the dishwashers. I also know that in early vaudeville—
1920-21—everybody played four beats.

"The top jazzman around 1919-20 was Jack Hatten, a
trumpet player. He had been in New York most of his life.
He played with a lot of power and a lot of flutter-tonguing.
He was very exciting. Yet his playing and that of the other
New York musicians of the time was different than the playing of men in Chicago, St. Louis, Texas and New Orleans.
New York 'jazz' then was nearer the ragtime style and had
less blues. There wasn't an eastern performer who could
really play the blues. We later absorbed how from the southern musicians we heard, but it wasn't original with us. We
didn't put that quarter-tone pitch in the music the way the
Southerners did. Up North we leaned to ragtime conception—
a lot of notes.

"Small dance bands played in cabarets like the Orient on
135th Street between Lenox and Fifth Avenues. It was a
characteristic gutbucket joint, and it was there that Mamie

Smith found her band. The instrumentation in the place was trumpet, trombone, clarinet, piano, drums, and sometimes saxophone. The trombone player, Dope Andrews, was Charlie Shavers' uncle. He had the style they called tailgate later on, but there was more beauty and control of tone in his work than in George Brunis', for example. All of Harlem had bands like that; if they couldn't get a clarinet, they used a saxophone. There was Jerry Preston's at 135th near Lenox; Leroy's at 135th and Fifth down in the cellar where all but one of them were. Edmund's with Ethel Waters (around 1921) was at 133rd and Fifth; it was there Ted Lewis met a cabdriver named 'Sipi. The cabdrivers were still wearing big plug hats, and Ted got the idea from him of incorporating it into his act.

"Most cabarets had a five-piece band and seven or eight singers. The singer would sing one chorus at each table and would make every table in the joint. If you didn't know the song when she started, you would by the time she'd completed her rounds. The pianists could improvise very well; for one thing, they got a lot of practice, working from 9:00 P.M. to 6:00 A.M. After each singer-entertainer, the band would play a dance number.

"My first year in New York I was a clerk, drove a truck, and was an elevator operator. On Sundays I rehearsed with a band from Florida. The way they played reminded me of my uncle's work in the circus band. They played real blues.

"Gradually, the New York cabarets began to hear more of the real pure jazz and blues by musicians from Florida, South Carolina, Georgia, Louisiana, etc. What they played was more expressive than had been heard in New York up to that time.

"Most of the Negro population in New York then had either been born there or had been in the city so long they were fully acclimated. They were trying to forget the traditions of the South; they were trying to emulate the whites. You couldn't deliver a package to a Negro's front door. You had to go down to the cellar door. And Negroes dressed to go to work. They changed into work clothes when they got there. You usually weren't allowed to play blues and boogie woogie in the average Negro middle-class home. That music sup-

posedly suggested a low element. And the big bands with the
violins, flutes, and piccolos didn't play them either. Like when
I was in Russia and suggested we do *The Volga Boatmen,* but
they said they wanted to forget that.

"You could only hear the blues and real jazz in the gutbucket cabarets where the lower class went. The term 'gutbucket' came from the chitterlings bucket. Chitterlings are the
guts of a hog and the practice used to be to take a bucket to
the slaughter house and get a bucket of guts. Therefore, anything real low-down was called gutbucket. So far as I know
the term was used in St. Louis, Kansas City, New York, Kentucky, Tennessee, many places.

"They improvised in the cabarets and what they played had
a different timbre from the big dance bands. What the white
man in New York called the blues, however, was just more
ragtime. The real blues used a special melodic line together
with a way of playing in between the quarter-tones like the
Irish cadences and the Indian quarter-tones combined with the
Negro's repetition of melody. And Indian music, incidentally,
also has a repetitive beat.

"I think the influence on jazz of the American Indians has
been underestimated. There were plenty of Indians back of our
house in Springfield, and part of my family is Indian. There
were Indians all through the South, Southeast and Southwest
—the Carolinas, Tennessee, Kentucky, Florida, Virginia,
Louisiana. When the slaves ran away, Indians would often
take them in because the Indians hated the white man too.
How do you think there came to be so many Negroes with
Indian blood?

"By the Irish cadence I mean the 1 5 4 5 7 1 sequence that
was somewhat like the blues. There were a lot of Irish in the
South.

"Now, about the piano music in New York around 1920.
I remember Alberta Simmons. She was in her thirties, and was
one of the first pianists I'd heard who played a style that
sounded a little different. I hadn't heard James P. yet. She
seemed to use fewer notes, was more expressive, and had
more drive. It was ragtime, but it was definitely her version of

it. She played a swinging bass line; tenths seemed the dominant pattern. It wasn't a walking bass.

"Then I heard Willie the Lion, James P., Willie Gant and
Freddie Tonsil. Fats at that time—the latter part of the twenties—wasn't in their class. They wouldn't let him play.

"Willie the Lion played more ragtime than James P. Johnson. James P. was cleaner and more inventive, as those early
QRS piano rolls demonstrate. He played things that were very
close to what pianists in Ohio and the West were doing. He
was getting away too from the ragtime of Joplin, adding to
what he retained, and expressing *himself*. The major influence on all of them was Abba Labba. He and Tonsil never
took a steady job. Abba Labba would come in and play thirty
minutes, cut everybody, and go out. They both dressed well
all the time.

"An important piano influence came out of Baltimore.
Players like Eubie Blake, Madison Reed, Edgar Dow were
early exponents of ragtime and came to New York. They
played modified ragtime—technically and musically more than
Joplin had done. The important banjo players came out of
Baltimore too.

"James P., due to the influence of Abba Labba and his own
capacity, was one of the few great pianists in New York.
Fats came to be another. When you heard James P. at his best,
that was Abba Labba, except that James P., who had studied,
played with a little more finesse and taste. When Ellington
came to New York with Elmer Snowden's band, he was playing like James P. He'd apparently heard the QRS rolls.

"Abba Labba used tenths in the bass, and he could swing.
They called it 'shout' in those days from the church when the
Baptist minister would start preaching and the congregation
would get all worked up emotionally. Negro church music had
great influence on jazz. They sang the blues in church; the
words were religious, but it was blues. They often had a
drummer and a trumpet player. You can still hear it in a
church like the one at Eighth Avenue and 123rd Street. The
Negro carried his troubles to church and talked to God about
them."

It was Bushell who took Fats Waller with him into vaudeville in 1922. Before that Bushell's first job in vaudeville had
been with singer Clarence Potter in the latter part of 1920.
"He did Harry Lauder songs. He was real dark but looked like
Lauder. He wore kilts in the act, but he was born on the East
Side and had a typical Brooklyn accent. There was nothing
Negro about him except his color. In those days, Negro instrumentalists were secondary in show business. The whites
wanted to hear the Negroes sing.

"My first recording date was in 1921 as part of a band
backing Daisy Martin for Okeh. We got $30 for two sides;
didn't matter how long it took to cut them; and we had to
wait months for the money. She was a singer—not a blues
singer—with a northern accent. In the band was Gus Aiken
on trumpet and Jake Frazier trombone, among others.

"Speaking of trombone reminds me that another influence
on northern musicians were the Jenkins Orphanage Bands out
of Charleston, South Carolina. They started going around the
country in 1910, and went to Europe in 1913. It was a swinging brass band—like one of those circus bands—that would
play in the street and then the hat would be passed. The bass
drum played four beats and the baritone horns would take
solos like trombones.

"By and large, the Negro musicians from the Southeast
were technically better than the musicians from the Southwest
and Louisiana. I except the New Orleans creole players. When
I hear youngsters trying to emulate the sound of the New Orleans players, I wonder if they realize that those men were
doing the best they could but weren't doing all they *wanted* to
on their instruments. I will say though that the musicians from
the Southeast—Virginia and Baltimore, etc.—had the blues
feeling but not the soul of the players from Louisiana, Texas
and Mississippi.

"I began to record with Mamie Smith in 1921. I lived back
of Perry Bradford's house; he heard me practicing one day,
and asked me if I wanted to make some records. He was
Mamie's manager. Up to then, I'd kept doing vaudeville. I
played in *Ol' Kentuck',* a book show, at 14th Street. We did

three shows a day and before each show, we went out front to ballyhoo. We played on the stage and improvised. We didn't have any saxophones; we did have three clarinets, tuba, three trumpets, two trombones, two upright baritone horns, and two drums (bass and snare).

"Mamie Smith wasn't like Bessie. Bessie was the real Mc-Coy. She didn't get in between the tones the way Bessie did. I soon went out on tour with Mamie, and Bubber Miley was in the band. Bubber replaced Johnny Dunn, the original trumpet player with Mamie. It was Dunn who first took a bathroom plunger and used it as a mute. When we were in Chicago, Bubber and I would go to the Dreamland and hear King Oliver every night. Bubber got his growling from Oliver. Before hearing Oliver, he never growled. That's where Bubber changed his style and began using his hand over the tin mute that used to come with all cornets. It was hearing Oliver that did it."

On the Road

"We went on the road with Mamie Smith in 1921. When we got to Chicago, Bubber Miley and I went to hear King Oliver at the Dreamland every night." Louis was not yet in the band, but Baby and Johnny Dodds were—together with Lil Armstrong and Honore Dutrey.

"It was the first time I'd heard New Orleans jazz to any advantage and I studied them every night for the entire week we were in town. I was very much impressed with their blues and their sound. The trumpets and clarinets in the East had a better 'legitimate' quality, but their sound touched you more. It was less cultivated but more expressive of how the people felt. Bubber and I sat there with our mouths open.

"We talked with the Dodds brothers. They felt very highly about what they were playing as though they knew they were doing something new that nobody else could do. I'd say they did regard themselves as artists, in the sense we use the term today.

"I remember that when Tommy Ladnier joined us in the Fletcher Henderson band in 1925, he clearly had the feeling that nobody could play trumpet like the guys in New Orleans.

"Before I went to Dreamland every night, I'd hear a New Orleans band that played at a lot where a carnival was taking place. It was the Thomas New Orleans Jug Band, and was more primitive than Oliver's. It included trumpet, clarinet, trombone, a jug, bass, drums, guitar. It had the same beat as Oliver's—what we called in Ohio the 'shimmy' beat. They played four beat—as did Oliver."

Mamie's troupe went on to Kansas City in that year of 1921. "We played the 12th Street Theater and that's where I first met Coleman Hawkins. They had added a saxophone to play the show with us in the pit. He was ahead of everything I ever heard on that instrument. It might have been a C melody he was playing then. Anyway, he was about fifteen years old—I remember that because one night we went to his mother's house in St. Joseph and asked her to let him go with us, and she said, 'No, he's only a baby; he's only fifteen.' He was really advanced. He read everything without missing a note. I haven't heard him miss a note yet in thirty-seven years. And he didn't—as was the custom then—play the saxophone like a trumpet or clarinet. He was also running changes then, because he'd studied the piano as a youngster.

"As for soul," Garvin continued, "he had soul, but it was less on the blues side. He had a lot of finesse.

"We heard music at several cabarets in Kansas City. I wasn't impressed. We felt we had the top thing in the country, so the bands didn't impress me. It may be, now that I look back, that I underestimated them. The bands in the Midwest then had a more flexible style than the eastern ones. They were built on blues bands. They had also done more with saxophones in Kansas City. Most bands included a saxophone. They just played the blues, one after another, in different tempos. It was good, but after we'd heard Oliver and Dodds, they were our criterion. I also heard blues singers in Kansas City, just like Joe Turner sings, and they did impress me."

Bushell returned in his conversation to Chicago, because he'd been asked about Jo Jones's contention that the musicians of the Southwest generally played with more drive. "I'd say

that all those blues bands did play with power, with everything
forte, and so did the bands from New Orleans. Joe Oliver,
however, never did have the power Freddie Keppard had.
Freddie could make the glasses on the bar jar—they'd bet
money on that. Freddie was more exciting than Joe. Joe played
things that hit you inside. Joe also had that lip shake or trill—
New Orleans trumpeters created it—that could make people
jump out of their seats.

"Freddie was in the band at the Sunset. There were about
twelve men, including Flutes Morton on flute and piccolo.
He's still in Detroit, and even then, he improvised jazz on the
flute. He sounded great, and still does. He had a big, loud
powerful sound on the flute—much louder than the guys get
today, and he still has it. The band had two trumpets, and
even though they were twelve, I'd say they often improvised
collectively. They could read—or some of them could, those
that played at the Vendome Theater. Chicago jazzmen had
the advantage in those years of having a crack at theater
music before the New York jazzmen did. They improved
their ability that way, and so could read a little better than
jazz musicians in the East.

"Fats Williams played first trumpet and Freddie did most
of the jazz solos. They played a lot of things together, but not
unison breaks the way Louis and Oliver later did. Fats and
Freddie were a better team though—more exciting.

"We were supposed to play Tulsa on that tour, but didn't
because they'd killed a lot of Negroes there. The refugees
came to Kansas City. In Detroit is where I first heard Jimmy
Harrison. Jimmy was just as unusual on trombone as Hawk
was on tenor. I'd never heard a guy before who got over the
trombone and ran changes as he did. We'd been hearing trombonists with the glissandos and the playing of one, five and
four harmony, actually doing mostly rhythm fill-ins. But
Jimmy was doing melodic things. I think that melodic style
on trombone mostly started in Indiana·or Kentucky. At least,
that's where I first heard it. They had a lot of five-piece bands
there in which the saxophone or trumpet would share the
front line with the trombone with piano, bass and drums. Fess

Williams from Kentucky had a band like that going in the early twenties. I heard them in Peoria when I was there with Ethel Waters. Anyway, because of the instrumentation, the trombone had to team with the alto, and he had to know how to move. It wasn't like the New Orleans style at all.

"Jimmy did have a lot of soul. He played everything well and with taste. I should point out again that, by and large, what they played in Louisiana and in the South in general was based primarily on the blues. In the East and Midwest, they played published things, improvised on pop tunes, and didn't do as many folk things. The musicians from the South, however, had their *own* music, and it was based on the blues."

Bushell went to work at Leroy's in New York, at 135th Street and Fifth Avenue, in 1922. The rest of the band were alumni of the Jenkins Orphanage Band from South Carolina. At various times the band included Gus Aikens, trumpet; Buddy Aikens or Jake Frazier or Geechie Fields, trombone; and Steve Wright, drums. "We were certainly influenced by New Orleans jazz by then. We played *Shake It and Break It* in typical New Orleans style. In general, by then, the Midwest had been influenced by southern players, like those from Louisiana and Texas. Some of the eastern players had been influenced by New Orleans men and also by that Jenkins Orphanage band.

"Sunday nights at Leroy's were the only times we wore tuxedoes, because on those nights, we'd play overtures. It was dress-up night in Harlem, and around midnight we'd play the *Poet and Peasant; Morning, Noon and Night,* etc.

"It was at Leroy's that I first saw piano battles. Players like Willie the Lion, James P., Fats, Willie Gant. They'd last for three or four hours. One man would play two or three choruses, and the next would slide in. Jimmy was on top most of the time. Fats was the youngest, but he was coming along. They played shouts and they also played pop tunes. You got credit for how many patterns you could create within the tunes you knew, and in how many different keys you could play. You had to know how to play in every key, because all those players had been baptized in cabarets. You never knew what kind of key the entertainer wanted.

"There'd be more controversy among the listeners than the participants. There was betting and people were ready to fight about who'd won. Jimmy played with the most originality. He'd create things the other guys hadn't thought up."

Garvin also recalls a Gabrielli-like (pre-Henry-Brant, pre-stereo) arrangement of instruments at Leroy's on occasion. "This happened only in Leroy's and I don't know how it came about, but often when we played blues, each instrument would be in a different corner. The trumpet at the far end; the clarinet in the back room, etc. You'd take a solo from where you were in the room, and then when it was time to start the ensemble, you'd come back to the bandstand.

"The Charleston was introduced in New York at Leroy's. Russell Brown came from Charleston and he did a Geeche dance they did on the Georgia Sea Islands. It was called a cut out dance. People began to say to Brown, 'Hey, Charleston, do your dance!' and they finally called it the Charleston.

"We didn't allow white people in Leroy's. The manager, Harry Pyles, said, 'They'll come in here and trouble is liable to start, so we'll just keep them out.' They were allowed in other places in Harlem though."

Also in 1922, Bushell made some recordings with Edith Wilson. "About the same style as Mamie, she wasn't like Bessie, and using Bessie as your definition, she wasn't a blues singer."

At the Lafayette Theater on 132nd Street and Seventh Avenue at that time, there was a woman's orchestra playing for the movies, the stage shows, and the Sunday concert and dance. Fletcher Henderson's wife, Bushell recalls, was on trumpet and Tyree Glenn's mother-in-law, he thinks, was on piano. "They could read jazz, but didn't improvise much. Well, we got a call to play in the pit there for the picture. I mean Johnny Dunn and his jazz band did, the band that had played behind Edith Wilson on the records. We had to improvise, because we couldn't read the music. They gave us a big score to follow the picture, and we got lost. We kept playing *Over the Hill* for *everything*—in different tempos. We were fired after the first show. Perry Bradford never let us forget that.

"Johnny Dunn was an individualist. He's the guy that made double time famous. And he introduced the wa-wa effects with the plunger. He thought differently than the other musicians. He had a lot of drive, and his sound was dynamic. Lew Leslie used him in the pits to drive the ensemble. He came from Memphis, and he played the blues so it moved you, but not as soulfully as those blues players out of Louisiana. Charlie Creath was the only non-Louisiana player I heard that played that style as well as they did, and even better. He was born in East St. Louis.

"Johnny Dunn was a very proud sort of guy. He always carried three to four hundred dollars in his pocket. He was much sought after for records and shows. He came to New York with W. C. Handy. I first saw him in 1921."

Bushell joined Ethel Waters in late fall, 1922. They made some Black Swan Records, a label owned by Harry Pace of publishers Pace and Handy. It was the first label owned by a Negro. Fletcher Henderson, who had been working as a song plugger for Pace and Handy, organized his first unit to back Ethel Waters on the Black Swan sides. Gus and Buddy Aikens were on the band; Joe Elder played tenor; and a man Bushell remembers only as Bill D. C. was on baritone saxophone, playing parts that usually would have been taken by the bass.

"Ethel Waters was a jazz singer. She didn't sing real blues; she was strictly a jazz singer. She syncopated. She'd been in cabarets all her life. She'd been influenced by the horns she'd heard and by church singing. She literally sang with a smile, and that made her sound wide and broad.

"She turned out to be an important influence. Mildred Bailey had some of Ethel; Lena Horne has a lot; and there were others. I'd say the three major influences in jazz singing have been Ethel, Louis Armstrong and Billie Holiday. Of course, in Ella Fitzgerald's case, Connie Boswell was the major influence.

"Fletcher didn't write out anything for Ethel's record dates.

You didn't have written music to back singers in those days.
The piano player did have music, and the trumpet player
would take the melody off the piano sheet. We couldn't use a
bass drum although sometimes we used the snare drum or a
wood block. Also we didn't use a bass. Therefore, when there
was no drum at all, the rhythm tended to get ragged. Then too
we'd be in awkward positions and scattered all over the place,
which would also make it hard to keep the rhythm together.
We'd spend the greater part of the day making two numbers.

"The records were 'race records,' and were bought by the
Negro population. This kind of music was strictly confined to
the race catalogue, until, for the most part, the time of Louis
Jordan. The white market did not know anything about them.

"We went on tour with Ethel, opening in Philadelphia. Jack
Johnson was on the bill with us. He'd just gotten out of
Leavenworth. He did some shadow boxing and some talking.
People just wanted to look at him.

"We stayed at a place where all the toughs lived. In those
days most musicians and performers carried a gun. In those
days a Negro didn't have much protection from the law and
so had to protect himself. We were still insulted in the streets
and couldn't always eat when we were hungry—right in New
York too. There was only one theater in Harlem with stage
shows in which I could sit downstairs, and that was the Lafayette, an all-Negro theater. Wherever there were whites, we
couldn't sit downstairs until 1927. That made us bitter.

"So in Philadelphia at the Horseshoe Hotel where we stayed,
they tried to rob me, but I pulled my gun and ran everybody
out of the room. You were supposed to have a license to carry
a gun, but nobody ever had one."

With Ethel Waters

"After Philadelphia, we went to Baltimore. At that time,
Baltimore had a great variety of jazz and many excellent performers. They came to New York in droves, and a large pro-
portion of the significant figures in early New York jazz turn
out to have come from Baltimore or near by. There were
pianists Eubie Blake, Edgar Dow, Bobby Lee, John Mitchell,

banjo, Jerry Glasgow, clarinet, etc. Chick Webb later came out of Baltimore and so did trumpeter Pike Davis.

"There was good jazz in just about every cabaret, no matter how low or cheap. They had more technique than the New York musicians; I don't know why. They were very fly, smart, creative improvisers. But they too didn't play the blues the way the musicians from the South did. Their jazz was based on ragtime piano practices, and piano ragtime influenced the way they played their horns—they tried to do what the pianists did. They also had the best banjo players in the world.

"New Orleans musicians, of course, were not the first to improvise. Perry Bradford went from Georgia to New Orleans in 1909. He says there were no technicians to speak of there then, and they didn't know much about ragtime. He claims ragtime came up the East Coast from Florida and Georgia and that when they did bring it to New Orleans, the musicians there put the blues to it.

"After Baltimore, we did one-nighters in and around Pennsylvania for about a month. I heard Joe Smith for the first time at the Grape Vine in Pittsburgh. He was out of New York, but I hadn't heard him until then. His style was similar to that of Johnny Dunn, but he had a much better sound. Joe actually played more like some of the white trumpet players. I mean that he was more lyrical and had a finer sound. Joe played for beauty rather than drive. He was a trained trumpet player; he had the right embouchure. You see, 90 per cent of the Negro musicians were self-taught. The opportunities for training were mostly for the whites, and that's why they generally had a better sound. Several Negro musicians of the time, however, had the talent and capacity to have become first-rate classical musicians—if there had been openings for them. There was Joe's brother, Russell Smith, for example, who was one of the best legitimate trumpet players in the business. Anyway, Fletcher Henderson was very impressed with Joe's sound, and he never forgot it.

"When we got to St. Louis, I heard the greatest blues player of his time—Charlie Creath. He played at Jazzland, a huge place with the bandstand up in the balcony. The bandstands in the dance halls at that time were usually near the ceiling; the musicians felt safer there. Gene Sedric, a big, fat kid was playing clarinet in his band. We were the invited guests and were asked to play.

"Creath had a Joe-Smith-like tone, but with much blues feeling and drive. He had beautiful sound and soul, and the blues were his forte. He had command of the high register too; most New Orleans players couldn't go above B flat. Tommy Ladnier, for instance. Louis Armstrong was an exception. He went up to C and D and later to F and G whenever he wanted to.

"There was great music in St. Louis then. New Orleans influences had come up the river, especially blues playing. The St. Louis musicians had a lot of originality and a great desire to broaden their music. There were many places to play, and they slept and ate music there. By contrast, the bands just out of New Orleans were limited.

"There was a battle of music and a lot of the people there said we outplayed the Creath band. In our band, Gus Aikens was a good trumpet player and his brother, Buddy, played somewhat in the style of Jimmy Harrison. He was a good legitimate trombone player and whatever he thought of, he could play.

"But Creath was a phenomenon. I've heard Tommy Ladnier say: 'When Charlie used to hit certain notes, the whores would just fall out and throw up their legs.' He made his biggest impression on women—not so much his looks as his playing. The way he played the blues mellowed you; people threw their glasses in the air. He'd hit a seventh chord and sustain it and the people fell out. He later committed suicide; a woman was involved in some way. His sister married Zutty Singleton.

"Creath didn't get to New York except maybe for a visit. Even then there was a myth about New York. A lot of groups were afraid to come here, because everything big seemed to come out of New York. Look how long Joe Oliver stayed in Chicago before he came to New York; and Louis Armstrong and Tommy Ladnier wouldn't have come if they hadn't been sent for. New Orleans people anyway believe in security; they don't usually take chances. And they're clannish; they prefer to be where other New Orleans people are.

"In Louisville, where we went next, the music was like the kind we'd heard in Peoria, the kind Fess Williams had played there. Fess was from Kentucky. It wasn't based on the blues, but was good, flexible, moderate tempo ragtime. It wasn't as corny though and they had a lot of tricks. The usual instrumentation was alto and trombone, trumpet and alto, trumpet and trombone, and rhythm section. Sometimes there were three horns in the front line. The saxophone—not the tenor though—was very popular in Indiana, Ohio, Kentucky and Tennessee. There wasn't too much clarinet.

"It was in Louisville that I ran into another kind of hazard you could meet on the road. Our show closed for a week, and there was a woman I'd met in Louisville who tried to shanghai me. She owned seven buffet flats (whorehouses), and had been giving me two to three hundred dollars a day. When the show closed, she put a razor to my throat and said, 'You're going with me.' So for four days I stayed. One morning while she was making eggs in the kitchen, I ran fifteen blocks to the railroad station. I'd had my bag packed in preparation, and ran with my clarinet case under one arm and my suitcase under the other. I hid in the men's toilet and told the porter, 'If you see a big woman, you didn't see me.' She came to the station, looking for me, but I escaped to Chicago where we were due to play the Grand Theater.

"The first day there, I met Gus Aikens and we went out to a buffet flat and stayed until four in the morning. (They called it a 'buffet flat' because they served all the liquor and food from a buffet.) As we were leaving, some white fellows crossed the street toward us. I pulled out my gun and Gus his knife. They said, 'Drop it!' I never saw so many guns in my life. They were cops. They kept us in jail for three days. Fletcher didn't know where we were, and Buster Bailey had to play my parts.

"It turned out a lot of cops had been killed in New York that year, and when they found out we were from New York, they held us until they communicated with the New York po-

lice. Buddy Aikens and Charlie Jackson, our violinist, finally
found us and we were bailed out. It took all the money I had
—about $600 or $700—to pay the bondsman, the fine, and
the lawyer. But all that saved me from that Louisville woman.
She had come to Chicago looking for me intending to kill me.
She left after two days while I was still in jail.

"That band behind Ethel, by the way, had Gus and Buddy
Aikens; Charlie Jackson; Bill D. C. on baritone sarophone;
Joe Elder, tenor; Raymond Green, xylophone and drums; and
Fletcher, piano. Like any band then that got on stage, we had
to do a specialty of some kind. So we had an act in which I
was a cop and Green was a preacher, by the way. Some of
the others were also armed. Jackson kept a .45 in his violin
case and Buddy had a .22 under his derby. When he took off
his hat, he meant business.

"Ethel was going South. Gus, Buddy, Jackson and I weren't
going. We left the band in Chicago. We had just enough
money for the four of us to get to Pittsburgh. We went to a
dance, were asked to sit in and were invited to pass the hat.
We got enough money to pay our fare to New York with
$1.50 left over. That wasn't much for food. While on the train
to New York, we started practicing. The sandwich man heard
us, and we were told by the steward, that if we'd play in the
diner, they'd feed us for free. Life on the road was like that.
There was no telling what conditions you'd have to adjust to.
Once in Illinois we slept in a church; we couldn't get a room.

"A lot of the traveling was on the T. O. B. A. 'Take Old
Bailey's Advice,' some of us called it. A man named Bailey
ran this theatrical circuit with headquarters in Atlanta. We
also called it 'Toby' and another way of spelling it out was
'Tough On Black Artists.'

"There were Negro theaters all over the South and Midwest. Many were very small former nickelodeons. They were
often dirty with dressing rooms in the cellar—except for the
biggest in Baltimore. Memphis, incidentally, was the headquarters for a lot of Negro performers.

"If a Negro musician or entertainer on the circuit was good, he came to New York, auditioned, and was put on the Independent, the Keith, Loew or Proctor circuits.

"The Negro theaters remained because Negroes couldn't go to white theaters in those towns. In some white ones, a Negro could go through the alley, up five or six flights, and sit in the gallery, above the balcony. But in those theaters he didn't get to see many Negro entertainers—and no Negro singers.

"There were local bands in the pits of the Negro theaters. They played jazz and had to improvise behind the singers. Bad notes didn't mean anything if the tempo was right.

"The tent shows played the theaters in the wintertime. These all-year-round reviews carried a comic, singer, dancer, piano, drums and maybe one horn. There were maybe thirty or forty stops for the season.

"With Ethel, we didn't bother much with T. O. B. A. We played auditoriums or big theaters whenever we could. An attraction like Mamie Smith or Ethel could do a tour and not have hardly any T. O. B. A. bookings at all.

"I never saw a white person in the T. O. B. A. theaters. The kind of music played there the whites and the 'higher class' Negroes hadn't yet accepted. They didn't want to hear the blues; the blues were 'low class.'

"The top pianist of that day in the South, by the way, was Eddie Heywood's father in Atlanta. He played in a T. O. B. A. theater there, the 88 Theater. He was modern for that day, I was told. They said Eddie played just like his father.

"Well, we were back in New York in February, 1923, and went back to Leroy's for a couple of months. Then, until October, 1923, I was part of a vaudeville act—Modern Cocktail—a singer and a dancer backed by a five-piece band—that went to the West Coast and back. The jazz on the West Coast was nothing compared to the Midwest, East and South. They were using tuba and two saxophones—not trumpet, clarinet and trombone, so far as we heard—and were trying a 'symphonic' approach to popular music. It was really ricky-tick orchestrations, and no blues.

"I then went with Adams and Robinson. Clarence Robinson, who was a singer and dancer, and I finally took the act over, and the pianist was Fats Waller. He'd been playing the organ at the Lincoln Theater on 135th and Lenox Avenue, and I asked him to join us. He was still a big kid; he used to come into the theater with an apple on a stick. The act was called Liza (she was Katie Crippen) and Her Shuffling Sextet. When Robinson and I split up, I took over the band, including Fats and Katie.

"It happened in Washington. Robinson had heard Elmer Snowden's band with Otto Hardwicke, Freddie Whetsel, Sonny Greer and Duke Ellington. He hired that band to join him on the circuit, and that's how Duke Ellington got to New York in 1923."

Don Redman, Jazz Composer-Arranger

by Frank Driggs

It has been close to twenty years since anyone has really paid much attention to the pre-modern composer and arranger. We live in the era of George Russell, Manny Albam and Gil Evans. It would seem from the recordings of the past decade that some of our greatest and most original minds have been all but forgotten: Benny Carter, Don Redman, Jesse Stone, Eddie Wilcox, Eddie Durham, and even later men like Walter Gil Fuller. For more than a decade, and for some much more, none of these men has been called upon by either major or minor firms for the quality and originality in composition and arrangement that is so necessary to sustain jazz. While the history books, and they are in many ways inadequate, have noted most of their contributions, they have done so without adequate recognition of their true significance. A series of articles may result from further research, but it is fitting to begin with the first and one of the greatest of all jazz composers-arrangers: Don Redman.

There may be a younger reader who will say, "Now, who is Don Redman?" But it is not only to him that this biography is addressed: there are many older people, followers and professionals in the field, who seem to have forgotten about Redman's talents.

Don Redman introduced arranged jazz in New York while with the Billy Paige band from Pittsburgh in 1922 and went on from there to be the jazz arranger in Fletcher Henderson's first great band, between 1924 and 1927. During those years he wrote arrangements for the Henderson library that pioneered many of the standard techniques of arrangers all dur-

ing the swing era of the middle and later thirties. In 1927 he took an average Midwestern band, McKinney's Cotton Pickers, with vague qualities of musicianship and showmanship and little individuality, and made it one of the four top jazz orchestras for the duration of his four-year stay, in competition with Fletcher Henderson's, Duke Ellington's and Alphonso Trent's. He scored some exceptional small group sides for Louis Armstrong during the same period and arranged for Paul Whiteman's and Ben Pollack's bands as well.

He formed his own orchestra late in 1931 and it was the equal in musicianship, inspiration and verve of any playing over the next several years. A series of wonderful recordings resulted. By 1940 he dropped his band and turned almost entirely to writing for others, turning out some notable hits, among them Deep Purple *for Jimmy Dorsey,* Five O'Clock Whistle *for Count Basie, and* Things Ain't What They Used to Be *for Cootie Williams. He was the first to take a big band overseas on a continental tour after World War II in 1946-47 to tremendous acclaim and upon his return continued free-lance commercial arranging. After several years he teamed with Pearl Bailey, leading a band accompanying her and writing her arrangements. Today he's still free-lancing for people like Sugar Ray Robinson, for CBS and for many transcription and record firms and still working with Pearl.*

He's always done such a professional job that hardly anyone has ever stopped to think that perhaps he has yet to realize his full potential in jazz. It would be a marvelous thing should one of the major recording firms give him the freedom they have extended to the younger arrangers and composers over the past decade.

A most welcome addition to the jazz library would be an LP from Victor and one from Columbia who hold the bulk of Don's best orchestral work. Victor has some twenty good sides of the 1938 through 1940 period, and Columbia has an even better and wider range of material from 1932 through 1937 on Brunswick, Columbia, Perfect and Vocalion dates. Only Decca in the Brunswick "Harlem Jazz" set (no longer in print) has ever issued anything by Redman; that was the su-

perior Chant of the Weed *and* Shakin' the African *from late
1931, just as the band was organizing. Victor's last Cotton
Pickers collection was ten-inch LPT 24.*

*Regardless of reissue, let's hope that Don Redman is plucked
out of the bland commercial atmosphere that he has been a
part of for such a long time and given an LP without strings
attached so that he can give us some more of the jazz that he
still has up his sleeve.*

F. D.

*What follows is Don Redman's story, told to Frank Driggs
in Redman's own words.*

I WAS A child prodigy you know. From the age of three I was
performing in public. I didn't have much of any kind of in-
struction, just started in playing. By the time I was fourteen
I was playing music regularly. In grade school I had charge of
the number-three band. They had several different bands, all
graded according to their ability. After a while I moved up to
be in charge of the number-two band, but I never did get to
the number-one spot, although at that time I was playing all
the instruments, especially cornet. I started working around
town (Piedmont, West Virginia) with a bunch of local musicians, none of whom ever left town.

Actually, I began writing arrangements for some of the
touring road shows that came to town, when I was in my
teens. Our band was only seven pieces and we'd back up the
acts, and occasionally I'd do an original tune. Being a country
boy I didn't know much about copyrighting songs and lost
Prohibition Blues that way. It was a pretty big hit later on.

After I finished high school I went to Storer College in
Harper's Ferry and majored in music, graduating in three
years. Then I joined Billy Paige's Broadway Syncopators from
Pittsburgh and spent the next year or two with them. They
were very popular around Pittsburgh in the early twenties, and
were considered, along with Louis Deppe's band, as the top
band from that part of the country. Earl Hines came to town

about the same time I did, and he was great even then. He joined Deppe's band.

Jim Fellman was our pianist and he was great. Earl got something from him then. Fellman couldn't read and he died by the time Billy Paige left Pittsburgh, so we sent to Boston to get Roy Cheeks. He's still around New York today, playing mostly exclusive supper clubs and that sort of thing, because he had a fair voice, just enough to get by with as an entertainer.

Bart Howard, out of Toledo, was another fine pianist around Pittsburgh then, and so was "Toodle-oo" Johnson, who played in all the sporting houses. He was a little hunchbacked guy, about the same size as Chick Webb, but he could really play in that style. Deppe's band got by because of Earl and himself, although both Joe Smith and his brother Russell were with him for a while. Deppe was a terrific singer and did some numbers with McKinney later on, when I was there; I remember Ben Bernie's theme, *It's a Lonesome Old Town*. He's out in Chicago now, doing mostly church work, but his voice is badly cracked. He was very big in show business back then, doing some of the "Great Day" shows and introducing *Without a Song*.

Our band became so popular that Paul Specht picked us up and brought us to New York under his banner. We were the first to play arrangements in New York and did very well for a while, but we broke up pretty quickly.

I wasn't in town but a few days after that when I got a phone call to come and make a record date for Emerson. I went down to the studio and found Fletcher Henderson on the date. There was a band there, but it wasn't his band. He didn't have a band then, but was kind of a house pianist for Emerson and he worked behind some of the singers like Edith Wilson. On this date, Florence Mills was singing. Fletcher had an in with W. C. Handy who knew him from the South. Handy had a publishing company, Handy and Pace, and also Black Swan records, and Fletcher was house man for them also.

On the Florence Mills date the band consisted of Howard

Scott and Elmer Chambers on trumpets, George Brashear on trombone, Fletcher, Charlie Dixon on banjo, and myself. I even played piano on some of them, and there were no drums, because they hadn't learned how to record them. I remember accompanying Baby Benbow on piano on one session. She was pretty popular at that time.

By the time we graduated to Columbia we added a man here and there. Coleman Hawkins came in from Mamie Smith's band, and Billy Fowler came in on baritone. Joe Smith made some of the early dates too, before he left and went out of town.

Columbia's studios were on Columbus Circle where the Coliseum building is now. On one date we were to make some instrumentals for them with the band, even though it still didn't belong to anyone. After we recorded that day, someone told us about an offer for an audition at the Nora Bayes Theater (Little Theater) on 44th Street in Shubert Alley. We didn't want to go because we didn't have any arrangements or any repertoire. The guy who told us about the job said we ought to use the same tunes we recorded that day. We didn't even have all the stuff with us, just some of the blues things we made with the singer. I remember we made the *Dicty Blues* that day, and went down and auditioned with that stuff and got the job, which was for the Club Alabam'. That was the Cotton Club of that era.

When we went into the Club we added Kaiser Marshall on drums, Ralph Escudero on tuba, Allie Ross, a violinist, as front man, and Heard (I forget his first name), a trombonist and a nice arranger. We decided to make Fletcher the leader because he was a college graduate and presented a nice appearance. We became popular right away and used to broadcast over WHN all the time. Edith Wilson was on the bill with us and she wanted Hawk to come out on stage and play the blues behind her. He didn't mind, but he wanted to get paid for it. George White was the manager of the club and he told Fletcher to fire Hawk. Since we were doing terrific business and had gotten other offers from Roseland and other places, we decided we'd give notice to a man if Hawk was fired. We moved over to Roseland and from there on we were the top band in New York. No one rivaled us then.

When I was in Pittsburgh I'd heard a lot about Louis Armstrong, and Fletcher wanted to get another good man in the band, so we got him away from Joe Oliver in 1924. Kaiser Marshall had a car and brought us downtown to meet Louis. He was big and fat and wore high-top shoes with hooks in them and long underwear down to his socks. When I got a load of that, I said to myself, who in the hell is this guy? It can't be Louis Armstrong. But when he got on the bandstand it was a different story. Joe Oliver sent along his book of tunes when Louis joined the band, and right away I picked out *Dippermouth Blues* as a framework for Louis. We called it *Sugarfoot Stomp* and it used to ·go over very big. In fact, Louis, his style, and his feeling, changed our whole idea about the band musically.

We used to have battles of music with Sam Lanin all the time. He was at one end of the hall and we were at the other, and in the middle was the arrangers' table. All the time both bands were there, the arrangers' table used to be full. We were always making up new arrangements trying to top theirs. They had Red Nichols, Miff Mole and Vic Berton in their band. We used to tear off the top of any new arrangement and put a fake title on it to throw them off . . . we'd be trying to see what the other was playing. They had one arrangement that really used to break up the crowds, and Fletcher sent his men all over town trying to get copies. They called it *Hole in the Wall* and we didn't find out for a month that it was really *Milenburg Joys* that they were playing. We had the best musicians in town playing with us then.

We needed another reedman and I wanted to get Vance Dixon in the band, but he didn't want to leave Virginia, so I sent for Milt Senior who was with the Cotton Pickers. When he wouldn't come to New York, Louis suggested we get Buster Bailey out of King Oliver's band. He joined us the night he hit town, and we featured him on numbers like *Dizzy Fingers* and *Tiger Rag,* and he broke up the place. Jimmy Dorsey was there that night and he came every night after that.

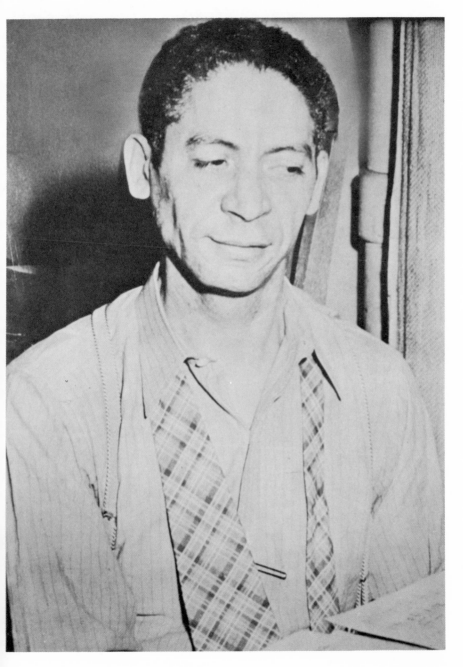

JELLY ROLL MORTON

MINOR HALL, HONORE DUTREY, KING OLIVER, LIL HARDIN, DAVID JONES, JOHNNY DODDS, JIMMY PALAO, ED GARLAND. California, 1921.

In the three years I was with Fletcher, the only other one to make any arrangements was Coleman Hawkins, and he'd bring in about two or three a year, because he was lazy. He did a terrific job on *Singin' in the Rain*. The only other arranger was Ken Macomber and he'd do the new hits from the Broadway shows which we had to do to satisfy the customers. After I left, Fletcher started writing, and Charlie Dixon did some too.

I wasn't getting but twenty-five dollars an arrangement in those days, until Paul Whiteman gave me a blanket order for twenty arrangements at one hundred dollars apiece, and paid me the two thousand dollars right then and there. I was out of this world then, because the usual twenty-five dollars was all anyone was getting. I did *Whiteman Stomp* for both him and Fletcher, as well as several others he recorded. Fats Waller sold Fletcher nine arrangements including *Henderson Stomp* for a dozen hamburgers.

Louis became pretty dissatisfied because he got all the hard work, all the high stuff, and Joe Smith was the pet of both Fletcher and his wife. When he left, we got Tommy Ladnier. He was a terrific soloist, but he couldn't read too well, and he had to go out and learn his parts. He was especially good on the low-down blues, I thought even better than Louis.

Fletcher's wife had been married to Russell Smith, and he taught her to play trumpet. He had the beautiful tone and was the first chair man. She used to play just like him, and whenever he was out for some reason, she used to do the first chair parts, and she did them well, too. She was in back of Fletcher in practically everything he ever did.

Around New York there were many good musicians then. When I first came to town, Johnny Dunn was *the* trumpet player. He was a terrific salesman for himself and he was the first one I knew to use any kind of mute. He'd set himself up in a show with just himself and dancers. His valet would come followed by all sorts of trunks, and I used to wonder if they were all for one man. The valet would set them up against the wall, and in them would be all kinds of pots and pans, flowerpots, cans, anything to get a different sound out of his horn. I

think he was an influence on Duke because he really did get a
lot of sounds out of his horn. In those days he used to be with
pit bands, and nobody was featured from a pit band, but him.
I don't think he was much of a musician technically. He later
went overseas with Florence Mills and the *Blackbirds*.

There was another guy around town called Brassfield who
was a sensational sax player then. He couldn't read a thing,
nothing. Nobody else could play his horn, and his mouthpiece
would be on the horn so that it would be a half note out of
tune. When he played it, it would be in tune. Everybody used
to marvel at him.

June Clark and Jimmy Harrison used to have a band uptown at Connor's on 135th Street, and all of us used to practically live in there. June was very good, but he couldn't read.
They used to play some great jazz together. When Jimmy was
in Fletcher's band later on, he was the best around.

Benny Carter's cousin, Cuba Bennett, was another terrific
trumpet player, and all he needed was a little more experience
to really make it.

In those days nobody had the knack of picking out talent
better than Chick Webb. He picked Johnny Hodges, Bobby
Stark, John Trueheart, Don Kirkpatrick and, of course, Ella,
and many others.

I had gotten an offer from Bill McKinney to run his band
for him, but since I was getting pretty good money from
Fletcher and was well regarded, I decided not to take another offer until it was better than what I was getting then.
We used to work the Graystone Ballroom in Detroit all the
time, while McKinney was at the Arcadia and he would come
over and tell me when he got in a position to make me the
kind of offer I wanted, would I take the job? I told him I
would.

When I joined the Cotton Pickers they were pretty much of
a novelty outfit of around ten pieces. John Nesbitt, an exceptional trumpet player, was doing all their arranging, and he
knew his music, but he was copying everybody else's records.
They had been known as the Synco Septette for years, ever
since they built their reputation at the Green Mill in Toledo.

I told Nesbitt to stop copying others' work because he had enough ability to do his own stuff, and he eventually did turn out some fine things for the Cotton Pickers.

He loved Bix and used to play a lot like him in his own way. I'm thinking of doing one of his things this year, *Will You Won't You Be My Baby?*

The Cotton Pickers wasn't a solo band, but a unit. I was trying to get a sound and a style a little different than the other bands. Out in Detroit we really had that town sewed up, and the people used to be wild over our stuff. The band became so popular at the Graystone that Jean Goldkette (who owned the Graystone and backed the band) wouldn't let me take all the men to New York with me when we got the offer from Victor to record. That's one of the reasons why there were so many different guys on those sessions.

While I was directing the Cotton Pickers we used to have Mondays off and I'd go to Chicago for some sessions with Louis Armstrong. He was featured with Carroll Dickerson's band at the Savoy Ballroom, and took a small group from the band to record for Okeh. At the same time I was doing some arranging on the side for Ben Pollack's great band with Benny Goodman and Jimmy McPartland.

The Cotton Pickers were so popular that we battled bands all over the country. I first met Count Basie when we went to Kansas City and battled Bennie Moten at 15th and Paseo. That's when I first heard *Moten Swing,* which is nothing but the "go" chorus from *You're Driving Me Crazy.* They also used to do a terrific job on *I Want a Little Girl* and I'm surprised they never recorded it. They really had a fine band and they used to give us a lot of trouble.

We went to Hollywood to play Sebastian's Cotton Club after Louis in 1930. The first week there I thought we were dead ducks, and nobody could figure out why. We didn't begin to click until Sunday night when all the bands were off and the hotels were closed. The musicians packed the joint and really put us over. They told us that nobody had heard a band playing arrangements up until that time, and after that it was smooth sailing. We played to a packed house for seven weeks.

There had been a lot of dissension building up in the band, not among the musicians, but with management, which was McKinney and Charlie Horvath, the manager of the Graystone. The boys wanted a raise, because their name was a big attraction then, but they were turned down. On that trip to the coast the management brought the announcer from Detroit and his whole family and a couple of other guys and their families along on vacation paid for with Cotton Pickers' money. The guys in the band couldn't get a five-dollar raise! That was it.

When we got back to Detroit, I got word that Tommy Rockwell and Sam Smith wanted me to take a band into Connie's Inn in New York. McKinney knew I was getting ready to leave and that I wanted to take some of his men with me. He told me I could take anyone I wanted except Cuba Austin and Billy Taylor the bass player. I picked Prince Robinson, Ed Cuffee, Ed Inge and Buddy Lee. They gave Cuffee and Prince a raise so they stayed on. I heard that Horace Henderson had a school band at Wilberforce that was very good but out of work, so I got to them and took six men plus Horace and got the band together.

I barely had the band organized when Irving Mills had gotten me a recording contract with Brunswick. Mills and Horvath were set to manage the band, but they were cut out when Rockwell took over. We rehearsed for two weeks and I didn't even have my trombone section set when we cut the first sides. Red Allen had to fill in for Sidney DeParis, because he was kind of temperamental and didn't show up for the date. Leonard Davis and Shirley Clay were with the band then, and so was Bennie Morton. Fred Robinson was also in the band but he quit after a while because he wasn't getting enough solo work. I thought Bennie was the best around in those days anyway.

We needed a singer and I was told to go around to the Rhythm Club because there were two guys there who were singing great. They turned out to be Harlan Lattimore and Orlando Robeson. I preferred Harlan because he had a deeper voice and was so handsome, and he was a fine performer. His idol was Bing Crosby and he used to sing like him. When Crosby heard him the first time, he changed his way of singing so that it would be closer to Harlan's. Claude Hopkins got Orlando and he was a big hit with him during the thirties.

Our records started doing very well, and I was doing a lot of writing, things like *Cherry, How'm I Doin'* and numbers like that. I never liked *How'm I Doin'* until I heard one of the singers in the show at Connie's Inn put it over big. Then the Mills Brothers recorded it and it sold very well. We were in Connie's Inn regularly for three or four years during the early thirties, and in 1932 were sponsored by Chipso in a package with the Mills Brothers. We were really hot then. We were on the air three and four times a week and the only time we went out was during the summer for a couple of months.

I'll never forget the night the Lindbergh baby was kidnaped. We were on the air from Connie's all night long, in between news flashes, until nine the next morning. We were really swinging. It's too bad someone couldn't have taken that down that night. Connie kept bringing up hot coffee and food and the place was jumping.

During those same years we made a short film for Warner Brothers with a racing background. It was called *Sweepstakes* and it won some kind of an award I believe.

We did a lot of traveling on the road and were almost always playing for white dances during the early years, and were considered a very commercial property then. We had a terrific band but I wasn't able to do the kind of jazz things I might have in the places we were playing. This was true even on the road. I did get one of my best men while we were on the road, however, after many other leaders had tried for years.

Down in St. Louis there was a band called Johnson's Crackerjacks that really used to make us work every time we hit town. They had a pretty good outfit, but one man was really exceptional. That was Harold "Shorty" Baker. Duke, Fletcher, Andy Kirk and others had been trying to get him for years, but no one had been able to turn the trick, because of his older brother Winfield, who was a pretty poor trombone man.

He told all the leaders if you wanted Harold you had to take him too, and nobody wanted that. One night he got pretty high and I got him outside after the dance and made him the offer, which he accepted. Some of the other guys who knew him said he'd never be there, but he was in time for the bus to leave the next morning and without his brother. He stayed with me until I reorganized the band in 1938.

Around 1937 we went under the Mills banner, although they never did much for us as far as records went. We started working the Savoy quite a bit around that time, but I was getting tired of the road. The excitement, the bright lights, the star billing, and all that I'd had, and I said, give me some money now. Actually, I always liked to write, and liked that part of the business best anyhow. I wasn't even playing too much myself then, and I never did go too much for Don Redman's playing. I could play parts, pretty things, arrangements, but there were guys like Benny Carter around, and I never fooled myself thinking I could play jazz like they could.

I still had offers from many sources to take over bands and to organize new bands, but I wanted to concentrate on writing. In fact, I turned down all kinds of offers. All the agencies would call and want me to go out on the road for them. They offered me very good money, but I didn't have anything ready, no repertoire, nothing.

I did go out a couple of times when Jay McShann came to town in 1942, and found the going tough after a while. They were getting ready to go back to Kansas City. I'd gotten an offer from the American Legion in Trenton for a two-week stand which I had to turn down, until my manager told me about McShann's band being around and struggling. He said they were organized and a pretty good outfit. I took them out under my name, and the first night on the job I told Jay to set up and play his own music, just like it was his own gig, and I'd just stand up in front of the band and direct and work with the people. I didn't pay them too much attention the first night, but on the following night they played an up-tempo arrangement of *The Whistler and his Dog,* and Charlie Parker took four choruses. That was it, I was sold. I told him to stay in New York even if the band did go back home, and he said he'd be glad if I could find him a job. I told him to go into any of the joints and start playing his horn and he'd get all the jobs he wanted. He did stay when the band went West again, but he would have made it anyway, with his unusual talent. Later on I took McShann's band out for another month, this time to the Tic Toc in Boston. After that I kept pretty close to my writing, and sold arrangements to all the bands then.

I did take a band out again in 1943 and we went in the Cafe Zanzibar on Broadway and recorded a couple of sides for V-Disc, *Redman Blues, Pistol Packin' Mama* and things like that.

After the war I was the first leader to take a band overseas and we did terrific business all over Europe. We were supposed to have gone over before the war, but things prevented that, and the same agency arranged this tour. I took Tyree Glenn, Peanuts Holland, Don Byas, Billy Taylor, and a lot of other fine musicians, and we recorded quite a lot while we were over there, both with the big band and with small groups. That was in 1946 and 1947. I've been free-lancing ever since then, with CBS and for many of the recording firms, and in the fifties I tied up with Pearl Bailey, and have been making all her arrangements and directing her orchestra ever since.

Most of the recordings I've made in the past year or so have been commercial things, for outfits like Sesac and groups like that. They all liked what I did for them, and I managed to get Hawk, Charlie Shavers and guys like that in on the sessions.

I haven't signed with anyone yet, because I want a free hand in composing and arranging, and most of the companies all have their things they want you to do. There's so much talent in town today that anyone ought to be able to make good records, but not too much of what's on the market is good.

Some of the younger musicians who are being recorded so much today just don't have the experience behind them to make good records. Look at a guy as great as Hawk is, he didn't really hit his stride until he was ready to go overseas in the middle thirties, and by that time he'd already been in the business for close to ten years.

I'm planning to do some remakes of some of the best things I did, like *Cherry, Milenburg Joys, Try Getting a Good Night's Sleep* and things like that. I think there's a market for them, and the public is going to want the big bands back pretty soon anyway.

Young Louis Armstrong

by Mait Edey

It was the Louis Armstrong who, in Redman's words, "changed our whole idea about the band," that Mait Edey had for review in the reissue album YOUNG LOUIS ARMSTRONG.

YOUNG LOUIS ARMSTRONG, Riverside RLP 12-101.
Alligator Hop; Krooked Blues; I'm Going Away to Wear You off My Mind (with King Oliver's Creole Band); *Mandy, Make Up Your Mind* (with Fletcher Henderson Orchestra); *Jelly Bean Blues; Countin' the Blues* (with Ma Rainey); *Terrible Blues; Santa Claus Blues; Of All the Wrong You've Done to Me; Nobody Knows the Way I Feel This Morning; Cake Walking Babies from Home* (with Red Onion Jazz Babies); *The Railroad Blues* (with Trixie Smith).

THESE OLD SIDES are of some importance historically, as repetition of a couple of familiar truisms will make clear. First truism: Few men in any art make a contribution important enough to affect the entire future of that art. Jazz has had its few: Louis, Prez, Bird, Dizzy, and not many others. Louis is the first in line, chronologically at least. Second truism: Just about everybody, including the great innovators, begins by playing like an admired predecessor, or several of them.

When you compare a man's later playing with that of his elders, you find out what, if anything, he has added. Louis' prime elder was Joe Oliver, and Louis' early development out of (or on) Oliver's style is what this album gives us. Riverside has included three tracks by the Oliver band in this set. Whatever their reasons were for doing so, it ends up a wise decision, as we can compare the two trumpeters side by side, hear how much Louis owes to Oliver and just how much he added himself.

Listening to records of very early musicians can be more of a chore than a pleasure, and I don't mean the low fidelity. An inept sense of time, unintentionally wavering pitch, and embarrassingly bad ideas mar the majority of early records to some degree or other. There are those that are free from these faults; in the others, you listen for the isolated moments which have remained good: a note, a phrase, sometimes a whole chorus. Because of its age, this set inevitably has its share of these failings which may unfortunately close the ears of somebody who hasn't built up the necessary tolerance, or at least patience. I say unfortunately, because this album has moments which rank with the best jazz of any period, though none of it was recorded later than early 1925. Predictably, most of the moments are Louis', a few Oliver's.

The album includes three tunes by Oliver's Creole Jazz Band, one by Fletcher Henderson, two by Ma Rainey, one by Trixie Smith, and five by the Red Onion Jazz Babies.

In spite of the fact that Louis plays a subordinate role, two of the Oliver tracks, *Alligator Hop* and *Krooked Blues*, are more consistently satisfying than any other performances on the album. This is partly because there is less bad playing, partly because the group has such a superior ensemble technique. In addition, Johnny Dodds is far preferable to Buster Bailey, who is the clarinet on most of the other tracks. Oliver, of course, is the dominant figure on his own records. He is in good shape here and plays very well. On *Alligator Hop,* taken moderately fast, Louis is barely audible; Oliver plays a straight, simple lead until the final two choruses (after an unremarkable Dodds solo) when he begins to shout magnificently. On the final chorus he reaches up and plays a couple of very impressive ideas. You can hear Louis' beginning in these phrases of Oliver's.

Krooked Blues is not a blues, but a pleasant sixteen-bar tune, moderately slow, with breaks between each chorus (by Oliver, Dutrey, Dodds, and Evans). Except for the breaks, it is all relaxed ensemble work. Oliver plays a series of strong, simple variations with the power and feeling that set him above his contemporaries. He is muted on the last two choruses. Louis is clearly audible, easy to follow, playing a fine second part with little runs and fill-ins.

The third Oliver track, *I'm Going Away to Wear You off My Mind* is one of those early recordings where low fidelity is a really serious handicap, and where grouping the musicians around the recording horn seemed to be a pretty hit-or-miss operation. What is salvageable of the music is mostly Johnny Dodds, who is not as good here as elsewhere, and brother Baby on wood blocks. There is a terrible piano solo by Lil Hardin. Oliver can be heard fairly steadily, though dimly, and he is hard to follow. Only a note here and there of Louis. The tune itself is a pleasant one, as it should be with its poignant title, but there is no reason for including it in a set under Louis' name.

The Henderson track is *Mandy, Make up Your Mind*. Louis and Henderson each have a chorus; Coleman Hawkins has three breaks; otherwise it's all ensemble. Not the blowing ensemble of the Oliver band, but written section work, and the writing is unspeakably bad throughout. Louis is audible in the trumpet section, though not playing lead; his chorus is in a clipped, abbreviated style less effective, for me, than most of his work on the rest of the album. Maybe the tune held him down.

The Red Onion Jazz Babies are two quintets, having Louis, Lil, and Buddy Christian (banjo) in common. On *Terrible Blues, Santa Claus Blues,* and *Of All the Wrong You've Done to Me,* they are joined by Buster Bailey and Aaron Thompson (trombone). *Nobody Knows the Way I Feel This Morning* and *Cake Walking Babies from Home,* Sidney Bechet (soprano only) and Charlie Irvis (trombone) complete the group. Buster Bailey is often inadequate, subject from time to time to all the ills mentioned above. Thompson is competent but dated. *Terrible Blues* is a good performance in spite of mediocre sidemen because Louis is so fine. Oliver is his model in the ensemble, but to Oliver's style he has added a subtler sense of time, a more imaginative structure to his lines, and the expert use of hesitations and grace notes completely foreign to Oliver's playing.

Louis' time and tone *might* derive from Bunk Johnson to some degree. Though denying him as a teacher, Louis did express an early admiration for Bunk, and the recorded evidence shows elements in Louis' playing (chiefly time and tone) which were like Bunk rather than Oliver. Bunk's status, both as an influence and as a player, has been made hard to assess fairly because of the quantities of undeserved praise and equally undeserved scorn that have been heaped on him, and also because he recorded only during the forties, making judgments about his earlier work open to legitimate question. His good records (unfortunately a small minority of the ones I have heard) like *Down by the Riverside*, show a trumpet with much in common with the early Louis, and his contemporaries.

To continue this digression, the point has been forcefully and correctly made, by Leonard Feather and others, that jazz was not born in New Orleans alone, that the music was the product of the entire (though predominantly southern) American Negro scene, To say this is one thing; it is not to say (as has been maintained as a corollary) that the New Orleans players and the New Orleans contribution were no more remarkable than those of other cities. Questions of taste creep in here, as well as questions of historical accident (i.e., who just *happened* to be recorded), but the recorded remains seem to indicate that of all the very early trumpeters, say those recorded before 1925, the best New Orleans men like, say, Oliver, Ladnier, and Louis were more advanced and have worn better over the years than those from Louisville, New York, and other towns who tended to be more raggy, ricky-tick, and less "soulful."

As a group, of course, the New Orleans men lost this superiority by the middle of the twenties, but only in the sense that they were joined by a host of others who were beginning to reach their level. And even during the early thirties nobody was cutting Louis and Red Allen. These two, though in some ways far removed from the styles of Bunk and Oliver, retained much contributed by the older men and built on the original styles rather than diverged from them (compare them with Joe Smith, Beiderbecke, Jabbo Smith, Bubber Miley, and other fine players outside this tradition). And strangely enough, listening to the Louis and Allen of this later period, Bunk, with his delayed attack and relatively subtle time, comes to mind as supplying roots as strong as or stronger than Oliver's.

The point of this digression is that Louis was not just a genius who sprung newborn from the brow of King Oliver, but the peak of an established and varied tradition of which Oliver was only a part, though a major part.

Terrible Blues also includes a chorus by Louis which is one of his earliest totally successful solos. It is in this solo that he is conceptually farthest from Oliver in this album. Oliver's solos (and Louis' with the Oliver band) had been in the ensemble lead style; they hadn't varied their phrasing just because they happened to be taking a solo. Like most pre-Louis New Orleans trumpeters, Oliver sounds more comfortable in the ensemble and is most effective there. In this solo, Louis' organization and climaxing are, as far as I know, something completely new and the beginnings of his great contributions as a soloist. His two breaks later in the record revert to the Oliver style, which is no real loss, as Oliver was excellent at short, simple breaks.

The same remarks apply to Louis' ensemble work on *Santa Claus Blues* and *Of All the Wrong*. On the latter, Louis has a muted solo over stop chords which doesn't quite come off.

Nobody Knows is entirely a vocal by Alberta Hunter under the pseudonym Josephine Beatty. Louis and Bechet function as unobtrusive accompaniments; neither has much to do, and Bechet is a little repetitious. Alberta Hunter's singing does not impress me. *Cake Walking Babies* is an excellent driving performance hideously marred by a duet vocal by Beatty and Todd in a style recalling burlesque and barbershops. Louis is first-rate throughout. Charlie Irvis is an effective trombonist, slippery but gutty. He preceded Nanton with Ellington and is one of the first sources of Ellington's fondness for muted brass. Listen to Louis on the first half of the chorus following the vocal, then turn back and listen to Oliver on the last chorus of *Alligator Hop.*

The remaining three tracks are vocals, two by Ma Rainey: *Jelly Bean Blues* and *Countin' the Blues;* one by Trixie Smith: *Railroad Blues.* The accompanying players are out of the Henderson band; the horns are Louis, Bailey, and trombonist Charlie Green who is solid and has a sense of humor. Ma Rainey's singing is somber with only slight vibrato. She sounds as though she could command a lot of volume; the old recording techniques probably didn't do her justice. Her phrasing is a little repetitious and dull rhythmically, especially next to Louis whose time is always so fine. Trixie Smith has a lighter, higher voice with a somewhat wobbly vibrato. She has Ma Rainey's faults without Ma's depth.

Louis is least effective on *Countin' the Blues* where he talks with a mute in Oliver fashion. His horn is open on *Jelly Bean* and *Railroad Blues,* both of which have beautiful openings. Of all the tracks in the album, it is *Railroad Blues* on which Louis sounds most like Oliver. Except for the unmistakable vibrato, it could be Oliver on the eight-bar introduction. Louis even closes up his tone a little and gets a bit of Oliver's acid sound. On his chorus he is more characteristic of himself, but it is not an example of his best work.

These records are typical of Louis as he was the year or so after he left Oliver. They are valuable both for their moments of beauty and for the information they supply about the development of the first great soloist. It seems to me that Louis' greatest contribution was rhythmic. Oliver had swung before him, but not consistently; Louis swung almost every note he played. In a way, the presence of lesser musicians in this album is a blessing; we are so used to hearing Louis' rhythmic contribution in all the players that followed him that we take them for granted. When we hear them here alongside men who didn't have the advantage of having absorbed Louis' example, we can be more properly impressed.

Louis Armstrong

by Martin Williams

This review is of a collection of Armstrong reissues, originally recorded in the thirties, and of a set of four LP records, most of them done in the fifties, in which Armstrong re-created his early career.

Louis Armstrong: COLLECTOR'S ITEMS, Decca D18329.
Shadrack; Jeepers Creepers; Old Man Mose; Shoe Shine Boy; Brother Bill; Now Do You Call That a Buddy; On the Sunny Side of the Street; Confessin'; Ain't Misbehavin'; I Can't Give You Anything But Love; Sweethearts on Parade; Baby, Won't You Please Come Home.

Louis Armstrong: MY MUSICAL AUTOBIOGRAPHY, Decca DXM-155.

APPARENTLY THE METHOD of selection for the COLLECTOR'S ITEMS set was to pick "best sellers"—with no thought about whom the records sold to or why. Thus the vocal performance of the pseudo-spiritual *Shadrack* (complete with "mixed chorus") is placed next to that splendid series of displaced accents in the trumpet chorus on *Jeepers Creepers;* and it isn't long after we have met *Brother Bill* that we hear such a magnificent harmonic variation as that on the Decca version of *I Can't Give You Anything But Love;* and not long after we have heard all about *Old Man Mose* that we hear that *Confessin'* on which grandstanding and art go hand in hand in the way that only Armstrong can bring off—and Armstrong not often.

The Armstrong on that set is the Armstrong heard in the AUTOBIOGRAPHY set—and that fact forces me to repeat the truism that Armstrong the soloist is not the Armstrong of

Canal Street Blues, Mandy Make up Your Mind, or even of *Muskrat Ramble.* That is, Louis the sublime soloist necessarily soon abandoned Louis the integrated lead ensemble voice and, despite his having played again with small groups for over ten years now, never relearned that role. The loss was a gain, the gain a loss, and all of it necessary to Armstrong's growth.

The omnibus has four LPs, has forty-eight selections, all but six of which (*New Orleans Function, Muskrat Ramble, Struttin' with Some Barbecue, My Monday Date, Basin Street Blues, Sleepy Time Down South*) were redone especially for it, and none of which dates earlier than 1947. Fully twenty-four of those forty-eight selections were originally done on records before 1929 (Armstrong for the time being is apparently as willing as a record collector to present his autobiography largely in terms of what happened in recording studios before that date).

There are further troubles. On all but six titles we are treated to the bouncy, monotonòus, unresponsive drumming of Barrett Deems—drumming to which the presence of Kenny John on two tracks and Cozy Cole on two others (even whopping after beats), and, of course, Sidney Catlett on one, is an enormous relief.

Armstrong introduces the collection with a pronouncement about "the music just the way it was played in those good old days." Hardly. And, of course, impossible.

Judged against the original records, the three Oliver Creole Jazz Band numbers are near travesties. Yank Lawson might seem a good choice (if one were in a hurry) at first, but he plays with what seems a monotonous affectation. Some effort (by Bob Haggart) was made to take parts off the 1920's recordings but, in every case, the original conception is soon abandoned for a string of solos—fairly conventional ones really—and there are such details as the Oliver choruses on *Dippermouth* being reduced to two, played in unison by the two trumpets at the beginning and then abandoned for some of Armstrong's familiar current blues style. Edmond Hall, a brick throughout and certainly the best clarinet Louis has had in ten years, should surely have been given another shot at *High*

Society. Canal Street is the sincerest effort at re-creation and in it the deep rocking swing and integration of parts of the Oliver band is totally absent.

The Clarence Williams Red Onion and Blue Five dates are referred to only by using some of the tunes made on them, and Louis' solo after the generally rejuvenated Trummy Young chorus on *Everybody Loves My Baby* is very good current Armstrong.

Next come four blues numbers. Admittedly Velma Middleton is not a Ma Rainey or a Bessie Smith or even a Trixie Smith or a Chippie Hill. Actually she is not a singer and is almost totally insensitive to the works done. Most of Louis' accompaniments are rather bland and nearly coast.

We go back to New Orleans for that 1950 night club act "New Orleans Function" on which Louis' playing of *Free As a Bird* was fairly straight and full of feeling. And what a relief this Hines-Cole-Shaw rhythm section is! On *Gut Bucket*, Louis' re-creation of that superb solo is a shadow and the performance ends on some light riffing.

On the third side begins a series of seven more numbers from the Hot Five-Seven period, and one ringer—a *Snag It*, spoiled from the start by the substitution of a trite and silly riff for the answering bass figure in the once plaintive introduction. Suffice it to say that Deems plays all the way through the stop-time sections on both *Potato Head* and *Gully Low* (*S.O.L.*) *Blues:* the powerful effects (even in the solos) of the original records are ignored, misapprehended, gone, and a good Armstrong solo on *Wild Man Blues* does not save an otherwise tricky, even superficial, performance. Of *Struttin' with Some Barbecue* we shall speak in a moment.

On *Cornet Chop Suey*, guitarist George Barnes, incongruously present on several of the small band numbers (imagine his taking Lonnie Johnson's role in *Hotter Than That;* that's the way they set it up!), has an inane guitar solo that all but characterizes the whole performance. (For *Heebie Jeebies*, Armstrong, incidentally, scatted, this time in nonsense words as "old-fashioned" as those Morton used.) *Muskrat* is repre-

114 JAZZ PANORAMA

sented by the "Symphony Hall" version. Of the astonishing *King of the Zulus,* a word later.

Next come three from the Armstrong-Hines period, one of them (*A Monday Date*) a really fine 1951 performance by probably the best permanent band Armstrong has ever had (individually if not collectively) with three major soloists in Teagarden, Hines (playing especially well), and Louis. The *Basin Street* here is the one from the "Glenn Miller" soundtrack: of it too, more later.

At this point, we have entered the period when Armstrong the great soloist has abandoned all pretense of being anything but that. Again, to discuss most of these records is to harp on details—the sublime way Armstrong incorporates a fluff in *Dear Old Southland;* Billy Kyle's excellent introduction to the vocal on *Body and Soul;* the fine vocal on *I Surrender Dear;* the banal riding on grandstand mannerisms on *Exactly Like You; Hobo, You Can't Ride This Train;* and *Sunny Side of the Street.* Of *Lazy River* and *Georgia on My Mind,* later.

Out of the research for the narration, done by Milt Gabler and Leonard Feather, comes the news that on *Gully Low Blues,* Johnny Dodds was too frightened by the recording horn to speak the line "Oh, play it, Pappa Dip"—of course, the story goes with *Gut Bucket Blues,* heard two LP sides earlier. Louis Armstrong also informs us what "leading trumpet men" Humphrey Lyttelton and Yank Lawson are. He is clear, however, about the fact that the sides for Clarence-Williams-led groups were made at separate sessions with different personnels, but the liner (which lumps them all as "the Blue Five in November and December, 1924") is not. The liner will also tell you that on *Memories of You,* Ed Hall is replaced by Hilton Jefferson. Jeff may have been there, but if that isn't Ed, it's his brother Herb.

The handsome, not to say garish, production begins with a biographical essay by, of all people, that collector of poetry and verse for the American middlebrow, Louis Untermeyer. He quotes everyone from critic William Russell to disc jockey Gene Norman to give Louis his credentials, and in a burst of phrase-coinage, wishes to add "a loud and fervent Amen." The essay is a tepid, facile rehash of some of the usual biographical sources.

There follows what is billed as "an appreciation" by Gilbert Millstein. It is skillfully slick anecdotal prose, initially built on a simile between Armstrong and (*n.b.*) Charles G. Finney's *Circus of Dr. Lao* plus the proposition that Louis is "beyond praise."

Am I calling this an uneven set, a mistake, a bad set with a few good moments, an effort to recapture what cannot be recaptured? I don't know, quite honestly, what it is on the whole, except that on the face of it, it is a bit imbalanced in favor of an 'Armstrong who now exists only on important reissue albums from Brunswick, Columbia, and Riverside. But about *Struttin' with Some Barbecue, Basin Street Blues, Lazy River,* and *Georgia on My Mind* and particularly *King of the Zulus* I do know something of which I would like to try to speak.

It is very well to talk about Armstrong's rhythmic conception, about his transformations of banal melodies, about the superb imagination on a harmonic variation like that in the 1938 *I Can't Give You Anything But Love,* about "the first great jazz soloist." It is also all very well to say that this *King of the Zulus* is not like the first. It happens to be better. On it, and on the other titles for which I have reserved comment, Armstrong is astonishing, and astonishing because he plays what he plays with such great power, authority, sureness, firmness, and commanding presence as to be beyond style, beyond category, almost (as they say of Beethoven's last quartets) beyond music. When he plays the trumpet this way, all considerations of "schools," most other jazzmen, most other musicians simply drop away as we listen. The show biz personality act, the coasting, the forced jokes and sometimes forced geniality, the perpetual emotional content of much of Armstrong's music past and present (that of a marvelously exuberant but complex child)—all these drop away, and we are hearing a surpassing artist create for us—each of us—a surpassing art.

Bix Beiderbecke

by Mait Edey

After Armstrong, one of the most original and influential musicians to appear in the twenties was Bix Beiderbecke, whose earliest recordings were reissued again in the fifties.

BIX BEIDERBECKE AND THE WOLVERINES, Riverside RLP 12-123. Bix Beiderbecke, *trumpet* (*piano* on *Big Boy* only); Jimmy Hartwell, *clarinet;* George Johnson, *tenor;* Dick Voynow, *piano;* Bob Gillette, *banjo and guitar;* Min Leibrook, *tuba;* Vic Moore, *drums.*
Oh, Baby; Copenhagen; Riverboat Shuffle; Susie; Royal Garden Blues; Tiger Rag; Tia Juana; Big Boy. With George Brunis, *Trombone* added: *Sensation Rag; Lazy Daddy.* With Al Gande replacing Brunis: *Fidgety Feet; Jazz Me Blues.*

RIVERSIDE HAS AGAIN made available, this time on a single twelve-inch LP, almost the entire recorded output of the Wolverine orchestra (one tune, *I Need Some Petting,* is not included), a group whose finest hours were in 1924, the year on these sides, and which is interesting today almost solely because of Bix Beiderbecke.

Almost all of Beiderbecke's records are plagued by inadequate sidemen. Depending on how you take these things, the men here may annoy you, or you may be able to function as a listener in spite of them. As a group the Wolverines were far from matching the rhythmic ease that the Oliver band, say, achieved at its best, but neither were they as bad as many other groups. Some momentum is generated on the medium tempo tracks (nothing is taken slow); surprisingly, a lot of it is generated by the banjoist, Bob Gillette, who in spite of corny rolls, is very steady, and occasionally gets a fine sprung-rhythm effect. The tunes are Dixieland standards, some of them new at that time, arranged with some care, and with rather more solo work than apparently was common in 1924. Only Beiderbecke provokes any interest as a soloist—or as a part in the ensemble passages, for that matter.

Bix himself was one of the four or five best cornetists or trumpeters to be recorded during the twenties, and the first white soloist we know of whose playing can be compared in quality to that of his best Negro contemporaries. He was one of the first men to develop, at least on record, a truly solo, as opposed to ensemble, concept for a horn; he was second only to Louis in the extent and quality of his contributions to solo trumpet playing before 1930. These contributions were harmonic and melodic, rather than rhythmic. Bix's time was based on the white Dixieland style; his rhythmic displacements were usually crude syncopations next to those of the most advanced Negro players of the twenties like Louis, Earl Hines and Jimmy Harrison. His time was excellent in one lesser sense, however; although he didn't conceive very sophisticated patterns, he managed to play the ones he did conceive absolutely perfectly. Not a note was ever misplaced to the slightest degree. I think it's this control, this, in the broad sense, *technical* brilliance which accounts for so much of the beauty of his playing. His tone was round and golden, with a fragile vibrato in all registers; each note, because of its attack and tone, was beautiful in itself; how it functioned in relation to the notes preceding and following it seems almost a secondary matter in Bix's case. There's a tremendous kick in listening to him skip a large interval flawlessly at a fast tempo, or make a subtle, lacy thing out of a Dixieland tune like *Sensation Rag* just through the delicacy of his slight variations and the perfection of his control, a control perhaps no greater than Louis', but more instantly striking.

Actually, their success in broadening the melodic and formal equipment of the soloist was just about the only thing Bix and Louis had in common; in other respects—time, tone, melodic concept—they were about as far apart as contemporary trumpeters could be. Louis' phrasing was based largely on that of

King Oliver, with the addition of grace and passing notes and short ornamental runs—full of hesitations, and saturated, even at fast tempos, with blues phrasing and inflections. When Louis was making something, he let you know it. There were the careful silences, then the exultant triumph of a note reached or a beautiful phrase executed. Bix, on the other hand, made everything with the same smooth, unhurried aplomb. Having developed the tone he apparently wanted, he never altered it to suit the moment; his tone was invariably beautiful, but it was not, as Louis' was, an expressive tool. Bix also lacked the blues, the primary element in Oliver's playing and only slightly less important in Louis'. This put him in the company of many northern and eastern players who sound hopelessly ricky-tick and trivial today; one of the most remarkable things about Bix was that he managed to play fine, lasting things without once drawing on the soulful southern tradition which ended up being the mainstream of that time.

These are Beiderbecke's earliest records. He was only twenty-one when he recorded them. But although they don't include his most ambitious solo work, they show a style which was already more than mature: it was radically advanced. The set is indispensable to anyone interested either in the development of early jazz or in the cornet (or trumpet, with its very similar problems and potential) as an instrument.

Andy Kirk's Story

by Frank Driggs

Andy Kirk's was one of the most famous of the southwestern bands, playing what came to be called "Kansas City style." But Kirk's career is a continuing one, and his comments on the current scene are one of the most provocative parts of his story, as he told it to Frank Driggs.

WHEN I GOT STARTED in music there was really only one good band in town . . . George Morrison's. He had a society band, but they had a beat, and for that reason he was the leader in the field. There weren't many Negroes around Denver then, only six thousand out of a total population of three hundred thousand. The best jobs in town were the country club, the city amusement park, and private lawn parties when the white people wanted live music for entertainment. We'd work for the colored dances too, but there weren't enough of them to keep you busy all the time. We'd go out on short tours as far as Cheyenne, Salt Lake City, Colorado Springs and places like that because we were well known around that part of the country. One season we played the Elks and Shriners indoor circuses playing behind the acts. After the show was over we'd play for dancing in another smaller room which was set up as a cabaret. At that time we had two others with the band who were later to become famous. Hattie McDaniel was singing with us and Jimmie Lunceford was getting started on alto sax then, just a kid. . . .

There were any number of musicians who came through Denver on tour with bands like Fred Waring's Pennsylvanians, Ben Bernie's band and those type of outfits, so I didn't hear any real jazz until Gene Coy and his Happy Black Aces came through. They had a real beat and upset the town. From that time on I kept my ear open for music like that. Jelly Roll Morton came through as a single and I liked his style. In fact he influenced me a great deal rhythmically.

I went with jazz full-time when I quit Morrison to join Terrence "T." Holder down in Dallas. We were working every night in a blood-and-thunder place called the Ozarks. It was just outside of town, a typical roadhouse, lots of bloody fights every night. Our band was really swinging and outside of Alphonso Trent's band ours was the most popular in Texas at that time. We had some terrific men in that band. Big Jim and T. on trumpets were two of the best jazzmen and the sweetest musicians I ever heard in my life, and when they used to play duets they'd break up any dance. Those two could play the prettiest waltzes too. T. had been with Trent's band before organizing his own. Eddie Durham's cousin, Allen, was on trombone, and we had a terrific alto player, Alvin "Fats" Wall. You never heard of him because he wouldn't travel. His wife was older than he was and she kind of ran his affairs. She knew what was best; a musician's life was a pretty unsettled one. They moved to Detroit and settled down, and all the name bands that came through that way would try to hire him. Fletcher [Henderson] always used him whenever he was short a man. He had a terrific style and so many ideas that I'd just sit down and write them out, adding harmony to them. By the time I'd taken over from T. he had formed his own group.

During those years we were just starting to write out arrangements, because playing for jitney dances as we were then, there wasn't any call for them. The idea then was to get the dancers on and off the floor. Two choruses was an arrangement then. To get around that, we'd make up an introduction that served as a bridge for the next chorus following, and we'd always make up a different ending for the same number. These things helped make it more interesting.

Jack Teagarden was around there with a group of his own, just six pieces. He was doubling on tuba as well as trombone. He was playing opposite our band at the Winter Garden in

Oklahoma City. We were carrying eleven pieces at that time. We played all the waltzes and the popular tunes, because they didn't play them, and they were considered the jazz band!

In those days all the bands went under trade names, the Gloom Dodgers, Blue Moon Chasers, the Blue Devils, the Southern Serenaders, etc. The bands used to travel a circuit from Tulsa, Oklahoma City, Little Rock, Fort Worth and Dallas to Kansas City. Kansas City was considered the center of that part of the country, the place for all those bands from the other cities to work to. That was because cities like Tulsa and Oklahoma City had only a few places to play in and most of the choice spots were being used by the big-name traveling bands then. . . .

I took over the T. Holder band in Oklahoma City in January, 1929. The entire band except for three men came with me. I fell heir to the band, because I wasn't even thinking about having my own band then. We had some trouble with T. when he ran out on the band after his wife left him. He went after her to Dallas and we were left without a leader. We were working for a man named Falkenburg who ran the Southwest Amusement Corporation. They had two ballrooms each in Tulsa and Oklahoma City. He asked me if I'd like to take over the band, and I told him we ought to try to get T. back, which he did. T. didn't stay long, and Falkenburg told me if I didn't take over the band, he'd get another one. That was it. . . . The last time I saw T. he was in his sixties and still had that beautiful sweet tone.

That summer we went to Crystal Park in Tulsa, and George E. Lee came down from Kansas City to replace us at the ballroom in Oklahoma City. One night he came out to Tulsa and did a few numbers with our band, and Falkenburg made an announcement that the people would soon be hearing Lee and his band. George liked our band and he told me one of his friends in Kansas City was looking for a new band, and not one of the Kansas bands because they were so well known. Lee contacted his friend in Kansas and he turned out to be the manager of the Pla-Mor Restaurant. The Pla-Mor was considered one of the finest ballrooms in that part of the country

and their manager evidently put some stock in what George
Lee told him about our band, because he came out to Tulsa
to sign us up for that winter season. In many ways that was
a turning point in my career. Because of the deal George Lee
had gotten me we became good friends and worked out a business agreement so that we wouldn't be cutting each other's
throats. We both agreed to forget about scale and ask for some
real money. Our bands were getting very popular locally then,
and there was plenty of work around for both of us, so we set
up a scale which neither would go under. We weren't concerned with what the other bands got because we were more
commercial and did a lot of novelties which the other jazz
bands like Bennie Moten's weren't doing. Many times the
managers of the different ballrooms would try to bargain with
either me or George by saying, "Well, look, we can get Kirk
for . . ." and it turned out to be the same price. We never
did consider Bennie Moten as our competitor because we
weren't playing the same kind of music or playing in the same
places. The last time I saw George Lee was some years ago
when he was managing a tavern in Detroit for a syndicate. His
sister Julia is still the big attraction back in Kansas City that
she was in the twenties when she was featured with George on
piano.

We had just started our engagement at the Pla-Mor when
Jack Kapp, Dick Voynow, and some of the scouts from Brunswick came to Kansas City with portable equipment looking
for talent. Kapp got in touch with me and told me he wanted
to hear my band at a rehearsal the following afternoon. I got
the boys together and told them to be on time, and the next
day they were all there, all except Marion Jackson, who was
playing piano with me then. He was somewhat of a ladies'
man and must have had something on that day. We waited
around for him a little while until Kapp started to get impa-
tient. I asked John Williams (he replaced Fats Wall) to call
his wife Mary Lou, who he had been telling me about and to
get her over to the Pla-Mor in a hurry so we could get on with
the audition. She came right over and sat down at the piano
and played everything we had just like she'd always been in

the band. John wasn't lying, she was terrific, had perfect pitch, a terrific ear, everything. We gave her some solos, and Kapp liked what he heard because he set up a date to record the following week at the radio station (KMBC). Because Mary Lou made the audition I felt it only fair that she make the record date too. She said she had some ideas she wanted me to hear so we sat up for two or three nights and put several things together. The records came off very well, because Kapp gave us an exclusive .contract. He also recorded George Lee's band and Walter Page's Blue Devils. They came up from Oklahoma City to make the date. Kapp told me any time I had numbers like *Messa Stomp* to call him up and he would make arrangements for us to record in Chicago where their main offices were.

In order to work toward that area, I'd just call up the local promoters in places like Hannibal, Missouri, and Quincy, Illinois, and tell them I wanted to play some dates in their area. They would just throw a dance; it was that simple.

The first time I went to Chicago to record a batch of new numbers I had Marion Jackson on piano. During rehearsals Kapp came in the studio and noticed Jackson and asked me where the girl was. I told him she stayed home. He said the band didn't sound the same without her and didn't want to record us unless I sent for her. I wired home and she came up to Chicago and made the sessions. She recorded that way without actually being a member of the band for a couple of years before I finally had to let Jackson go . . . this was around 1931 or so.

My records were selling well and got around East as well as the Midwest. Charlie Buchanan, the manager of the Savoy Ballroom, heard them and wanted to have us work there. The spring of 1930 Fletcher Henderson came through Kansas City on tour and he heard our band and wanted us to replace him at Roseland while he was working our part of the country. He wired Lou Brecker, the owner of Roseland, and told him to hire us as his replacement which Brecker did . . . for six weeks. Then we went into the Savoy and from there all over

New York State, New Jersey, and Pennsylvania, and spent almost two years in the East before we came home again.

There were so many ballrooms and hotels to play in those little towns in Pennsylvania like Sunbury, Lancaster, Scranton, Pottsville, and Allentown that we were kept busy all the time. We worked the Savoy again in 1931 and worked down to Philadelphia where we became the house band at the Pearl Theater. Blanche Calloway, Cab's sister, was doing a single there, and Sam Steiffel, the manager of the theater, decided she looked good with the band behind her and tried to take the band away from me to give to her. I was playing tuba then and we didn't have a front man except Billy Massey, our vocalist.

We recorded several numbers under the name "Blanche Calloway's Joy Boys" for Victor that year, because we were under contract to Brunswick. Steiffel placed two extra men in my band who were supposed to try to talk them into going with Blanche and leaving me. Just about that time, Bennie Moten came through on tour and told us the union was looking for us. They had a job for us back home at Winwood Beach, a summer resort, while Bennie was going into Fairyland Park. We continued working the theaters around Washington, Baltimore and Philadelphia with Blanche out in front directing, when I got wind of the band that Jap Allen had formed back home with Ben Webster, Booker Pittman and other younger up-and-coming musicians. Many of the guys in his band wanted to come East, so I wired him to come out and take this job with Blanche, which they were happy to get, while I went back to Kansas City. They recorded with her, but it didn't work out for them because they broke up not too long after I left.

We just got back to Kansas City before everything dropped dead in the East. The work was still good in and around Kansas City even though the depression was going full blast. After that summer we went on tour through Arkansas and Oklahoma for the Malco Theater chain. They had a great many houses around the Southwest but nobody had any money to go into the theaters with. That was just around the time Roosevelt called in the gold, right in the middle of the depression. We gave a final concert in Memphis, which was John Williams' home, and just did get back to Kansas City.

When we got back home, there was no depression. The town was jumping! We got back on a Friday and the following Monday I went into the Vanity Fair night club, a plush new spot right in the center of town and did good business. We stayed right around Kansas City, working all the other good spots in town like the El Torreon Ballroom. We'd get the finest acts out of Chicago to play in the night clubs in Kansas City, because they weren't working regularly.

By 1934 Roosevelt had things straightened out a little, so we took an offer to go into the Blossom Heath, the biggest night club in Oklahoma City. Ben Webster had joined our band then and so had Mouse Randolph, on trumpet, and Ben Thigpen on drums. We were really swinging and there was a lot of activity in Oklahoma then on account of the oil. We had a CBS outlet and were heard down South all the way to the bottom of Texas. Radio was getting big then and because of the fan mail we were getting, I decided to get in touch with Kapp and to make some more records. We finished up our engagement at the Blossom Heath and worked through Wichita and other parts of Kansas before going back to Kansas City.

There was a young boy who was a band follower, named George Crowe, who had gotten in touch with Joe Glaser and told him about our band. Glaser got in touch with me, and I asked him if he could get me some bookings that would take me East because we wanted to work New York again. He set us up with an engagement at a night club in Baltimore. By this time Ben left to join Fletcher Henderson, taking Lester Young's place after Fletcher let him go. I got Buddy Tate to replace Ben. We were upstate in New York when Bennie Moten died on the operating table back home. Things weren't going our way too well and we had to come back home for a while before trying to go back East. Buddy left and went back to Texas, and I got Dick Wilson from Gene Coy's band. This time we got some bookings that made us some money and made it to New York.

Kapp told us it wasn't called Brunswick any more, but
Decca, and we made a whole gang of records for him that
year. He specifically wanted us to make thinks like *Froggy
Bottom, Blue Clarinet Stomp,* and numbers like that. We were
getting set to record when he got something he wanted to record right away. That was *Christopher Columbus* and it was
hot then. I told him okay we'd made it, but that I wanted him
to listen to something special we had. He said to make his
tune first and then we'd talk about it. We made *Christopher
Columbus* and it became a big hit for us. While he was bragging to everybody about what a fine job we did with that tune,
I told him I had a couple of ballads I wanted him to listen to.
He looked at me like I was crazy, and asked me what I was
trying to do, go high hat on him? He said he had plenty of
bands for that and not to waste the talent we had, but to keep
on making the type of numbers we had made our reputation
with. I finally got him to listen to one chorus of *Until the Real
Thing Comes Along.* He flipped, and from then on I had a
hard time getting him to record any more jazz; he wanted
everything schmaltz. We had a lot of good tunes in our book,
but he wanted the opposite of what he said before . . . *Dedicated to You, Poor Butterfly,* and things like that. I was always hoping to get in some more jazz numbers, but the other
things were commercial then and they made a lot of money
for us.

Pha Terrell's vocals helped make our band successful right
from the start when we were getting big nationally. He was a
Kansas City boy, working as a hoofer and muscle man front-
ing for some joint on 18th Street owned by one of the syndi-
cates in town in the early thirties. Leo Davis, who was with me
in Morrison's band back in Denver, and who is now a music
teacher in Kansas City, told me about him and to go down
and listen to him. I heard him do one number and thought he
would go well with the band, and asked him if he would like
to join us. He was very happy that I asked him because he
was just around twenty-one then. I made him the front man
and he could sing a good jazz tune when he wanted, but all
he had to do was to hear those girls swoon when he sang

ballads like *Dedicated to You,* and that was it; he didn't sing
anything else then. The boys in the band used to kid him
about his high voice, and they thought he was soft because of
that, but they soon found out. He wouldn't say much, just
went into action, and that was it. He was a real ladies' man,
and a great singer. He died in 1945.

I've had some terrific musicians in all my bands. In my first
band, Big Jim [Harry Lawson] was playing most of the trumpet solos and he was compared to Ed Lewis. Floyd "Stumpy"
Brady was considered an outstanding trombonist in those days
and I had him in the early thirties. Stumpy got an offer to
join Fletcher Henderson that he wanted to take, but asked to
stay in my band so that he could break in Ted Donnelly,
whom we called "Muttonlegs." Donelly stayed with me a long
time, through the war, and played a lot of good solos. He died
just recently.

Before Ben Thigpen was on drums, I had "Crackshot" [Ed-
ward McNeil] and there was none greater. He died of a heart
attack in 1930. Fletcher Henderson tried to get him away from
me several times. He should be mentioned because he was one
of the early greats. He was what you call a percussionist. He
worked with Ringling Brothers Circus. He was the only colored drummer I know that they hired for their big band, and
they featured him in their sideshow. He had such an easy
crush roll, and that gave us a smooth feeling, and he could
play bells and chimes. He was a finished musician, could read
anything, and this was during the time when most drummers
just beat the drums. He died too soon. I should give Ben Thigpen more credit, because I never paid too much attention to
what he was doing, because my ear was tuned to "Crack's"
drumming. Ben was very dependable. I got him from J. Frank
Terry's band in Cleveland on Mouse Randolph's recommendation.

I had some of the best brass men like Mouse Randolph,
Paul King, Clarence Trice and Harold Baker. I knew Baker
back in the early thirties when he was featured with Johnson's
Crackerjacks in St. Louis. That was a trumpet town because
they were all influenced by Charlie Creath. Jesse Johnson, the

local promoter, used to book us in on the riverboats on Monday, our day off. I tried to get Baker for years, so did Fletcher, Don Redman, Duke and all the others. Don got him first, and I got him after Teddy Wilson's great band broke up. He had such a beautiful tone, open and big. Then I got Howard McGhee. He was young and had a new style at that time. He was a big influence on Fats Navarro, who was in my big band during the war. Fats was one of the best I ever had; it's a shame what happened to him.

All my reedmen were good and could solo. John Harrington was a fine clarinetist, and Dick Wilson, besides being handsome and a great lady-killer, could play tenor with anyone then. He was way ahead of his time and died very young, of tuberculosis, in 1941. Then I had Don Byas on tenor and Buddy Miller on alto; both were very good soloists. Later on, Charlie Parker played with me for a short while. One of the guys who was with me right from the start and never received credit for all he did was Merle Boatley. He called himself Earl Thompson, but we didn't learn his real name until the war broke out. He was a terrific musician, and many of the things Mary Lou got credit for were actually done by him, but he was taken for granted.

Floyd Smith came into the band right here in New York, although I first heard him with Jeter-Pillars as a kid of seventeen in St. Louis. He was with the Irvin C. Miller show, "Brown-Skin Models," which had split off from the Sunset Royals band out of West Palm Beach, Florida. They were playing in a theater in Flatbush, and I caught Floyd and hired him right away. He was a big hit and one of the causes for Mary Lou's leaving the band. She had been the baby and was featured all those years, until Floyd came along and he was the baby. Then I got June Richmond, and she always upset the crowd wherever we played. Whenever she'd do *Hey, Lawdy, Mama* that broke up the house, and Mary Lou although she was appreciated, would never get that kind of applause, because of June's showmanship.

Mary Lou started giving Floyd some of her solos, and I got used to him playing a lot of her stuff. The night she quit the

Courtesy of Donald Silverstein

DON REDMAN

LESTER YOUNG

band in Washington, I didn't even know she had gone. She'd usually walk off the stand to have a smoke, and with Floyd's amplifier turned way up I didn't notice a thing. She caught the train for Pittsburgh. I wanted to get young Billy Taylor to replace her, but he was out of town when my call came through.

Ken Kersey fitted fine in the band and he stayed until he was drafted. Then Johnny Young of Chicago took his place. He could copy Kenny's *K. K. Boogie* note for note. Ken was in Camp Kilmer in Special Services all during the war, and whenever I'd play the Apollo Theater he'd come up to New York and I'd bring him on stage in his uniform and the place would go wild.

When I think back, I realize we had several offers to leave Kansas City just before we made the big time. Both John Hammond and Willard Alexander, who had come to Kansas City to hear Basie at the Reno Club, heard my band at Fairyland Park. The same night, Craig, the owner of the Blossom Heath in Oklahoma City, asked me to open the winter season for him, and Charlie Buchanan of the Savoy called me long distance from New York. They all wanted *Until the Real Thing Comes Along*. Joe Glaser was staying at the Muehlbach Hotel and told me not to sign with anyone until I'd thought his offer over. He wired me plane tickets from Chicago and that was it. We had a working agreement with the Grand Terrace in Chicago, and we alternated with Fletcher, Louis Armstrong and Earl Hines from 1936 until 1939. I'll tell you how that worked. Ed Fox owned the Grand Terrace, but Joe Glaser owned the building premises that housed the Grand Terrace, so that was the working arrangement. . . .

The broadcasts we made from the Grand Terrace went down South and we were swinging. It seemed as if we weren't making any records but ballads, but on the broadcasts we were jumping, so the promoters down there wanted us, because they didn't know we played so much jazz.

I played all the best spots in the South. In Atlanta we played the Piedmont Driving Club, the Brookdale Country Club, the Druid Hills Country Club, and a lot of colored dances. I

played all four seasonal proms at Emory University, Texas
A & M, Oklahoma A & M, played Arkansas University any
number of times. The guys at those colleges would take us
right into the frat houses then. Why, every time you'd look
up, you'd see our band at Kentucky University! In Birming-
ham we'd always play a very swanky club called the Five
Points. We'd play the Tiger Hotel at the University of Missouri many times. In fact we played more big places in the
South than we did in the North. The college kids who'd heard
our records would come up to us and say, "We didn't know
you could play so hot, why don't you make some more records
that way?" We never did get as much recognition for our jazz,
but no band worked more than we did. We'd play everything
with a little bounce, always swinging, while the other bands
were always shouting, with high brass, etc. Our stuff was
muted much of the time, but always rhythmic. Up North we'd
play Yale, Harvard, Cornell, Syracuse, University of Connec-
ticut, Franklin & Marshall. Marshall Stearns was at Yale, and
George Frazier was at Harvard, so we got plenty of attention
from them. . . .

Since civil rights went into effect, we had hardly any places
left to play up North where we used to work so much. In
Pennsylvania where I used to work all those small towns, I
had only two places left, Philadelphia and Harrisburg. One of
the managers in a theater where I used to do some of my best
business wouldn't rehire me after civil rights because of the
Negro business it would bring in. Even though he liked me
and wanted me, and the white audiences loved the band, his
boss didn't want Negro business. Before that there was so
much work in these small towns. They all quit hiring Negro
bands. . . . Civil rights worked in reverse in the music business. . . .

During the war I had to enlarge my band because the styles
then called for it. I had to meet the competition then, even
though it was a fad. I had seven and eight brass . . . it was
loud and wrong. My style is built around twelve pieces, although you can still do a good job and get away with ten.
Toward the end of the war things started to fall apart. I made

my last records for Decca, and *I Know* became a big hit. We were booked on a theater tour.

We made a one-nighter in Durham, North Carolina, and jumped from there to Fort Worth, Texas. We made three thousand for the one-nighter, but the jump ate up a lot of it. Then we jumped from Texas to Denver, Colorado, and from there to Brandon, Saskatchewan. From Brandon to Winnipeg, and from Winnepeg to Minneapolis, and from there to Kansas City. When I finally got back to New York, I was seventeen hundred dollars in the hole. The promoters were all but ruined. They had been broken by the booking agents who told them they couldn't get Hampton if they didn't take Armstrong, etc. So the promoters would go ahead and book Armstrong when they didn't need him, in order to get Hampton. All those little operators in Louisiana and Florida and places like that went broke trying to fill four and five dances when they couldn't raise enough to fill one. That's what happened to the band business, so I gave it up. . . .

Today I'm dividing my time between managing at the Hotel Theresa and taking a band out occasionally. I used seventeen men on a date recently, because there are so many places in New York where you can't work with less than twelve. Up until the last year or so I've been using Big Jim, but his teeth went on him. I like to use Ray Copeland because, although he's modern, he's not wild. I introduced him to Don Redman because I felt he had it and should be working regularly with his horn. I've got another terrific man in Allen Smith. Wait until he gets around a little more, he's really got it.

We're still the Clouds of Joy and still play the same basic style. The audiences seem to go for it, in spite of all the changes in music. . . .

Jimmie Lunceford

by William Russo

Another very successful band of the thirties and the forties was—as Danny Barker indicated in the beginning of this book —Jimmie Lunceford's. The first comment on the band comes from Bill Russo, composer-arranger, who virtually grew up with Lunceford's music.

THE DECCA ALBUM, JIMMIE LUNCEFORD AND HIS ORCHESTRA (DL 8050), is made up of 78's originally recorded between 1935 and 1940. The Capitol album, JIMMIE LUNCEFORD IN HI-FI (TAO 924), is a "reconstruction" of Lunceford. It was produced with great love and care by Billy May who used top Los Angeles players, including four or five men who held important chairs in Lunceford's band during the thirties.

The music itself in the first album is far from fine art. It is nowhere near, say, Ellington's work in quality, but it does, however, have great charm and an open, almost ingenuous flavor. The portions of compositional validity do not usually extend for any length. One passage may be lovely and complete, followed by another passage as good but bearing no relationship (not even contrasting relationship) to the first passage. Worse, an imaginative and spontaneous passage may be followed by a passage of utter nonsense.

Impromptu is excellent writing, but too much writing; the result is confused. The saxophone background on *By the River Saint Marie* is worse than that on a stock orchestration. The voice-leading of the saxophones on *Annie Laurie* is inept, as it is frequently in this album. (The brass voice-leading is not much better, but brass cover up internal trouble more easily than saxophones do.)

The first two sections of *Yard Dog Mazurka* are excellently connected; the contrapuntal *pot pourri* is great. How sad that the guitar bridge was inserted. Even worse is the attempt (right after the guitar solo) to pick up where things left off.

Hell's Bells is the most uneven piece of music in the album. The use of wood blocks is delightful. They help create a gay macabre tone—a touch of Halloween. This goblinesque is heard on *Stratosphere* also.

Perhaps the most serious compositional flaw is the way the pieces are ended. Somerset Maugham said, "Anyone can begin a good book but not anyone can end it." The endings of more than half the pieces are incomplete or brutalized. The most incomplete is *Saint Marie,* which begs for two more quarter notes—on the fourth and first beats following. The most brutal ending is that of *Annie Laurie,* one of several which are "buttoned" with a choked high-hat.

The improvised solos in this album are on the whole not good. Only Trummy Young comes anywhere near making an organic and developed statement. On a different level, however, several of the alto saxophone and trumpet solos are very good "band" solos. That is, they are not of great compositional importance in themselves. but they fit the general tone of the preceding and following material; they mark time graciously (the alto solo on *Marie* for example) and connect with the prevailing nature of the piece.

The worst of the improvisation is an absurdity. It is like the incoherent rambling of a "third" alto man who writes some of the vocal charts and gets three chances a night to express himself—at our expense. See the clarinet solo on *Siesta at the Fiesta.*

Although I approve of pre-LP solo length, not believing that Sonny Rollins has gone beyond Lester Young on any level, the cut-up solo segments in these pieces would hamper even the good improviser. He is here asked to play for sixteen bars, lay out for a bridge, and then pick up the chain of thought.

In addition, the whole setting of the music is not particularly conducive to improvisation. The chord progressions do not suggest melodic connection, the backgrounds are too prominent or too jerky, and the music is basically orchestral rather than soloistic.

As a performing group the band is a marvel. It is not as good as good could be, *but it is something!* The brass as a unit and the trumpets as a section know moments of fire and spontaneity and art and cohesion. The plunger brass passages on *Pigeon Walk* are wonderful. Do listeners who don't play brass instruments know the difficulty of a passage like this? The trumpets call to God on *Annie Laurie*. They are loud and brassy, but they do not attack the world—they sing of love and sunlight. The stiff strutting of *Yard Dog Mazurka* is not a caricature. It is affirmative.

This band at times plays with an untouchable ensemble— with good attack and release, matched articulation throughout the winds, and beautiful shadings of volume.

However, the intonation is often bad (especially in the saxophones) and the section balance of saxophones or of trombones is rarely uniform (the fact that these were recorded before our era of Enlightened Stereophony will not excuse this). The drums are badly tuned throughout, and the drummer's playing is often sloppy.

On the whole, though, this band can teach us much. Few groups play with the enthusiasm and *élan* of Lunceford. The glory of being an ensemble player is not even comprehensible to most musicians now. Good-by to a sweeter day!

There are two ways to approach old material. One is to extract and re-form. Since this is often done so badly, it is less popular but is still tempting. This is what Shorty Rogers did in his Basie album. He recast Basie in his own image— giving Basie higher brass, better individual playing, some new harmonies, more players, and more uniformly good soloists. He lost, though, the best qualities of Basie. What is more important, he did not come up with an art object as good as Basie's band (the old one, in this case; the new one has made even greater errors than Rogers did).

A really deplorable example of this approach was Georgie Auld's Broadwayizing of Lunceford. Auld took Lunceford's charm and turned it into a species of Bronx showbiz. His tribute to Lunceford was loud, fast, fierce, and filled with trumpet screams and trombone splats.

May, on the other hand, has tried to produce a Lunceford sound as it would be if recorded today. He has been scholarly, perhaps excessively so. He has added a couple of men but I don't think he has added actual parts. (I'm not positive, of course, since not all the original versions of these pieces are available to me.) In general, May has stuck with the letter and the spirit of Lunceford.

The defects of the music noted in the above Decca album are, of course, still here. But the performance is different.

The drummer is not quite right for the music but he gets a lovely lightness at times especially with the high-hat. The brass shakes on the introduction of *Uptown Blues* are fantastic. On this *Annie Laurie* the brass play three different types of eighth notes (roughly: [a] even, [b] dotted eighths and sixteenths, and [c] quarter and eighth triplets) with cohesion and sensitivity. The intonation throughout the album is impeccable.

When I played this album for Paul Desmond he commented: "Wouldn't Lunceford have loved to take these guys (Conrad Gozzo, Pete Candoli, *et al.*) on the road!" The players here are superb. Man for man they are better than those Lunceford had.

May's band is a better band but they don't play better than the Lunceford band. They could, I'm sure, if they spent three years or even three months together. But they haven't the sound a group gets through night-after-night performance with little change of players, and just about the same music is not to be gotten any other way.

The moral is, of course, that superb players should in some way be held together so that the heights of large jazz orchestra performance could be reached. These two albums direct us toward the heights, certainly.

Jimmie Lunceford: A Reply

by *Albert McCarthy*

This second comment is a letter from Albert McCarthy, who is an expert discographer, long-time Lunceford admirer, and the proprietor of the British critical magazine, Jazz Monthly.

BILL RUSSO'S REVIEW of the Lunceford records was honest and motivated by sympathy, but it still missed the point of the Lunceford band. It is an arranger's view, valid to a degree, but touching only the fringe of the subject.

I heard the Lunceford band a few times in person. I realize that we tend to look back and think things were better than they were, but I also heard Ellington, Teddy Hill, and Edgar Hayes in person, and they did not leave the same impression, so I don't think my attitude is pure romanticism. I am not claiming that the Lunceford band was better than Ellington's, but I expected a certain degree of brilliance from Ellington. Lunceford was a shock. There are lessons to be learned from Lunceford, and it is a pity that only the superficial aspects of the band have been used in the numerous "re-creations."

To begin with, the Lunceford band, almost more than any other, found the secret of pleasing several audiences at once without, except in a few instances, lowering musical standards. To the dancers it was a fine dance band; to the people who went to see a show it was a good theatrical spectacle; to the jazz fan it was a good jazz group. I don't think any other band succeeded so well in engaging diverse audiences. I am concerned with it as a big band from a jazz viewpoint and, leaving out Ellington and Henderson, I don't think it was equaled.

The Lunceford style was really the Sy Oliver style, I suppose—a story goes that Sy Oliver used the same sort of scores with Zack Whyte, but that band never recorded them. The swing of the band was always there, but whereas Basie featured a style that elevated the swing to the point where one could never miss it unless one were deaf, Lunceford utilized it as a necessity but did not feel it necessary to drive it home in the same fashion.

Humor was never far from the surface—even on the dreariest pop complete with a Dan Grissom vocal—and it is instructive to note the contradictory band passages once the vocal was over on so many records—contradictory in the sense that while the vocal was in the accepted sentimental pattern of the day, the band passages were often quite the opposite in mood. Also, on such a pop number as *Linger Awhile,* some of the most interesting scoring (in this case a fine use of three trumpets) can be found.

Paul Desmond is quoted as saying that Lunceford would have loved to have taken musicians like Conrad Gozzo and Pete Candoli on the road, while Mr. Russo says that man for man the musicians in the May band are superior to those Lunceford used. This shows a lack of appreciation of the subject. Gozzo and Candoli *may* be all-around better *technicians* to the Lunceford men (one wonders if this is so why Candoli needed a four-bar help-out to take the solo that Paul Webster managed quite ably on his own on the original version of *For Dancers Only*), but as *personalities* they fall well below their opposite numbers in the Lunceford band—Paul Webster and Eddie Tompkins. The strength of the Lunceford band was based on the individual members of the band as personalities, and, as is so often the case in jazz, the sum total was greater than the score one would get by considering each man on his own. Gozzo and Candoli may be fine musicians, but I have yet to hear any strength of personality in anything they play. They, of course, live in an era of conformity in jazz, and their playing reflects that fact. Such men, excellent in a Hollywood studio group as they might be, represent the antithesis of what Lunceford needed in his band. One might as well say that

Maynard Ferguson would have been better than Paul Webster by virtue of his ability to play higher high notes, but the point is that as a personality it is ludicrous to think of him in the Lunceford band. Too many musicians today, technically flawless though they may be, sound like musical machines, and their music comes out that way. There were only two major soloists in the Lunceford band—Willie Smith and Trummy Young—and yet compared to so many of today's soloists people like Joe Thomas, Sy Oliver, Ted Buckner, etc. sound outstanding. They were not, of course, but by virtue of a certain individuality they almost convince one to the contrary.

The LP Russo was reviewing was a poor selection of titles on the whole—Lunceford has been served badly by his reissues—including some of the most ephemeral numbers made at a time when the band was past its best. (But despite the lack of major soloists that I have mentioned, it is interesting to note how individual the band sounded as against Basie today, when a similar position prevails.) I doubt if any technically equipped studio men could take a piece of rubbish like *Organ Grinder's Swing* and do with it what Sy Oliver and the Lunceford band did. The technique may be there, but the spirit is a different one.

It is this that caused the Lunceford band itself to collapse in the end, for it is not often realized that Lunceford himself was re-creating in the last few years of the band. The effects, high-note exhibitionism, etc. that originally were used with humor and were never taken seriously began to be used with deadpan gravity. It is no accident that the first Kenton band sounded like the latter-day Lunceford, for Lunceford himself lost his own individuality when he began to copy the worst aspects of the "progressives" of his day.

If he had lived, he might even have ended up like a rather poor Kenton.

Lester Young: Paris, 1959

by François Postif

François Postif's interview with Lester Young deserves a special note. The original version of this exceptional conversation appeared in the French magazine Jazz-Hot. *We wrote to editor Charles Delaunay for permission to reprint it, and were able to get a copy of the original tape recording of the exchanges from M. Postif. Thereby, with the help of Frank Driggs and Wen Shih, we published a rather different version, including several portions which had to be omitted from the* Jazz-Hot *version because they all but defied translation.*

Although he wasn't free until five o'clock in the morning, I was determined to interview Lester. I knew he wasn't very talkative, but he wanted the interview to be taped, and that encouraged me.

One afternoon at six o'clock I knocked at his door. Lester told me to come in: he had been waiting for me.

When he saw my tape recorder he shouted happily. He asked me: "Can I talk slang?" I agreed, and from then on he relaxed. I felt during the interview that he was pleased to be able to speak freely.

Q. You weren't really born in New Orleans?

A. Uh, uh. Should I really tell you? I could tell a lie. I was born in Woodville, Mississippi, because my mother went back to the family; so after I was straight, you know, everything was cool, she took me back to New Orleans and we lived in Algiers, which is across the river.

I left when I was ten. They had trucks going arouhd town advertising for all the dances, and this excited me, you know? So they gave me handbills and I was running all over the city until my tongue was hanging out. From there I went to Memphis and then to Minneapolis. I tried to go to school and all that . . . I wasn't interested.

The only person I liked on those trucks in New Orleans was the drummer, you dig?

Drums now? No eyes. I don't want to see them. Every time I'd be in a nice little place, and I'd meet a nice little chick, dig, her mother'd say, "Mary, come on, let's go." Damn, I'd be trying to pack these drums, because I wanted this little chick, dig? She'd called her once and twice, and I'm trying to get straight, so I just said, I'm through with drums. All those other boys got clarinet cases, trumpet cases, trombone cases and I'm wigging around with all that stuff, and Lady Francis, I could really play those drums. I'd been playing them for a whole year.

Q. How did you get started on tenor?

A. I was playing alto and they had this evil old cat with a nice, beautiful background, you know, mother and father and a whole lot of bread and like that, you know, so every time we'd get a job . . . this was in Salinas, Kansas, so every time we'd go see him, we'd be waiting ninety years to get us to work while he fixed his face, you know, so I told the bossman, his name was Art Bronson. So I said, "Listen, why do we have to go through this? You go and buy me a tenor saxophone and I'll play the m-f and we'd be straight then."

So he worked with this music store, and we got straight, and we split. That was it for me. The first time I heard it. Because the alto was a little too high.

Q. When did you learn to read music?

A. When I first came up in my father's band I wasn't reading music; I was faking it, but I was in the band. My father got me an alto out of the pawnshop, and I just picked the m-f up and started playing it. My father played. all the instruments and he read, so I had to get close to my sister, you dig, to learn the parts.

One day my father finally said to me, "Kansas, play your part," and he knew goddam well I couldn't read. So my sister played her part and then he said, "Lester play your part," and I couldn't read a m-f note, not a damn note. He said, "Get up and learn some scales." Now you know my heart was broke, you dig, and I went and cried my little teardrops, while they went on rehearsing. I went away and learned to read the music, and I came back in the band. All the time I was learning to read, I was playing the records and learning the music at the same time, so I could completely foul them up.

I don't like to read music, just soul . . . there you are.

I got a man in New York writing music for me right now, so when I get back it'll be for bass violin, two cellos, viola, French horn and three rhythm. I'll just take my time with it, if it don't come out right, I'll just say no. This is the first time, and I always wanted to do that. Norman Granz would never let me make no records with no strings. Yardbird made million of records with strings. When I was over here the last time I played with strings, the first winners, I think they were. Germans. Anyway I played with them, and they treated me nice and played nice for me.

Q. Who were your early influences?

A. I had a decision to make between Frankie Trumbauer and Jimmy Dorsey, you dig, and I wasn't sure which way I wanted to go. I'd buy me all those records and I'd play one by Jimmy and one by Trumbauer, you dig? I didn't know nothing about Hawk then, and they were the only ones telling a story I liked to hear. I had both of them made.

Q. Was Bud Freeman an influence?

A. Bud Freeman??!! We're nice friends, I saw him just the other day down at the union, but influence, ladedehumptedore-bebob . . . ! Did you ever hear him [Trumbauer] play *Singing the Blues?* That tricked me right then and that's where I went.

Q. How about Coleman Hawkins?

A. As far as I'm concerned, I think Coleman Hawkins was the President first, right? When I first heard him I thought that was some great jazz I was listening to. As far as myself, I think I'm the second one. Not braggadocious, you know I don't talk like that. There's only one way to go. If a guy plays tenor, he's got to sound like Hawk or like Lester. If he plays alto, he's got to be Bird or Johnny Hodges. There's another way, the way I hear all the guys playing in New York, running all over the place.

In Kansas City, when I was with Basie, they told me to go and see Coleman Hawkins, and how great he is; so I wanted to see how great he is, you know. So they shoved me up on the stand, and I grabbed his saxophone, played it, read his clarinet parts, everything! Now I got to run back to my job where there was thirteen people and I got to run ten blocks. I don't think Hawk showed at all. Then I went to Little Rock with Count Basie, and I got this telegram from Fletcher Henderson saying come with me. So I was all excited because this was big time, and I showed it around to everyone and asked them what I should do. Count said he couldn't tell me, so I decided to split and went to Detroit. But it wasn't for me. The m-f's were whispering on me, every time I played. I can't make that. I couldn't take that, those m-f's whispering on me, Jesus! So I went up to Fletcher and asked him, "Would you give me a nice recommendation? I'm going back to Kansas City." He said, "Oh, yeah" right quick. That bitch, she was Fletcher's wife, she took me down to the basement and played one of those old windup record players, and she'd say, "Lester, can't you play like this?" Coleman Hawkins records. But I mean, can't you hear this? Can't you get with that? You dig? I split! Every morning that bitch would wake me up at nine o'clock to teach me to play like Coleman Hawkins. And she played trumpet herself . . . circus trumpet! I'm gone!

Q. How did you first go with Basie?

A. I used to hear this tenor player with Basie all the time. You see we'd get off at two in Minneapolis and it would be one in Kansas City, that kind of stuff, you dig. So I sent Basie this telegram telling him I couldn't stand to hear that m-f, and will you accept me for a job at any time? So he sent me a ticket and I left my madam here and came on.

Q. How did you get along with Herschel?

A. We were nice friends and things, but some nights when we got on the stand it was like a duel, and other nights it would be nice music. He was a nice person, in fact I was the last to see him die. I even paid his doctor bills. I don't blame him; he loved his instrument, and I loved mine. . . .

Q. Why did you leave the Basie band?

A. That's some deep question you're asking me now. Skip that one, but I sure could tell you that, but it wouldn't be sporting. I still have nice eyes. I can't go around thinking evil and all that. The thing is still cool with me, because I don't bother about nobody. But you take a person like me, I stay by myself, so how do you know anything about me? Some m-f walked up to me and said, "Prez, I thought you were dead!" I'm probably more alive than he is, you dig, from that hearsay.

Q. You've known Billie for a long time, haven't you?

A. When I first came to New York I lived with Billie. She was teaching me about the city, which way to go, you know? She's still my Lady Day.

What people do, man, it's so obvious, you know? If you want to speak like that, what do I care what you do? What he do, what he does, what nobody do, it's nobody's business! Man, they say he's an old junkie, he's old and funky, all that, that's not nice. Whatever they do, let them do that and enjoy themselves, and you get your kicks yourself. All I do is smoke some New Orleans cigarettes, don't sniff nothing in my nose, nothing. I drink and I smoke and that's all. But a lot of people think I'm this way and I don't like that, I resent that. My business is the musical thing, all the way. . . .

Q. Do you think you play modern today?

A. In my mind when I play, I try not to be a repeater pencil, you dig? Always leave some spaces—lay out. You won't catch me playing like *Lester Leaps In* and that shit, but I always go back.

I can play all those reed instruments. I can play bass clarinet. If I brought that out, wouldn't it upset everything? I know both Coltrane and Rollins. I haven't heard Coltrane, but I played with Rollins once in Detroit. I just made some records for Norman with clarinet. I haven't played it for a long time, because one of my friends stole it. That's the way it goes. I made them in 1958, in the Hollywood Bowl. Oscar Peterson and his group.

I developed my tenor to sound like an alto, to sound like a tenor, to sound like a bass, and I'm not through with it yet. That's why they get all trapped up, they say "Goddam, I never heard Prez play like this." That's the way I want them to hear. That's *modern,* dig? Not what you played back in '49 —it's what you play today, dig? A lot of them got lost and walked out.

Q. Do you play the same thing every day?

A. Not unless you want to get henpecked.

Q. What kind of group would you like to have?

A. Give me my little three rhythm and me—happiness . . . the four Mills Brothers, ha, ha. I can relax better, you dig. I don't like a whole lotta noise no goddam way. Trumpets and trombones, and all that stuff. I'm looking for something soft; I can't stand that loud noise. Those places, in New York, the trumpets screaming, and the chicks putting their fingers in their ears. It's got to be sweetness, you dig? Sweetness can be funky, filthy, or anything. Whatever you want!

The blues? Great Big Eyes! Because if you play with a new band like I have and are just working around, and they don't know no blues, you can't play anything! Everybody has to play the blues and everybody has them too. . . .

Am I independent? Very much! I'd have taken off the other night if I had five hundred dollars. I just can't take that b-s, you dig? They want everybody who's a Negro to be an Uncle Tom, or Uncle Remus, or Uncle Sam, and I can't make it. It's the same all over, you fight for your life—until death do you part, and then you got it made. . . .

Republished from *Jazz-Hot* by permission of Charles Delaunay, *redacteur.*
Transcribed from tapes of the interview.

Billie Holiday

by Glenn Coulter

Certainly Glenn Coulter's appreciation of Billie Holiday should follow Lester Young's words. Miss Holiday's mother has said that, from the next room, she could not tell the difference between the sound of her daughter's humming and Lester Young's tenor saxophone.

LADY IN SATIN, Columbia CL 1157. Ray Ellis and his Orchestra: *I'm a Fool to Want You; For Heaven's Sake; You Don't Know What Love Is; I Get Along Without You Very Well; For All We Know; Violets for Your Furs; You've Changed; It's Easy to Remember; But Beautiful; Glad to Be Unhappy; I'll Be Around; The End of a Love Affair.*

BODY AND SOUL, Verve MGV 8719. Jimmy Rowles, *piano;* Barney Kessel, *guitar;* Ben Webster, *tenor sax;* Harry "Sweets" Edison, *trumpet;* Alvin Stoller, *drums.*
Body and Soul; Darn That Dream; Comes Love; Moonlight in Vermont.
Same personnel except Larry Bunker, *drums:*
They Can't Take That Away from Me; Let's Call the Whole Thing Off; Gee, Baby, Ain't I Good to You; Embraceable You.

THE BLUES ARE BREWIN', Decca DL 8701. Sid Cooper, Johnny Mince, *altos;* A. Drelinger, Pat Nizza, *tenors;* Bernie Privin, *trumpet;* Billy Kyle, *piano;* Jimmy Crawford, *drums;* Joe Benjamin, *bass;* Everett Barksdale, *guitar;* Louis Armstrong, *vocal;* on first two tunes.
You Can't Lose a Broken Heart; My Sweet Hunk of Trash; Now or Never.
G. Dorsey, Pete Clark, *altos;* Fred Williams, Budd Johnson, *tenors;* Dave McRae, *baritone;* Shad Collins, Buck Clayton, R. Williams, *trumpets;* G. Stevenson, Henderson Chambers, *trombones;* Horace

Henderson, *piano;* Wallace Bishop, *drums;* J. Benjamin, *bass;*
E. Barksdale, *guitar:*
Do Your Duty; Gimme a Pigfoot and a Bottle of Beer.
G. Dorsey, J. Mince, *altos;* Fred Williams, Budd Johnson, *tenors;*
Ed Barefield, *baritone;* B. Privin, Tony Faso, Dick Vance, *trum-
pets;* H. Chambers, M. Bullman, *trombones;* H. Henderson, *piano;*
G. Duvivier, *bass;* E. Barksdale, *guitar;* drummer unidentified:
Keeps on Rainin'.
G. Dorsey, Rudy Powell, *altos;* Joe Thomas, Lester Young, *tenors;*
Sol Moore, *baritone;* Jimmy Nottingham, E. Berry, Buck Clayton,
trumpets; G. Matthews, Dickie Wells, *trombones;* H. Henderson,
piano; Shadow Wilson, *drums;* G. Duvivier, *bass;* M. Lowe, *guitar:*
Baby Get Lost.
Lem Davis, *alto;* Bob Dorsey, *tenor;* Bobby Tucker, *piano;* D.
Best, *drums;* John Simmons, *bass;* R. Reese, *trumpet:*
The Blues Are Brewin'; Guilty.
Joe Guy, *trumpet;* Billy Kyle, *piano;* Kenny Clarke, *drums;* T.
Barney, *bass;* Jim Shirley, *guitar:*
Baby, I Don't Cry over You.
Joe Springer, *piano;* Kelly Martin, *drums;* Billy Taylor, *bass;* Tiny
Grimes, *guitar;* Joe Guy, *trumpet:*
Big Stuff.
Milt Yaner, *clarinet* and *alto;* John Fulton, *flute, clarinet* and *tenor;*
Bernie Leighton, *piano;* Bunny Shawker, *drums;* J. Lesberg, *bass;*
T. Mottola, *guitar;* Bobby Hackett, *trumpet;* and five strings:
Somebody's on My Mind.

THE LADY SINGS, Decca DL 8215.
*Deep Song; You Better Go Now; Don't Explain; Ain't Nobody's
Business If I Do; God Bless the Child; Them There Eyes; Good
Morning Heartache; No More; No Good Man; I'll Look Around;
Easy Living; What Is This Thing Called Love.*
On 1, 2, & 11, orchestra directed by Bob Haggart; on 6, orchestra
directed by Sy Oliver; on 8, orchestra directed by Camarata; 10,
Billy Kyle and his Trio; orchestra unidentified on others.

HOLIDAY CLASSICS, Commodore FL 30008. Frankie Newton, *trumpet;* Tab Smith, *alto sax;* Kenneth Hollon, Stanley Payne, *tenor
saxes;* Sonny White, *piano;* James McLin, *guitar;* John Williams,
bass; Eddie Dougherty, *drums.*
*Yesterdays; I Gotta Right to Sing the Blues; Strange Fruit; Fine
and Mellow.*
Eddie Heywood, *piano;* Doc Cheatham, *trumpet;* Lem Davis, *alto
sax;* Vic Dickenson, *trombone;* Teddy Walters, *guitar;* John Simmons, *bass;* Big Sid Catlett, *drums:*
*I'll Be Seeing You; I'll Get By; I Cover the Waterfront; How Am
I to Know; My Old Flame.*

Eddie Heywood, *piano;* John Simmons, *bass;* Big Sid Catlett, *drums:*
Lover, Come Back to Me; She's Funny That Way; On the Sunny Side of the Street.

Langston Hughes: THE WEARY BLUES, MGM E 3697. Langston Hughes, *recitation;* Red Allen, *trumpet;* Vic Dickenson, *trombone;* Sam Taylor, *tenor sax;* Al Williams, *piano;* Milt Hinton, *bass;* Osie Johnson, *drums.*
Blues Montage; Testament.
Langston Hughes, *recitation;* Horace Parlan, *piano;* Jimmy Knepper, *trombone;* Shafi Hadi, *tenor sax;* Charles Mingus, *bass;* Kenny Dennis, *drums:*
Consider Me; Dream Montage.

LADY IN SATIN is the name of a new Columbia record of twelve more or less insipid songs done by Billie Holiday against the neon arrangements of Ray Ellis. It is very nearly total disaster. The fault is not wholly that of the arranger, though one is tempted to say so. Still, the ideal accompaniment for a jazz vocal is a many-noted commentary which does not interfere with what the singer is doing, but rather provides a texture of the utmost contrast and a springboard of rhythm. Ellis provides the hit-record approach, slow, sleek, insufficiently subordinated counterpoint, as rugged as Reddi-wip and so continuous that Billie's timing is thrown off, for want of anything to brace itself against. The instrumental richness (to say nothing of the heavenly-choir effect furnished from time to time: it is at any rate simply *aah*, not *doo-aah*) also cancels out her own unique sonority, that rasp or snarl which in itself preserves her from expressing mere self-pity.

It is a burden to hear the Ellis arrangement systematically frustrating Billie's intentions through every measure of *Easy to Remember*, which might have been, in any but this chenille setting, a real accomplishment. But whoever selected the material for this date is as much to blame as Ellis. True, Billie (like Armstrong, Toscanini, and most established performers) usually prefers to handle the same few numbers over and over. Doubtless someone designed this record to introduce her, as the phrase has it, to a wider audience, and also to a broader repertoire. The results are not happy. At best, Billie must contend with songs for the most part of indifferent quality, on which her grasp is too uncertain to allow any exercise of power or insight—anything that might make them worth attention. At worst, she has not even taken the trouble to find out how they go: *Glad to be Unhappy* (and it is the most substantial tune in the set) is a discreditable travesty which should never have been released.

With these stimuli to unease, it is no wonder that Billie's voice fails her. Nowadays, whenever she has to fight undesirable circumstances—inappropriate accompaniment as here, or uncongenial surroundings as at Newport II—she mistakenly responds by forcing, with a result that must make every listener's throat ache sympathetically. (On the other hand, when there is no untoward pressure, as at Lenox in the summer of 1957, her voice is intact. Critics lately have praised her for showing "flashes of the old brilliance" so frequently that one might well mistake hers for the eternal fire of the Arc de Triomphe.) It is no pleasure to describe most of these performances, the gritty tone, the wavering pitch, the inability to control an instrument that is nothing without control; many times one can't name with any certainty the notes she is striving for. Billie's superiority (I am sure it remains, and will remain after this record has been deleted) has always rested in transcending her materials: hacking off melodic excess, and attacking the words with, alternately, deeper conviction and greater contempt. The ambiguity is, in her best performances, elusive and unpredictable, gives even rather foolish songs a startling resemblance to real existence, and, since the process is just as musical as it is verbal and operates like opposing mirrors, results in fascination rather than monotony. Naturally, when sheer articulation becomes difficult, none of this can come into play. It does in this set only once: *You've Changed* is remarkably free of flaws, and one is likely to play it over several times in delight without realizing how absurd the text is.

In a better world than this, Columbia, on its side, would have reissued more of the Wilson-Holiday masterpieces, now more than twenty years old. On her side, Billie might better have stayed with Granz. For the last of her Verve records to be released, BODY AND SOUL, is a better product in every way. Here are eight tunes suited to Billie, and in place of the heavenly choir Webster and Edison supply obbligatos and solos. Webster is particularly good; his sonority alone is music to read F. Scott Fitzgerald by. Billie's voice is as clear as it can be these days, though there is a straining after high-lying passages, as in the title song, and the amplification of her voice, though necessary, is excessive, yielding a sound darker and coarser than the reality. *They Can't Take That Away from Me* demonstrates the advisability of having the instruments get out of her way early: she begins like the guillotine blade in slow motion, and Webster, when his turn comes, has a solo that is all jaunty nostalgia. Billie teases *Comes Love* along: just imagine how arch another singer would be, or how self-consciously sultry. (Next to Billie, others singing of love sound like little girls playing house.) It was not to be expected that Lady should surpass her 1944 *Embraceable You,* but she has. Her second chorus is more than an embellishment of the melody; it is a new melody, a sort of inversion of the original or shadowy melody that offsets its descent by overleaping the climactic note. It is a striking line indeed, and her commanding manipulation of it exceeds the ability of every other active singer of jazz.

Billie Holiday's desire to phrase like a horn, not just to sing, enhances words as well as music. It is a strategy that involves attacking each note separately, a vocal approximation of the instrumentalist's bowing or plucking or whatever it is, and stifling the voice's natural vibrato in favor of one that is rare and eccentrically placed. These characteristics of her style mean that each syllable seems unnaturally distinct, as if each were a stone plopped into a pool of still water, and, because she delights in staying well behind the beat, critics have been fooled into dismissing her as a kind of precious *diseuse,* momentarily interesting but not to be compared with a real jazz artist, like, say, Sarah or Anita.

This misunderstanding might be most readily cleared up if such critics would try listening to Lady's voice as they would to a horn, to the way it burns through *Fine and Mellow* (when Blesh ridiculed this he must have been too busy beating time to notice how the angry wail blazes throughout—or does he think the tone of a buzz-saw enervated?)—but then, it would be too bad to overlook what happens to the text.

Fine and Mellow is one of twelve songs done for Commodore now newly reissued on LP. Even God gets tired of too much alleluia, and it would be fruitless to invent fresh ways of commending performances which Commodore rightly calls classic. Among others which are better known, I would single out two: *My Old Flame* is done with a jauntiness not often associated with Billie and beautifully in keeping with the spirit of the text. It would be difficult to imagine an emptier song than *How Am I to Know;* yet Billie seems to charge it, from the release on, with some fleeting but true significance.

A jazz collection without these performances would be a poor thing indeed.

Billie Holiday's work for Decca (1946-49) has been transferred to LP, and two of the records which make up this praiseworthy venture afford an amusing and instructive contrast. As might be expected, the last issue, THE BLUES ARE BREWIN', is the least in merit, the bottom of the bin. Two tunes linked to the name of Bessie Smith—*Gimme a Pigfoot* and *Do Your Duty*—remind us of what Billie's work lacks: informality, joy, spontaneity. A pair of duets with Louis are well sung but disfigured by stale ad libs. None of these should be taken seriously anyhow; they are music-hall material, only incidentally jazz. The rest of the set contains mediocre pop tunes performed with due (but unintentional) insipidity—except for a Leonard Bernstein tune which it would be better to deal with further on.

Most of the backing for both sets is supplied by sizable bands. Brasses make the kind of din that is, science tells us, fatal to mice, yet the arrangements are not bad as support and they are idiomatic.

THE LADY SINGS is the other Decca, and indeed she does. It seems wasteful to attempt any description of these performances: anybody of a certain age must have taken cognizance of them when they were first issued. (The sound, incidentally, has paled in the transfer.) What was not so apparent when they were released two by two was their expressive variety: the cold dismissal of *No More,* the contorted pathos of *You Better Go Now,* the perhaps excessive virtuosity of *Ain't Nobody's Business.* *I'll Look Around* is a lesson for all who would be jazz singers, the line sustained from first to last, the approach to it just suspenseful enough to make it live, the words forced to generate real meaning. But there is no pat explanation of how Billie can make a quite common interval, say a major third, seem an unusual and difficult leap, nor of how she can isolate and break down for analysis the counterwords in her lyrics.

This unique method—of course the word is misleading; I do not suggest any gnawing consciousness that the words are trash—of battling the weakness of the material is only intermittently successful. So are the attempts of writers to break away from the greeting-card accomplishments of the ordinary popular song and create something the average intelligent adult can stomach. No escape has been devised so far, save into a pretentious rhetoric (see *Deep Song*), or a supper-club smartness the only true merit of which is an unintended status: the payoff is Mabel Mercer. Worst of all, perhaps, is a text like Bernstein's *Big Stuff,* a post-Freudian attempt to evoke the blues, only less insulting than the deplorably successful *West Side Story* because it is, happily, brief.

The failure of lyricists to keep pace with the refinement and development of jazz may be one reason why so few singers of jazz exist. It is the more surprising when one considers the affinity of jazz with poetry or with any sort of spoken word. Jazz instrumentalists are complimented for making the horn talk, and the two arts are alike in their approach to rhythm: they both delight in stress variation and in substituting length for accent. It is not necessary to glance at Hopkins' sprung rhythm (which of course he didn't say he invented) to understand this relationship; even the heroic couplet, in the hands of Pope, becomes a flexible measure, and one can hear that a line like "lulled by soft zephyrs through the broken pane" needs

to be declaimed like Bill, not Roy, Harris. Classical music, at
least that century and a half of it represented on most concert
programs, derives rhythmic complexity from the varied length
of phrases and from the timing of instrumental entrances; it
seeks to establish a larger structure than jazz does and is less
concerned with instantaneous excitements. For this reason
classical songs that have a care for poetic declamation appear
more fragmentary than songs that merely use the texts to suggest a mood: more fragmentary, but more venturesome.

This digression attempts to hint at a possible reason for the
most recent experiments in combining jazz with spoken poetry.
The experiments need not be faddy, though it is tempting to
dismiss them as that. On the contrary, they seem a reasonable
way of trying to cope with the suggested difficulties.

MGM's release of THE WEARY BLUES with Langston Hughes
(the title could have been spared) is the first recorded fruits
of the idea. It comes off easily, perhaps too easily. The poetry
of Hughes (his reading is too offhand) never strays far from
the blues form and the blues idea, though occasionally it attempts, with success, to reflect a conscious social attitude with
an oblique delicacy that is no part of the intention of a real
blues. Since William Empson, we have learned to call this a
form of pastoral poetry; it is really a defensive type of ghetto-
ism; the in-group counterpart to it is, say, a Perelman burlesque. The trouble with such verse is that it does not attempt
to do much more than jazz already can do; a Hughes reference
to Lenox Avenue, or to Count Basie, is equivalent to such
things as the Hot Seven *Squeeze Me,* in which Louis beautifully interpolates a phrase from *High Society,* or to a hundred
such interpolations. Poems which mean to evoke a jazz expressiveness are even less likely to be enhanced by competing
with the very source of their inspiration. *Six Bits Blues,* accompanied by a boogie-woogie train piece, cancels itself out,
and the music behind *Weary Blues* suffers from being talked
about—more accurately, the listener suffers in both instances
from having his own response anticipated and confined.

The blues I have mentioned form a part of the less effective
collage, in which Hughes goes snacks with a "traditional"

group—Red Allen, Dickenson, and so on. Hinton has a good solo, the best moment on the side, as well as the most imaginative use of words and music. It was an excellent idea to bring in a contrasting group—the Mingus unit—for the other side, even if the results show us nothing new. There has been more of an attempt to integrate the words and music, though in no mimetic way: "the boogie-woogie rumble of a dream deferred" is not accompanied by anything of the kind, and the brief reference to Basie is really witty, not a misguided literalism. The requirements of the situation appear to curb Mingus somewhat, though his *Double G Train* figure is a good thing, reminiscent of Ellington as the notes suggest, and once or twice everybody gets hot.

There are bound to be many more recordings of this sort in the future, but it seems doubtful that either poetry or jazz will benefit from the association. After all, no art can feed on another this way, however many successful momentary matches are arranged. It would be interesting to try reading some highly formal verse to jazz accompaniment; the French stanzas or even the complicated syllabic patters of Welsh verse which have occasionally been tried in English. And someone ought to try cueing in the spoken words as another rhythmic instrument. But however it is done, the words will have to be subordinated to the music, as they are in the few classical experiments of this kind: the Sitwell-Walton *Façade* and the Ramuz-Stravinsky *Histoire du Soldat*. Perhaps, after all, jazz will be obliged to assimilate new expressive devices and instrumental techniques, and the speaking of poetry in this context will disappear, having served its purpose.

Stan Getz

by Martin Williams

*Lester Young had many followers, several of whom were able
to work out very personal styles using his basic language as
their guide. The most celebrated and famous of them is Stan
Getz. (But of course, before Getz arrived, there had already
been Charlie Parker.)*

Stan Getz: THE SOFT SWING, Verve MG V-8321. Stan Getz, *tenor;*
Mose Allison, *piano;* Addison Farmer, *bass;* Jerry Segal, *drums.*
*All the Things You Are; Pocono Mac; Down Beat; To the Ends of
the Earth; Bye Bye Blues.*

ABOUT THREE YEARS ago the Jazztone club issued a collection
of Stan Getz's Roost recordings. I wrote a review of it which
I had better quote from. "These . . . have a surface excitement and motion, an immediately appealing tone. They have
been highly praised, and Getz's reputation greatly depends on
them. They certainly reveal a large talent and possibly an individual voice, however obviously derived in some respects
from Lester Young.

"But under the surface there are other things. The first is
the structure of some of Getz's solos: despite the apparent
flow, they aren't always melodic and may consist merely of
runs and riffs—mostly swing licks and riffs—carelessly strung
together, sometimes with a certain hesitation between licks,
rather different from the effective pauses of, say, Miles Davis,
however much they may sound like them. Also, he knows that
nowadays one is supposed to make transitions from one chorus
to the next, not stop dead at the end of one and begin the
next as a very separate unit; he is therefore always ready with

a phrase which crosses from, say, bar 31 to bar 2. . . . But there is sometimes an awkward moment before he gets that phrase, and it amounts to his stopping a chorus dead at bar 30 and beginning a new one at 32 or 2. . . . Again, his sometime efforts at Parkeresque double-timing can be badly fumbled. Most important—and I am frankly subjective—is the emotional element. It seems to me that despite the 'cool' surface . . . there is sometimes an almost harrowing frustration and excruciating tenseness (not tension) under the surface . . . like a man walking down a very steep hill trying desperately to move at a steady pace."

That is the feeling about Getz's work which I brought to this record. Almost none of it applies here, and for the first time I was able to enjoy rather than merely "appreciate" Stan Getz's wonderful musicianship, ear, and melodic spontaneity.

The reason, chiefly, is that he is relaxed and the music simply flows out of him. One of the things that comes through beautifully here is what a master of his own rhythmic idiom Getz is. It matters little that basically he is "old-fashioned," that he has taken the metric conception of the more "advanced" men of the late thirties as his basis, made it more "regular," and been little affected by Parker rhythmically. Here, without the usual inside pressure, he almost rolls around in his rhythmic idiom, teases it, coaxes it with an almost astonishing sureness.

There is very good stop-time on the two blues, *Pocono Mac* and *Down Beat* (that admission comes from one who still resents having heard Getz play *Lester Leaps In* almost note for note off the Basie-Young record at a public concert three years ago), and that second chorus on *To the Ends of the Earth* comes very close to being one of those brilliantly wrought improvisations that jazz records were made to preserve—and there's no whining either.

Allison's solos seem almost listless to me. Some Philly Joe-ish things that Segal does fit beautifully as a kind of rhythmic countervoice to Getz.

As you can deduce, this record (made, by the way, in 1957)

is, for me, *the* Stan Getz record. I tried it on a square friend. Comment: "That sounds lovely." I tried it on a friend who lost interest in jazz about 1940. Comment: "Is that modern jazz? I *like* it." I tried it on a critic. Comment: "But he sounds like Zoot."

King Pleasure and Annie Ross

by Hsio Wen Shih

During the fifties the practice of setting words to previously recorded jazz solos had a kind of boom. And two of its early recorded examples, by King Pleasure and Annie Ross (later of Lambert, Hendricks, & Ross), were reissued. Wen Shih's review of them was one of our "Reconsiderations."

RECENT REISSUES OF some King Pleasure and some Annie Ross recordings on Prestige 7128, and the recent revival of interest in vocal versions of famous instrumental performances, suggest a review of critical standards for assessing such records. Though their immediate popularity is based on the appeal of novelty, that novelty is soon exhausted. Their survival must depend on more solid merits which should at least include musical fidelity to their model, lyrics that reinforce the expression of the music, and an end result in performance that shows, as the Marxists would say, surplus value added by labor. Musical fidelity is no more than the duty which an adapter owes the originator, and since the singer is both adapter and interpreter, the lyrics set to the musical line should interpret and reinforce the musical content. Finally, if the performance does not intensify the impact of the music, there is no justification for the vocal version except novelty.

Few tracks on this LP would sustain examination along these lines. Even a comparison of the most interesting tracks, *Parker's Mood* and *Twisted,* to their models seems like harnessing butterflies to the plow. Still, some interesting conclusions appear.

The largest obstacle to musical fidelity is technique. Take

the selection of tempo: Parker played *Parker's Mood*[1] at about 165, Pleasure at 130; Gray's[2] *Twisted* is 192, Miss Ross's is 155.

Reducing the tempo is legitimate enough, but if the whole performance is limited to the running time of a ten-inch 78 rpm record, some cuts must be made. Pleasure made the simplest and safest cut. He was working with a no-theme blues, and he simply cut out the one-chorus solo that followed the piano solo, and went right into the out-of-tempo tag. Miss Ross's method was more elaborate and harder to understand. Gray's *Twisted* was structured like this: a single chorus of theme running into a three-chorus improvisation; three contrasting choruses, two by piano and one bass; another improvised chorus that contains a short drum solo running into two closing theme choruses. Miss Ross altered this into two theme choruses, the three solo choruses, one instrumental chorus, and two closing theme choruses. She deleted only two choruses, but she substituted a repeat of the theme for the interesting improvised chorus that included the drum solo. The result has lost the smooth flow of the first four choruses which Gray was careful to emphasize by building theme and improvisation of the same kind of phrases, and the admirable asymmetrical structure has been turned into a duller symmetrical one.

Technical problems affect other purely musical elements too. I am reminded of Josephine Tey's comment after hearing two children practice piano, "Ruth puts in all the tiddly bits and the expression and doesn't care how many wrong notes she strikes, but with Jane it's accuracy or nothing." King Pleasure knew the importance of producing the tonal quirks, the slurs and inflections, that were an important part of Parker's blues expression, but he does not seem to have had control enough to imitate Parker's gradually increasing volume on ascending melodic lines. He understandably omits the fluff in the fourth bar and the grace note in bar 14, but he hardly even approximates the runs in bars 8 and 9, and he seriously weakens phrases ending at bars 7, 11, 15, 17, and 23 by

---

[1] CHARLIE PARKER MEMORIAL—Savoy MG 12009.
[2] WARDELL GRAY MEMORIAL—Prestige 7009.

altering the last note to easier intervals. Miss Ross was more successful in singing all the rhythmic nuances of Gray's line, but she ignored the tonal inflections that liven Gray's solo, as she neglected almost everything in his playing that cannot be scored—one almost suspects that she worked from a transcription rather than the record itself. She never suggested the power or the twang of Wardell's tone, as she hardly could have with her small pure voice, and the loss is serious, for they were among Wardell's chief jazz strengths.

Setting words to jazz solos is also technically demanding, but the lyricist needs more than ingenuity; he needs musical sympathy enough to interpret the expressive intent of the original soloist. Since musicians tend to exercise their sense of irony in titling instrumentals, the titles often offer a misleading clue. King Pleasure again followed a simple method; he set the most difficult passages to snatches of traditional blues lyrics and wrote a "continuity" to hold them together. The result is a set of lyrics that, like many older blues, depends on emotional rather than logical cohesion; a collage of great unity.

Miss Ross started from the title rather than the music. She superimposed over Gray's celebration of masculine vitality another whole view of life: a cute, elaborate, and rather tricky spoof. The conflict is obvious only when her version is compared with the original, for she has removed all masculine traces from her version. The scale is reduced, and the intention is much less serious. The relation between the words and the music has become mechanical rather than organic.

Perhaps we should conclude that predominantly solo records like *Parker's Mood* and *Twisted* are not the most suitable material for singers to adapt. The complicated phrasing and the elusive and personal expressive qualities seem more than most singers can sustain. Less ambitious efforts like the recent Basie band adaptations, with more diffuse and impersonal content, seem to offer a better chance for success. Perhaps the whole school is doomed to a degree of aesthetic failure, for the best re-creator on these recordings is John Lewis, who played his solo of five years earlier and managed to extract more meaning from the same notes by slight rhythmic displacements.

Our final impression of *Parker's Mood* is a mixture of admiration, pleasure, and exasperation. King Pleasure has done something difficult. He has managed to write and sing a blues lyric that reinforced the meaning of Parker's solo. Our pleasure is increased by the quotes which give the same kind of snobbish satisfaction as an identified reference in Joyce or Eliot. The few rhythmic lapses and the substitution of easy intervals for interesting ones exasperate us in this otherwise fine recording.

Our feeling about *Twisted* is more ambiguous. We are convinced of the merits of Wardell Gray's *Twisted,* and we feel that Miss Ross, rather than reinforcing them, has eliminated many of their strongest qualities. This is aesthetically unforgivable, yet we are still charmed, not so much by the record, but by hearing her sing it in person. In the end we can only regard our feeling for *Twisted* as a bad habit, like the cigarettes we forswear every night and light up every morning.

An Afternoon with Miles Davis

by Nat Hentoff

Co-editor Hentoff's visit with Miles Davis was a part of our second issue.

MILES LIVES IN a relatively new building on Tenth Avenue near 57th Street. The largest area in his apartment is the living room. Like the other rooms, it is uncluttered. The furnishings have been carefully selected and are spare. Miles has a particular liking for "good wood" and explains thereby why his *Down Beat* plaques—and even his Four Roses Award from the Randall's Island Festival—are all displayed. He has a good piano and an adequate nonstereo record player.

The idea of the afternoon—the first of a series of observations by Miles to be printed at regular intervals in this monthly —was to play a variety of recordings for him and transcribe his reactions. This was not a blindfold test, for while I find those adventures in skeet shooting entertaining, I doubt if they serve much purpose except transistory titillation.

First was Billie Holiday's 1937 *I Must Have That Man* with Wilson, Clayton, Goodman, Young, Green, Page and Jo Jones. "I love the way Billie sings," Miles began. "She sings like Lester Young and Louis Armstrong play, but I don't like all that's going on behind her. All she needed was Lester and the rhythm. The piano was ad libbing while she was singing, which leads to conflict, and the guitar was too loud and had too much accent on every beat."

Miles was asked whether he agreed with most of the writers on jazz that the Billie of twenty years ago was the "best" Billie and that she is now in decline. "I'd rather hear her now.

She's become much more mature. Sometimes you can sing words every night for five years, and all of a sudden it dawns on you what the song means. I played *My Funny Valentine* for a long time—and didn't like it—and all of a sudden it meant something. So with Billie, you know she's not thinking now what she was in 1937, and she's probably learned more about different things. And she still has control, probably more control now than then. No, I don't think she's in a decline.

"What I like about Billie is that she sings it just the way she hears it and that's usually the way best suited for her. She has more feeling than Ella and more experience in living a certain way than Ella. Billie's pretty wild, you know.

"She sings way behind the beat and then she brings it up—hitting right on the beat. You can play behind the beat, but every once in a while you have to cut into the rhythm section on the beat and that keeps everybody together. Sinatra does it by accenting a word. A lot of singers try to sing like Billie, but just the act of playing behind the beat doesn't make it sound soulful.

"I don't think that guys like Buck Clayton are the best possible accompanists for her. I'd rather hear her with Bobby Tucker, the pianist she used to have. She doesn't need any horns. She sounds like one anyway."

Miles's reaction to Clifford Brown's *Joy Spring* as played by the Oscar Peterson Trio on THE MODERN JAZZ QUARTET AND THE OSCAR PETERSON TRIO AT THE OPERA HOUSE (Verve MG-V 8269) was intensely negative. "Oscar makes me sick because he copies everybody. He even had to *learn* how to play the blues. Everybody knows that if you flat a third, you're going to get a blues sound. He learned that and runs it into the ground worse than Billy Taylor. You don't have to do that.

"Now take the way he plays the song. That's not what Clifford meant. He passes right over what can be done with the chords," and here Miles demonstrated on the piano, as he did frequently during the afternoon. "It's much prettier if you get into it and hear the chord weaving in and out like Bill Evans and Red Garland could do—instead of being so heavy. Oscar is jazzy; he jazzes up the tune. And he sure has devices, like certain scale patterns, that he plays all the time.

"Does he swing hard like some people say? I don't know what they mean when they say 'swing hard' anyway. Nearly everything he plays, he plays with the same degree of force. He leaves no holes for the rhythm section. The only thing I ever heard him play that I liked was his first record of *Tenderly*.

"I love Ray Brown. As for Herb Ellis, I don't like that kind of thing with guitar on every beat—unless you play it like Freddie Green does now. You listen and you'll hear how much Green has lightened his sound through the years. If you want to see how it feels with a heavy guitar, get up to play sometimes with one of them behind you. He'll drive you nuts.

"Back to Oscar. He plays pretty good when he plays in an Art Tatum form of ballad approach. And I heard him play some blues once at a medium tempo that sounded pretty good. But for playing like that with a guitar, I prefer Nat Cole. I feel though that it's a waste to use a guitar this way. If you take the guitar and have him play lines—lines like George Russell, Gil Evans or John Lewis could make—then a trio can sound wonderful."

The next record was a track from KENNY CLARK PLAYS ANDRÉ HODEIR (Epic LN3376). It was Miles's own *Swing Spring* and these are Hodeir's notes on the arrangement: *"Swing Spring* is also treated as a canon, after an introduction featuring an elaboration of the main element of the theme, the scale. Martial Solal's brilliant solo is followed by a paraphrase with integrated drum improvisations. Both Armand Migiani (baritone sax) and Roger Guerin (trumpet) take a short solo."

Miles hadn't looked carefully at the liner notes and was puzzled for the first few bars. "That's my tune, isn't it? I forgot all about that tune. God damn! Kenny Clarke can swing, can't he? That boy Solal can play, but the pianist I like in Europe is Bengt Hallberg. Damn! You know, I forgot I wrote that. That's the wrong middle—in the piano solo—why does he do that? Because it's easier, I suppose. The arrangement is terrible. It was never meant to be like that. It sounds like a tired modern painting—with skeletons in it. He writes pretty good in spots, but he overcrowds it. Kenny and Solal save it. I think I'll make another record of this tune. It was meant to be just like an exercise almost." Miles went to the piano and played the theme softly. "It was based on that scale there and when you blow, you play in that scale and you get an altogether different sound. I got that from Bud Powell; he used to play it all the time."

Miles started to talk about his strong preference for writing that isn't overcrowded, especially overcrowded with chords. He found some acetates of his forthcoming Columbia PORGY AND BESS LP which Gil Evans had arranged but for the scoring of which Miles had made a number of suggestions. He put *I Loves You, Porgy* on the machine.

"Hear that passage. We only used two chords for all of that. And in *Summertime,* there is a long space where we don't change the chord at all. It just doesn't have to be cluttered up."

From the same Verve OPERA HOUSE LP, I played the Modern Jazz Quartet's version of *Now's the Time.* "If I were John," Miles began, "I'd let Milt play more—things he'd like to get loose on—and then play these things. It would be all the more effective by contrast. You can do a lot by setting up for contrast. Sometimes I'll start a set with a ballad. You'll be surprised at what an effect that is."

The conversation turned on pianists. "Boy, I've sure learned a lot from Bill Evans. He plays the piano the way it should be played. He plays all kinds of scales; can play in 5/4; and all kinds of fantastic things. There's such a difference between him and Red Garland whom I also like a lot. Red carries the rhythm, but Bill underplays, and I like that better."

Miles was at the piano again, indulging one of his primary pleasures—hearing what can be done with voicings, by changing a note, spreading out the chord, reshaping it. "You know, you can play chords on every note in the scale. Some people don't seem to realize that. People like Bill, Gil Evans and George Russell know what can be done, what the possibilities are."

Miles returned to the MJQ recording. "John taught all of them. Milt couldn't read at all, and Percy hardly. All John has to do is let Milt play with just a sketch of an arrangement. That's what we do all the time. I never have anybody write up anything too difficult for us, because then musicians tighten up.

"I love the way John plays. I've got to get that record where he plays by himself. I usually don't buy jazz records. They make me tired and depressed. I'll buy Ahmad Jamal, John Lewis, Sonny Rollins. Coltrane I hear every night. And I like to hear the things that Max Roach writes himself. A drummer makes a very good writer. He has a sense of space and knows what it feels like to be playing around an arrangement. Philly Joe plays tenor and piano, and he's starting to write."

The talk came to Coltrane. "He's been working on those arpeggios and playing chords that lead into chords, playing them fifty different ways and playing them all at once. He's beginning to leave more space except when he gets nervous. There's one frantic tenor in Philadelphia, by the way, Jimmy Oliver."

Then came Louis Armstrong's *Potato Head Blues* of 1927 with Lil Armstrong, Kid Ory, Johnny Dodds, Johnny St. Cyr, Baby Dodds, and Pete Briggs on tuba. "Louis has been through all kinds of styles," Miles began. "That's good tuba, by the way. . . . You know you can't play anything on a horn that Louis hasn't played—I mean even modern. I love his approach to the trumpet; he never sounds bad. He plays on the beat and you can't miss when you play on the beat—with feeling. That's another phrase for swing. I also love the way he sings. He and Billie never made a record, did they?" Miles was informed they had, but the material was poor (*c.f.* Billie's THE BLUES ARE BREWIN', Decca DL 8701).

"There's form there, and you take some of those early forms, play it today, and they'd sound good. I also like all those little stops in his solo. We stop, but we often let the drums lay out altogether. If I had this record, I'd play it."

Before four bars of Ahmad Jamal's *But Not for Me* on

Argo LP 628, Miles said happily, "That's the way to play the piano. If I could play like Ahmad and Bill Evans combined with one hand, they could take the other off. Jamal once told me he's been playing in night clubs since he was eleven. Listen to how he slips into the other key. You can hardly tell it's happening. He doesn't throw his technique around like Oscar Peterson. Things flow into and out of each other. Another reason I like Red Garland and Bill Evans is that when they play a chord, they play a *sound* more than a chord.

"Listen to the way Jamal uses space. He lets it go so that you can feel the rhythm section and the rhythm section can feel you. It's not crowded. Paul Chambers, incidentally, has started to play a new way whereby he can solo and accompany himself at the same time—by using space well.

"Ahmad is one of my favorites. I live until he makes another record. I gave Gil Evans a couple of his albums, and he didn't give them back. Red Garland knew I liked Ahmad and at times I used to ask him to play like that. Red was at his best when he did. Bill plays a little like that but he sounds wild when he does—all those little scales."

Miles by now was back at the piano, talking with gathering intensity about the need for more space and less chord-cluttering in jazz. "When Gil wrote the arrangement of *I Loves You, Porgy,* he only wrote a scale for me to play. No chords. And that other passage with just two chords gives you a lot more freedom and space to hear things. I've been listening to Khachaturian carefully for six months now and the thing that. intrigues me are all those different scales he uses. Bill Evans knows too what can be done with scales. All chords, after all, are relative to scales and certain chords make certain scales. I wrote a tune recently that's more a scale than a line. And I was going to write a ballad for Coltrane with just two chords.

"When you go this way, you can go on forever. You don't have to worry about changes and you can do more with the line. It becomes a challenge to see how melodically inventive you are. When you're based on chords, you know at the end of thirty-two bars that the chords have run out and there's nothing to do but repeat what you've just done—with variations.

"I think a movement in jazz is beginning away from the conventional string of chords, and a return to emphasis on melodic rather than harmonic variation. There will be fewer chords but infinite possibilities as to what to do with them. Classical composers—some of them—have been writing this way for years, but jazz musicians seldom have.

"When I want J. J. Johnson to hear something or he wants me to, we phone each other and just play the music on the phone. I did that the other day with some of the Khachaturian scales; they're different from the usual Western scales. Then we got to talking about letting the melodies and scales carry the tune. J. J. told me, 'I'm not going to write any more chords.' And look at George Russell. His writing is mostly scales. After all, you can feel the changes.

"The music has gotten thick. Guys give me tunes and they're full of chords. I can't play them. You know, we play *My Funny Valentine* like with a scale all the way through."

The next record was *Ruby, My Dear* with Thelonious Monk, Coleman Hawkins, Wilbur Ware and Art Blakey (from MONK'S MUSIC, Riverside RLP 12-242).

"I learned how to play ballads from Coleman Hawkins. He plays all the chords and you can still hear the ballad. Who's playing bass? He doesn't know that tune. As for the performance as a whole, the tune wasn't meant to be played that way. I guess Hawkins figured that with young cats, he should play 'young.' It's a very pretty ballad and should be played just even. This way you can't hear it the way it is; I'd play it more flowing. Monk writes such pretty melodies and then screws them up.

"You have to go down to hear him to really appreciate what he's doing. I'd like to make an album of his tunes if I can ever get him up here.

"Monk has really helped me. When I came to New York, he taught me chords and his tunes. A main influence he has been through the years has to do with giving musicians more freedom. They feel that if Monk can do what he does, they can. Monk has been using space for a long time.

"The thing that Monk must realize is that he can't get everybody to play his songs right. Coltrane, Milt Jackson and maybe Lucky Thompson are the only ones I know that can get that feeling out of his songs that he can. And he needs drummers like Denzil Best, Blakey, Shadow, Roy Haynes, and Philly.

"I love the way Monk plays and writes, but I can't stand him behind me. He doesn't give you any support."

The final record was Bessie Smith's *Young Woman's Blues*, 1926, with Fletcher Henderson, Joe Smith and Buster Bailey.

"Listen to Joe Smith's tone. He's got some feeling to it." Miles laughed while listening to the lyrics. "They're pretty hip. This is the first time I've heard this record. I haven't heard much of Bessie, but I like her every time I hear her. She affects me like Leadbelly did, the way some of Paul Laurence Dunbar's poetry did. I read him once and almost cried. The Negro southern speech.

"As for those lyrics, I know what she means about not being a high yellow and being a three-quarter brown or something like that. In those days high yellow was as close to white as you could get. It's getting more and more mixed though, and pretty soon when you call somebody an m.f., you won't know what kind to call them. You might have to call them a green m.f.

"I'd love to have a little boy someday with red hair, green eyes and a black face—who plays piano like Ahmad Jamal."

Miles Davis

by Dick Katz

This review is one of the very few developed pieces of criticism of Miles Davis' recordings.

Miles Davis: BAGS' GROOVE, Prestige 7109. Miles Davis, *trumpet;* Milt Jackson, *vibes;* Thelonious Monk, *piano;* Percy Heath, *bass;* Kenny Clarke, *drums.*
Bags' Groove (take 1); *Bags' Groove* (take 2).
Miles Davis, *trumpet;* Sonny Rollins, *tenor sax;* Horace Silver, *piano;* Percy Heath, *bass;* Kenny Clarke, *drums:*
Airegin; Oleo; But Not for Me (take 2); *Doxy; But Not for Me* (take 1).

Miles Davis: WALKIN', Prestige 7076. Miles Davis, *trumpet;* J. J. Johnson, *trombone;* Lucky Thompson, *tenor sax;* Horace Silver, *piano;* Percy Heath, *bass;* Kenny Clarke, *drums.*
Walkin'; Blue 'n Boogie.
Miles Davis, *trumpet;* Davey Schildkraut, *alto sax;* Horace Silver, *piano;* Percy Heath, *bass;* Kenny Clarke, *drums:*
Solar; You Don't Know What Love Is; Love Me or Leave Me.

Miles Davis: BEMSHA SWING, Prestige 10″ 196. Davis, Jackson, Monk, Heath, Clarke.
Bemsha Swing; The Man I Love.

THE ARTISTS PERFORMING on the recordings considered here have earned the reputations to qualify them as "stars," to use the term employed by the jazz press. Therefore, these albums are all-star collections.

The current concept of all-stars has its origin in the frontier days of bop in the forties. It was not unusual then to find extraordinary talents like Charlie Parker, Dizzy Gillespie, Max Roach, J. J. Johnson, Bud Powell, Al Haig, Miles Davis,

Kenny Clarke, Oscar Pettiford, Fats Navarro, Don Byas, Lucky Thompson, Art Blakey, Sonny Stitt, George Wallington, Milt Jackson and Thelonious Monk working together in various combinations. The prewar, prebop emphasis on collective or ensemble playing with its need for group rapport was being replaced by virtuoso solo playing, which reached new heights.

However, because these key figures, particularly Parker and Gillespie, had had extensive big-band experience, *their* ensemble playing reflected maturity and sensitivity to each other. But their younger disciples, deprived of this type of experience that their idols had, often degenerated into a kind of waiting-in-line-to-play type of jazz which is too prevalent, even today.

Since those eye-popping days, all of the above people have gone their separate ways. Parker and Navarro are dead. Byas emigrated to Europe. Bud Powell is ill. The others all have emerged as strong individual personalities. Along with some outstanding jazzmen in the idiom who have arrived more recently, like Sonny Rollins, Kenny Dorham, and later Horace Silver, they all lead their own groups or function mainly as soloists. It gradually became economically unfeasible for them to work together steadily. And as the all-star concept had grown, so had the problems. Things like "prima-donna-ism" appeared, and it rarely worked out. Too many chefs "cooking" at the same time, and the stew will boil over, or worse— the fire will go out.

The albums reviewed here are notable exceptions, musically, an exciting glimpse of future possibilities. And certainly *Walkin'*, *Blue 'n Boogie*, and *Bags' Groove* are among the outstanding jazz releases of the past ten years.

Everyone involved in the BAGS' GROOVE album is an individualist. Miles Davis has an economical, fragile, but powerfully emotional style, devoid of superfluities. His only problem seems to be an occasional technical lapse. Indeed, he remarkably converted his limitations into assets, the true mark of the creator, as opposed to the player who interprets others' ideas. Much of the same applies to Thelonious Monk, who is truly a "homemade" artist. Milt Jackson is a virtuoso with a relatively sym-

metrical and less abstract approach. Kenny Clarke revolution-
ized the concept of rhythm playing. He and Percy Heath, an
extremely graceful player, came to the studio already a finely
developed team as members of the Modern Jazz Quartet, and
this fact turns out to be the cornerstone of the success of these
recordings.

The theme of the title tune is a choice example of Jackson's
gift for creating unique, memorable blues melodies. When
played properly, as it is here on take 1, it insures the perfect
mood and point of departure for the soloists. The balance between trumpet and vibes is very effective and is enhanced by
their juggling of the parts. Miles's solo is near perfect—a beautiful, unfolding set of memorable ideas, each a springboard
for the next. His sound or tone has real vocal-like quality of
expression. His interpretation of the blues here is deeply convincing, and it is without exaggerated "funk." He establishes
a mood and sustains it. His purported rejection of Monk's
services as an accompanist is irrelevant. The end result is
superb. And when Jackson enters with Monk behind him, the
contrast is strikingly effective. Milt constructs an impeccable
and soulful solo complete with long sustained lines and many
interesting effects. Monk's unorthodox accompaniment hinders
Milt not at all—on the contrary—it provides him with just
the right color. Curiously, Jackson sounds relatively straight
and formal here when contrasted with Monk, whereas in the
context of the MJQ *he* appears more angular with John Lewis'
more formal style of playing. Monk's solo on this piece is one
of his best on record. By an ingenious use of space and
rhythm, and by carefully controlling a single melodic idea, he
builds a tension that is not released until the end of his solo.
Every drummer could learn from him here. His sense of structure and his use of extension is very rare indeed. And it *sounds*
good. It could be called, almost paradoxically, a series of un-
derstatements, boldly stated. Miles returns to stroll another
solo, the theme returns and the piece ends cleanly. An extraordinary performance by all.

The ensemble in the beginning of take 2 is not as clean.
Davis' solo contains several "pops" which sound like saliva in

the horn, and which mar an otherwise fine solo. Also, this version is not as concentrated as take 1, but Jackson's solo maintains the high level of the first—take your pick. Monk surprises with a completely different solo—different in approach and feeling. Here he is more concerned with playing the *piano,* less with developing a motif, and is much more extravagant with his ideas. A fine solo, but take 1 was exceptional. During the rest of the take there were obvious technical defects in the performance.

I'm reviewing *Bemsha Swing* here because it is from the same session as *Bags' Groove.* It has a typical Monk melody and harmonization—direct, and with a slightly oriental flavor rhythmically. This performance apparently preceded *Bags' Groove,* because Monk plays behind Davis. Miles seems quite distracted by Monk, and it breaks the continuity of his solo. His discomfort is finally expressed by his quoting a couple of well-known Monk phrases. Monk in turn acknowledges Miles's sarcasm (or compliment?) and, lo and behold, they end up by playing a duet. Jackson follows Miles for a set of variations on the melody of the same quality as *Bags' Groove.*

Note how Monk's pieces almost *demand* a constant awareness of the melody; one can't rely on "running the changes." Monk's solo is a fine example of his ability to construct variations on a theme (in this case his own), rather than discard it and build "lines" on the chords as is the style of improvising of the majority of contemporary jazz players. In this respect, Monk resembles such earlier jazzmen as Art Tatum and other "stride" oriented pianists, and horn players—Johnny Hodges, Armstrong, Ben Webster, to mention a few. Miles Davis also has this gift of embellishing an existing melody, but he also utilizes the "running the changes" technique. Sonny Rollins, too, uses both approaches. Virtually all the superior players are never *chained* by the chord structure of their material. The chords are merely signposts. The sophistication in Monk, Rollins and Davis lies in the fact that after years of "making the changes" they now often only imply them, leaving themselves free to concentrate on other aspects of improvisation, such as expression, rhythm, etc.

In some ways *The Man I Love* is the most fascinating piece on the date. After a lovely Jackson introduction, Miles unfolds an exceedingly lyrical abstraction of the melody. His use of rhythm and completely original manner of phrasing here should continue to enrich a listener for years. Jackson doubles the tempo with a four-bar break and takes a fine solo which does not quite sustain interest all the way, probably because of its length. Monk follows with the *pièce de résistance* by getting carried away with his own self-made obstacle course. He tries to rearrange the melody rhythmically by extending the sequences over a number of bars. However, he gets lost (or so it sounds to me), and comes to an abrupt halt about the twenty-eighth bar or so (long meter). What follows is a model duet between Heath and Clarke which could serve as a lesson in graceful walking for anyone. Along about the fourteenth bar of the bridge, Miles leads Monk back on the track, and he comes roaring in in his best 1947 style. Miles comes in on his heels with a delightful bit and then surprises by quickly jamming a mute into his horn and continuing—an electrifying effect. A return to the original tempo at the bridge halts this discussion between Monk and Miles and the piece ends on a note of agreement. This performance would be absolutely impossible to repeat. God bless Thomas Edison. (This ten-inch LP has not yet been transferred to a twelve-inch.)

Airegin (on 7109) is a rhythmically interesting melody by Sonny Rollins. Miles plays more conservatively here, possibly due to Horace Silver's presence and style. Davis is extremely sensitive to other players and, consciously or not, adapts himself to prevailing circumstances. His solo here is a little drier and is rather formless by comparison to the others considered here, but his time is perfect. Rollins also almost plays it safe and shows little of what evolved in him not long after this session. Bird's influence is very strong in this particular solo. However, Rollins does attempt to build to a climax. An uncertain return to the theme ends an unrealized performance.

Oleo is a very good Parker-style melody, reminiscent of *Moose the Mooche* and other compositions based on one of the points of departure of so much jazz: *I Got Rhythm.* Davis and Rollins state the theme cleanly and with conviction. What distinguishes this performance is the intelligent work of the rhythm section. Only Heath supports the front line until Silver and Clarke enter at the bridge. During the solos, Silver plays only the bridges. The pattern is repeated on the last chorus, except that Clarke remains in. This device proves extremely effective and was and is used with variations by Miles in his subsequent working groups—but "strolling" in its various forms is, of course, as old as jazz. Miles makes effective use of a mute here and thereby previews his current style. (The device even became a commercial asset when he combined it with some of Ahmad Jamal's ideas about playing rhythmically in "two.") This solo is beautifully integrated and concentrated —with delicious time and taste. Miles's playing is elegant—I can think of no better word for it. Sonny Rollins is thoughtful and straightforward in his variations—almost as if he were reviewing and reminding himself what he had absorbed before embarking on the daring course he is on now. He seems a bit uncomfortable with Clarke's pure, even and unbroken cymbal line, so Kenny obliges on Rollins' second chorus by emphasizing the second and fourth beats—and does it tastefully and unobtrusively. Silver follows Sonny with a typical solo . . . percussive and with a powerful beat. However, his ideas sound overstated—at least in comparison to Rollins and Miles in this context. Kenny Clarke is superb on this piece. He truly accompanies each soloist so as to enhance the feeling each is trying to project. He has a beautiful cymbal sound, and propels a warm, very strong pulse, without ever being too loud. His sense of dynamics and volume is acute. Notice how he switches to brushes behind Silver, and how he prepares each soloist. He wields his sticks and brushes like a painter, making sure there are no superfluous strokes. He has the kind of emotional radar that Sid Catlett had—a genuine warmth and musical sensitivity to anticipate the *music*. Percy Heath's line is satisfying, his sound is very distinctive, and he has a wonderful beat. He works exceptionally well with Clarke. *Oleo* is by far the best performance on the date.

I don't see the point in releasing both takes of *But Not for*

Me. For celebrated performances the documentary value of such releases is real, but in this case, neither take is up to the standard of the rest of the date. This song is not the type that readily lends itself to the kind of perfunctory interpretation evidenced here. Miles respects the melody and embellishes it carefully—and he would have been even more effective in a more sensitive setting. Rollins sounds like one of his imitators here, a good solo, but not up to his usual standard. Silver makes a very good entrance on the break and he develops it nicely, but is out of character with the song. His percussive, so-called angular style seems to clash with Miles's particular brand of lyricism in this type of song. His strong individuality, which makes him an important jazzman, works against him here, because he bathes Rollins and Davis in an all-pervading percussive atmosphere. One might say, "But what about Monk?—he's percussive and rough, too." I think it's important to remember that Monk's redesigning of a song is so complete that he establishes his own point of reference. And his role above with Miles and Jackson was mainly that of a soloist—his accompaniments were usually behind Jackson—not Davis. Note also that in *Oleo* Silver plays only on the bridges, leaving Miles and Sonny free to create their own moods. Silver's style is not unorthodox enough to create his own point of reference—in other words, his conception is not "far out" enough for him to escape comparison with some other so-called mainstream pianists, and a few of them would be more compatible with the various subtleties in Miles Davis' playing, particularly on ballads. The *content* of Silver's playing often fits well, but his *manner* of playing is not always right for Davis. In the last chorus here, played by Miles, the rhythm is undistinguished, and the ending is rather sloppy.

Take 2 is taken at a slower tempo, as if Miles sensed this would help lessen the harshness, and it does somewhat. Miles's solo is characteristic and a moving melodic statement. Rollins is less successful and sounds a little indifferent. Silver does not match his solo on take 1; but he accompanies intelligently though with the same hardness. The rest of the take is uneventful, and releasing both takes has the effect of heightening the defects in each and dulling their good points.

Doxy is a light, spiritual-like sixteen-bar melody by Rollins stated in "two" by Miles and Sonny in unison. This piece comes off rather well and in this instance Horace fits like a glove—this type of piece is his forte and he has written similar ones himself. After an informal, almost casual, solo by Davis, Rollins constructs a very straightforward line completely in character with his tune. It's fascinating to see how Rollins has absorbed the elements he used at this stage of his development (1954) into the much broader palette he utilizes now. Silver's solo is typical of the many he has recorded in this vein.

Walkin' and its companion *Blue 'n Boogie* are acknowledged to be classics. To me they represent a sort of summing up of much of what happened musically to the players involved during the preceding ten years (1944-54). It's as if all agreed to get together to discuss on their instruments what they had learned and unlearned, what elements of bop they had retained or discarded. An amazing seminar took place.

If this seems a sentimental idea, think of the countless recorded jam sessions where nothing was discussed—musically or verbally—and resulted in the players mumbling to themselves on their horns (and knees). Relatively little of the jazz being played today qualifies as art, mostly because the level of communication is so low—between the players and between the player and listener. Much of it resembles sport—even to its terminology—but that question needs an essay of its own.

This record is artistic and of lasting value.

The main theme of *Walkin'* is unusually strong, and the use of the flatted fifths and the way they resolve should remain as a particularly good example which one could point to twenty years from now to illustrate that otherwise much overworked device. It is played in unison—and this particular combination of sonorities, trumpet-tenor-trombone, *sounds* good and feels good because of the specific players involved.

Miles's solo is as good as any he has recorded, before or since. His sound ideas and execution, and the feelings he projects, are prime examples of his art. Every idea that Miles states here is clearly formed and will remain with the listener afterwards. (How many times have you listened to a long, "exciting," jet-propelled "cooking" solo and gone away without being able to recall a single thing the man played?) Johnson's solo is also superior, but it is slightly marred by intonation trouble, perhaps due to a "cold" horn—I am judging this by J. J.'s own very high standards. But he sounds completely at ease in this setting and his playing is convincing. Lucky Thompson shows his wonderful sense of structure in a beautifully formed solo, which also demonstrates how he has absorbed some of Ben Webster's ability to build to a dramatic climax. He is helped when the other horns back him with the theme. Silver's solo contribution is overshadowed by his role as an accompanist. He provides a series of variations behind each soloist that creates a moving backdrop—and just the right feeling. Heath and Clarke are superb.

Many of the things said above apply to *Blue 'n Boogie*. The controlled intensity contained both in solo and ensemble is remarkable. The Gillespie theme remains as fresh as it did when first recorded in 1945—a real tribute to his talent. Miles's solo in this instance is less introspective and more extroverted—compatible with the forceful playing of the rhythm section. His variations are more elaborate, and his agile use of neighboring tones and chromatic scale passages is very effective. Also, he contrasts these with the wider spaced intervals and diatonic ideas he often favors to insure variety. Miles's spelling out of triads and general diatonic approach is reminiscent of early and middle Armstrong. Further, his precise, split-second sense of timing and swing are not unlike those of that early master. Each is a master of economy—few, if any of their notes are superfluous. Of course, there the comparison stops. The feelings and conception each projects couldn't be more different—for obvious reasons—age being one and Miles's much larger musical vocabulary being another. It appears that Freddy Webster also influenced Miles, especially in regard to sound or tone quality. J. J. Johnson's solo is good, but unfortunately intonation still seems a problem here. That he conquers this distraction and creates a moving solo is an indication of his stature. Many letter trombonists would have collapsed in a pile of clinkers. Lucky Thompson doesn't match his solo on *Walkin'*, and sounds a little forced at times, but he maintains his taste, control, and sense of melody nevertheless. The figures played by Davis and Johnson behind Lucky's solo are a kind of anthology in themselves. Horace Silver's solo is rather tense, if exciting, and his accompaniment is once again peerless. Clarke and Heath couldn't have been better.

This record date was an important one and provides fresh insights with each rehearing.

The date on the reverse of 7076 is a different matter. Davis and the rhythm section are in good form, but saxophonist Davey Schildkraut, a very gifted but erratic player, sounds ill at ease, and there is a lack of rapport between the two horns. The session is notable mainly as a superb example of Kenny Clarke's brushwork.

Solar opens with a nice Davis melody stated by him alone with the rhythm section. His variation is nice, but indifferent in comparison to his work on many other records. Schildkraut's alto solo is characterized by a lonely, but pure and beautiful sound. His ideas are interesting, but not integrated, and here he lacks authority. After a fair Silver piano solo, Miles returns to stroll a chorus before ending the piece. A rather aimless performance.

You Don't Know What Love Is begins with a beautiful, muted Davis solo rendition of this poignant song. Miles concentrates on probing the melody and again demonstrates his unique interpretive gift. I would have preferred a more legato accompaniment than Silver plays here. Schildkraut does not play on this track.

Love Me or Leave Me is played at a fast tempo. Very good Horace Silver solo kicked off by a sloppily played figure by the horns. Pretty good Miles, but Schildkraut has his troubles. His ideas are quite disconnected—it's hard to determine if his lagging behind is intentional toying with the meter or inability to keep up with the precise, almost anticipated articulation of the beat by the rhythm section. Silver relieves him to churn out another two choruses.

In summing up it should be emphasized that the unifying element in all the sessions reviewed here is Kenny Clarke. He literally holds them together and at the same time animates each player as few, if any, other drummers could. With playing of this caliber on the part of the horns, any lesser drummer would have destroyed these performances almost entirely. The other gratifying factor in these recordings is a total lack of the tricks and "hip" devices that have marred the work of some recent groups (such as trying to make a small band sound like a big one). There is musical honesty here and by and large a mutual respect among the players all too rare these days.

Charlie Parker and Dizzy Gillespie

by Ross Russell

As proprietor of Dial records, Ross Russell began recording Charlie Parker in the mid-forties in Hollywood, and pursued him to New York. Russell's novel The Sound *was recently published by Dutton.*

Incidentally, with the September 1960 issue of The Jazz Review *publication began of "The Charlie Parker Papers," a series of interviews Bob Reisner collected from everyone he could find who knew Parker. Reisner's work has subsequently appeared in a Citadel Press book,* Bird: The Life of Charlie Parker.

DIZ'N'BIRD IN CONCERT, Roost LP 2234. Dizzy Gillespie, *trumpet;* Charlie Parker, *alto;* John Lewis, *piano;* Al McKibbon, *bass;* Joe Harris, *drums.*
A Night in Tunisia; Dizzy Atmosphere; Groovin' High; Confirmation.

CHARLIE PARKER IN HISTORICAL RECORDINGS, VOL. I, Le Jazz Cool JC-101.
Ko-Ko; 'Round about Midnight; Cool Blues; Ornithology; Move; White Christmas; Ornithology; Hot House; Groovin' High; Theme.

CHARLIE PARKER IN HISTORICAL RECORDINGS, VOL. II, Le Jazz Cool JC-102.
Cheryl; Salt Peanuts (II); How High the Moon; Rifftide; Big Foot; Salt Peanuts (I); Out of Nowhere; Perdido.

The collective personnel for the two Le Jazz Cool LPs has been given by G. H. Jepsen in his Discography of Charlie Parker *as* Charlie Parker, *alto;* Miles Davis, Fats Navarro, Kenny Dorham, *trumpets;* Bud Powell, *piano;* Tommy Potter, *bass;* Max Roach, Roy Haynes, *drums.*

THE ADJECTIVE "GREAT" gets thrown around rather freely these days by writers and commentators on jazz. By rigid standards the last musician to whom *great* could rightly apply was Charlie Parker. The Bird had some important contemporaries, but there was no one in his time that he did not cut, outinvent, and outplay. Viewed against the entire profile of jazz history he was one of three or four soloists of unmistakenly major stature and influence—nor is there anyone today of whom quite as much may be said. Therefore it is welcome news when some new fragments of his record work come to light.

Ironically enough, Parker is not much played on the air these days. Many of his commercial recordings are no longer in the catalog and the rest have become old hat to the so-hip disc jockeys. These fellows can only survive on the New. Then, too, although the Bird was required listening for a whole generation of working musicians, he was not always easy listening. On the good nights the listener had the uneasy impression not so much of notes, as a stream of molten metal showering from a crucible. Hearing him on those occasions could be a numbing, even shattering, affair, often taking on the overtones of a religious experience; a phenomenon that may account for the fanaticism of his followers who, after his death in 1955 (at the age of thirty-four), went around writing on the walls and posts of the New York subways: "Bird Lives!"

The new issues are an unexpected windfall. From dark places have come three whole LPs of Parker previously unavailable, at least to any large audience—real vintage Parker!

Acoustically all three suffer in various degrees from semi-professional or amateur engineering, but even with these handicaps they are worth almost any quantity of jazz LPs which pour forth in such dreary sameness today. Still one must put up with disadvantages. For reasons best known to the manufacturers, no dates or personnels are given, so a little detective work was required on the backgrounds.

The Roost sides derive from a near scandalous Carnegie Hall concert dated September 29, 1947. Gosh, that long ago? I was pleased when I found the concert program intact in my files. The occasion was the first attempt to present pure bop

to a large audience in concert. Remember, this was 1947, and
the big names of jazz were Roy Eldridge, Don Byas and Bill
Harris. Bop was very much a poor relation, husbanded by a
hard-core claque, more annoying than effective. By divine
right, according to these hipsters, the Bird should have been
the main attraction, but there were a number of very good
reasons for building the concert around Dizzy. Old Diz was
then experimenting with the first of his big bands and of
course ranked as an outstanding practitioner of the new style.
More important, he was eminently employable, which at no
stretch of the imagination could be said about Parker. It was
often a matter of pure chance if Parker showed up for a booking at all (an advance was usually a fatal mistake), let alone
with his horn, and the promoters had understandably put their
money on the jovial and reliable trumpeter. The Bird was
strictly an added starter, "Guest Artist" according to the program, and was allotted a single twenty-minute spot just before
the intermission.

As things turned out, the Bird showed up all right; really
bugged—hopping mad, offended at having been passed over,
and loaded with aggression for his old friend and protector.
The concert, with its *auld lang syne* overtones, developed into
something more than scheduled; not so much a formal presentation of the new music, as an embittered duel between its
two leading exponents; the weapons were trumpet and alto
saxophone; the common ground such established but still cryp-
tic bop classics as *Night in Tunisia* and *Ornithology;* and the
seconds, if you will, the dismayed members of Gillespie's big-
band rhythm section, big bemused Al McKibbon on bass,
bomb-dropping Joe Harris on drums, and cool, wiggy John
Lewis. Add a bewildered audience, and a small, vociferous,
near-lunatic Parker claque seated well down in front, and you
have a very weird backdrop for the creation of music. And
indeed, weird music it is that one hears on these Roost grooves.

But before turning our attention to the music, a word about
the history of these records. There's a choice footnote to the
story there, too. Originally these same sides appeared on the
market around 1949 on a label whimsically called "Black

Deuce"! The private recordings were made by a studio located in the Carnegie Hall building which offered this service to artists, mainly recitalists, performing there. Obviously, in this instance, they fell into the hands of someone with an eye for the market, and it is to this nameless rogue that the jazz collector is presently beholden. The records appeared in a few jazz-specialty stores and enjoyed a brief, limited, almost clandestine sale. No effort was made to compensate the artists or clear contractual difficulties. (Dizzy was under contract to Musicraft at the time.) But a rumble of protests soon arose, and the sale of the records came to a halt, the result of a threatened injunction, or perhaps because of possible prosecution under a statute then before the state legislature which would make it a felony to sell pirated recordings for profit. (There was then no legislation covering such shenanigans—one gifted entrepreneur had just startled the industry by bootlegging an entire Verdi opera broadcast from the Met!) In any event the "Black Deuce" sides disappeared from the market. They became, in a matter of months, collector's items, much to the delight of their few proud possessors. Now, some thirteen years after the event, the sides are available to the general public.

In some respects they are still pretty sensational performances which managed to capture some of the electricity that broke loose, like chain lightning when Charlie Parker was putting out. *Night in Tunisia* opens with all hands joining in for a routine opening chorus—everyone except Parker, that is; the Bird plays strange riff figures, somehow connected with the theme, in an incredible kind of Chalumeau lower register. The phrasing and intonation were intended to unnerve and confound, and a lesser musician than Dizzy would have been routed at the outset. Dizzy wisely retires to gather his forces after the ensemble bit. There follows one of Bird's breathless four-bar breaks, then a long chorus played with fierce, hard, professional brilliance. The trumpet reprise is of the same quality, lustrous, chiseled, perhaps even more accurately articulated. This exchange sets the style of the following performances.

The duel is at its hottest on *Dizzy Atmosphere* (*Dynamo*) which is taken at a precipitous tempo. The feinting, surprise twists and musical gambits there are heady stuff. Parker is always the aggressor and Dizzy the counterpuncher. All this is the more remarkable when it is recalled that these liberties were being taken with material which only a handful of musicians had mastered at all in 1947. Variations upon variation, and the theme itself pretty far out at that! While the salient quality of the performances is one of brilliant jousting, striving to trip up and to surpass, there are some very moving passages, too. Despite their animus, Parker's solos retain that completeness of form and melodic continuity that marks his best work and makes it unique. He was the first jazz improviser to think in terms of *total melody*, as Dick Katz pointed out here. Previously the player had been bound by the restrictions of bar divisions. The Bird created new melodies which stretched over the bar framework like a shining piece of fabric. And this of course is why he is one of the really great improvisors of all jazz, as well as one of the great innovators.

Except for the music they have to offer, the Le Jazz Cool LPs are amateur productions, but the music is simply tremendous. This writer supervised some thirty-six sides of what are considered to be among Parker's finest commercial records for Dial, but he was never able to capture the sweep and force that distinguishes these performances. This is how small-band jazz really sounded in that day when the chips were down, and the quality and the inspiration were on the bandstand. So again, we are beholden to some, here, nameless one and his recording machine. The technical difficulties include distortion, faulty balance, damage done by playings, and they are trying. But they do not cancel out the music. Generally the tracks are tolerable, and certainly those on Volume I are. This seems to me one of the finest examples of the modern style. The trumpet player here is almost certainly Fats Navarro and, if this surmise is correct, it marks the sole occasion that this very wonderful musician recorded with Charlie. (Like Bird, he was in his later years a junkie; a shy, nocturnal character of unpredictable humors and lamentable reliability.) Yet, in many respects, Fats was the ideal brass companion for Bird. Fats was a player of impeccable taste, faultless execution, at home at any tempo, and his ravishing veiled tone has never been equaled. So this LP is a rare meeting of kin. They perform *Move* in a wildly ebullient fashion, and their version of *Ornithology* is, I must admit, superior to the famous Dial. The fact remains that Parker, when confronted with a bare recording studio and its cold, impersonal microphone, was as much a slave to conservatism as any other jazzman. But here he plays in one of the free-wheeling moods that came on him those certain evenings when everything, the time, the place, the crowd and above all, the quality of his musical companions, was just right. There is a rousing reading of *Koko,* a very fine *Cool Blues,* and Parker's only performance on record of Monk's beautiful *'Round about Midnight.* Parker's solos are not rationed to a parsimonious thirty-two bars, as happened in the recording studio. He lets go here and really blows. On the first *Ornithology,* for example, there are four straight choruses, with surprise heaped on surprise. And the chase fours between Bird and Fats are thrilling indeed. Hearing them play together one realizes how close Fats was on the horn to Bird and how much more suitable complement his trumpet was than Miles's or Dizzy's.

Miles seems to be on Volume II. The material includes *Out of Nowhere* and *Giant Swing* (*Big Foot*), which Charlie worked up for the Dial recording dates in the fall of 1947, just before the Petrillo recording ban (or one of them) shut down the recording industry. The group also plays *Cheryl,* probably recorded about the same time for Savoy (Savoy never gave out the dates), *Perdido, Rifftide* (Bird's earlier *Street Beat*), *How High the Moon* and two versions of *Salt Peanuts.* The mood and performance of these tracks is quieter than those on Volume I. The trumpet often has a round tone and is used mostly in the middle register, and there is a preference for oblique statements. But perhaps these sides will seem superior to those who have grown up on a diet of cool jazz. Comparison of the two volumes will interest those trying to trace out the "birth of the cool" and Miles's essential role in the movement.

The last Dial and Savoy recordings brought to a close the great period of Charlie Parker's recording career. During the Petrillo embargo period his group lost its spirit and began to disintegrate. An unhappy incident followed in the foyer of a leading night club in Detroit with the result that Charlie found himself on a trade "don't book" list. He was dropped from the circuit where instrumental jazz stars were being featured and paid prices usually reserved for name vocalists. Unable to record, he confined his activities to playing gigs around New York. Key men like Max and Miles drifted away. When he resumed recording, under the royalty-fund system, the price of Petrillo's peace, Parker signed with Granz and such productions as CHARLIE PARKER WITH STRINGS and SOUTH OF THE BORDER soon resulted. He seemed abandoning the trail blazed with the help of Dizzy, Max and a few others. The existence of these "amateur" recordings raises the very interesting possibility that there are undoubtedly more of them still around. This might be a good time to broadcast a general alarm for such material. Several of the better independent jazz labels (Riverside, Prestige, Atlantic, Blue Note, Pacific, Contemporary) would no doubt be only too happy to assist in the evaluation, renovation and release of such recordings.

Gil Evans on His Own

by Don Heckman

Alto saxophonist–composer Don Heckman's first contribution to The Jazz Review *was a letter about Gil Evans, and he later contributed this extended review.*

Gil Evans: GREAT JAZZ STANDARDS, World Pacific WP—1270. Johnny Coles, Louis Mucci, Danny Stiles, *trumpets;* Jimmy Cleveland, Curtis Fuller, Rod Levitt, *trombones;* Earl Chapin, *French horn;* Bill Barber, *tuba;* Ed Caine, *woodwinds;* Steve Lacy, *soprano sax;* Budd Johnson, *tenor* and *clarinet;* Ray Crawford, *guitar;* Tommy Potter, *bass;* Elvin Jones, *drums;* Gil Evans, *piano.*
Chant of the Weed, Joy Spring, Ballad of the Sad Young Men, Theme.
Coles, Mucci, Allen Smith, *trumpets;* Fuller, Bill Elton, Dick Lieb, *trombones;* Bob Northern, *French horn;* Barber, *tuba;* Al Block, *woodwinds;* Lacy, *soprano sax;* Chuck Wayne, *guitar;* Dick Carter, *bass;* Dennis Charles, *drums;* Gil Evans, *piano:*
Davenport Blues, Django, Straight No Chaser.

Gil Evans: GIL EVANS AND TEN, Prestige 7120; reissued as BIG STUFF, New Jazz NJLP 8215. Gil Evans, *piano;* Steve Lacy, *soprano sax;* Jimmy Cleveland, *trombone;* Louis Mucci, *1st trumpet* (replaced on *Remember* by John Carisi); Jake Koven, *2nd trumpet;* Bart Varsalona, *bass trombone;* Willie Ruff, *French horn;* "Zeke Tolin" (Lee Konitz), *alto;* Dave Kurtzer, *bassoon;* Paul Chambers, *bass;* Nick Stabulas, *drums* (replaced on *Remember* by Jo Jones):
Remember, Ella Speed, Big Stuff, Nobody's Heart, Just One of Those Things, If You Could See Me Now, Jambangle.

AFTER A NUMBER of years, Gil Evans has re-established his position as one of the most prominent composer-arrangers in jazz. His work for Claude Thornhill has been known and ad-

mired for years, but the limitations inherent in the requirements of dance bands prevented any major achievement. Although he was one of the important figures in the '49-'50
Miles Davis Capitol sides, the strength of the various personalities involved (Davis, Mulligan, *et al.*) was such that no
individual could predominate. In fact, these sessions may have
been of less importance than was generally considered at the
time, since a variety of economic and social conditions prevented them from exercising the influence which they un-
questionably deserved.

As with most artists who take pride in their craftsmanship,
Evans is able to transcend the limitations of any given assign-
ment, no matter how mundane. If it is required that he favor
his soloist, Evans can do so, as he did in the Davis albums
MILES AHEAD and PORGY AND BESS. But the relationship between soloist and composition is, by nature, extremely delicate and susceptible to a strain in either direction, and the
relative failure of Gil's World Pacific LP NEW BOTTLE, OLD
WINE may well have been caused by Cannonball Adderley's
disassociation from the context of the arrangement. In a sense,
when the arranger places himself in a supporting role, he
hitches his wagon to a star. The results may vary as much
as the star's temperament, and the fact that the Evans-Davis
recordings turned out so superbly is a testimonial to the rapport between the two men.

Many critics praise Evans as an orchestrator but refuse to
acknowledge him as a real composer. The conclusion is in-
valid. Rubens is no less an artist because he chose to paint
portraits from life, nor is Shakespeare's *Hamlet* any less masterful because the plot had been used before him. One of the
functions of art is to create a symbolic *illusion* of life. Evans
does not accept the limitations in style, form and expression
of his model, but rather uses it as à motif, a point of origin
from life. The manner in which he personally contributes to
the growth of this motif is as significant as if he were to use
original thematic material. And his pieces reflect a viewpoint
which is essentially optimistic, but never maudlin or cloying;

in them a full spectrum of emotion is encompassed by a very large and human love of life.

In his most recent recording for World Pacific, Evans has finally made a statement completely his own. It is probably pertinent that on it and on an earlier Prestige, he plays piano. (It was true of NEW BOTTLE, OLD WINE, but that record was hampered by the problems mentioned earlier.) From his seat in the heart of the rhythm section, Evans manipulates the sound units as though they were extensions of his finger tips. The direct personal involvement of the composer in the performance of the composition may be far more important in jazz than it is in "classical" music, a maxim which has been demonstrated by composers ranging from Jelly Roll Morton to Charlie Mingus.

The instrumentation on both recordings is similar, except that the World Pacific sides have been slightly augmented by the addition of more brass, a guitar, woodwinds, and Budd Johnson on tenor and clarinet. The Prestige record reflects the fact that it is Evans' first major jazz enterprise since the Capitols. As a result, the thematic content develops in a less complex manner than on the World Pacific recording. There are also more ballad settings on the Prestige which, although beautifully orchestrated, are limited by this dance-band style; a much stronger emphasis is placed upon sonorities than upon rhythmic content. BIG STUFF, for example, is practically a study of the sounds obtainable from the bottom register of bass instruments. The last open fifth between the two trombones rings with the richness of the implied overtones. *Nobody's Heart* demonstrates the use of bassoon in a register first made notorious by Stravinsky. In this case Dave Kurtzer's rich, full sound completely overcomes the difficulty involved in producing such high notes. Evans' voicings are superb. There are places where soprano sax, horn, and muted trumpet produce an excellent approximation of a symphonic woodwind section. Tadd Dameron's lovely *If You Could See Me Now* features Jimmy Cleveland who plays with a particularly resonant quality in his middle register. Evans' accompaniment is generally oriented around the French horn and is quite adequate in the frame of a dance-band style. One minor irritant is the occasional use of a triplet tied to a quarter note and repeated on the first beat of the bar—an amazingly corny figure for someone of Evans' stature.

All the ballads are organized generally into two slow sections surrounding a double-time center. *Remember* is very much in the Thornhill tradition, but Evans' piano playing is far more pleasant than Thornhill's. Lacy plays well in the up-tempo middle section. His use of time is very similar to Coltrane's, involving a superimposition of rhythmic multiples of nines, sevens, etc., and using the appropriate derivations as part of his basic rhythm. Lacy also stands out on *Ella Speed,* a *Georgia Brown*-type tune attributed to Leadbelly. Cleveland's work here is not so good, however. At this stage in his development he still retained an annoying tendency to overreach runs in his upper register and play on top of the beat. Evans has included a written paraphrase in the style of his *Donna Lee* chart for Thornhill; it's mostly successful, except that the thickness of some of the voicings tends to detract from the rhythmic propulsion. Again, too, he uses four repeated eighth notes on the first and second beat of the bar similar to the triplet figure I mentioned earlier. *Just One of Those Things* is all Lacy. The arrangement consists mostly of supporting figures for the solo, although some of the brass punctuations suggest Evans' use of trombone comping on the Davis recordings. Lacy makes extensive use of sequential patterns here, a practice which could be disastrous in a lesser jazzman, but which he brings off admirably.

Jambangle, the other up-tempo, is an Evans original, a sort of updated boogie woogie. Solos by Lacy and Cleveland are good enough, but the arrangement is probably the least interesting on the recording.

The World Pacific LP differs from the Prestige in several important aspects. The band is superior as a unit and the soloists are better individually; Cleveland and Lacy are featured again, but they have now gained in maturity and expressiveness. The choice of material is also far better, and its treatment is much more in the character of jazz composition than dance-band scoring. Evans' refusal to bow to the demands of fashion in solo style has also worked well in the choice of Budd Johnson as soloist for *Chant of the Weed* and *Theme*. Johnson's clarinet style is uniquely affirmative and self-confident in these days of the instrument's decline as an important solo voice. His warm, strutting interpretation of *Chant of the Weed* makes a pleasant contrast to Don Redman's angular whole-tone lines. Evans' re-creation of the old Cotton Club theme lacks some of the nervous vitality of the original but replaces it with a tongue-in-cheek good humor. There is an interesting spot directly before the ending which typifies Evans' concern with every last vestige of sound. Johnson plays some chromatic swoops over a climactic build-up which eventually returns him to the primary theme; yet as he does so, a last, persistent chromatic echo cascades down through Lacy's soprano, adding a tiny fillip to the dissipating climax.

Ballad of the Sad Young Men is the only tune here which corresponds to the ballads on the Prestige set. There is an obvious difference of interpretation, however. Evans' textures seem to be far more orchestral in character and less reminiscent of sectionalized dance-band voicings. His employment of the flute as an integral component of the massed body of sound differs from the usual dance-band practice of having it lead the woodwinds, or else function in unison with muted trumpets or saxes. Jimmy Cleveland's poignant trombone solo soars over a beautiful mass of shifting sound. Listen to the long, held woodwind notes in the second eight which leads into a tingling trombone smear. It is this kind of concern with detail that makes Evans' music so interesting to hear.

Bix Beiderbecke's *Davenport Blues* is another example. The 1927 work serves as a vehicle for the contemporary trumpet of Johnny Coles, yet, as is true throughout the album, no contradiction exists between the source material and the soloist. The consistent integration between the soloist and composition far exceeds the limitations of any "school" or "period." Coles plays with a warm, open sound somewhat similar to Miles's. His solos, however, are made primarily of short phrases that do not necessarily have a strong organic relationship to each other, a practice which Miles assiduously avoids in favor of interrelated melodic lines. The choice of *Straight No Chaser* is a good one, and Evans chooses to emphasize the humor that is implicit in so much of Monk's work. Listen to the gleeful piano and cymbal trills and the moaning flute in the opening sections. The theme is stated by a driving, orchestral unison—a tricky device to use, since it depends upon the jazz feeling of every member of the orchestra—and that was one of the main reasons that the same kind of unisons were unsuccessful in the Thornhill band. Steve Lacy's excellent solo further indicates his ability to interpret Monk's lines properly, an attribute shared by too few jazzmen. Lacy's talent is genuinely musical, and its expression is helped rather than impeded by the fact that he has chosen a difficult instrument. *Joy Spring* is a wistful bow in the direction of Clifford Brown's largely unfulfilled potential as a composer. Evans allows the melodic line to evolve from thematic material which precedes it, a sort of theme and variation in reverse. It works out well, and the theme is stated as in *Straight No Chaser* by an orchestral unison. Ray Crawford's guitar closes the chart with a quietly elegiac cadenza.

Theme is an original Evans riff tune written while the band was playing a date at Birdland. Budd Johnson contributes a tenor solo that is a model of virile, big-band blowing. Evans weaves a complex array of brass rhythms around Johnson, and the tenor man uses them to create a polarity between their complex character and the solid 4/4 of his own rhythm. The final choruses employ a climactic effect similar to *Straight No Chaser*, thickening the harmonic texture into an almost unbearable tension. The release into quieter harmonies then provides an effective denouement.

The most interesting piece of all to my taste is the magnificent setting of John Lewis' *Django*. There are so many things to listen for: the majesty of the opening brass statement (faintly recalling Sibelius' *Finlandia*); the delicate obbligato between French horn and flute, and the carefully woven interplay of piano and soprano sax, played over a gently strumming guitar. Johnny Coles executes a well-organized solo over

Don Hunstein, courtesy of Columbia Records

BILLIE HOLIDAY, MILES DAVIS

MILES DAVIS, GIL EVANS

a rhythm pattern that shifts in and out of double time. Then comes a positively rocking build-up as Evans lets out all the stops. Lacy improvises a line under Coles, the reeds play tremolos, and the brass punches out rhythmic explosions. As the tension dies down, there is a short improvised passage in which Lacy softly echoes Coles's lines; and finally, a brief horn echo of the theme.

These recordings have given me many happy hours, and I strongly recommend them as basic items in any comprehensive jazz library, particularly the World Pacific LPs. And they are not like those "important" records that remain untouched on the shelf as source material. Evans' music on both of these records is vibrantly alive and, unless I am drastically wrong, will be as enjoyable ten years from now as it is today.

In a recent issue of *The Jazz Review*, Steve Lacy speaks of the Evans band in glowing terms. "Sometimes when things jelled, I felt true moments of ecstasy; and recently, when a friend of mine who worked with the Claude Thornhill band in the forties . . . said that some nights the sound of the band around him moved him to tears, I knew exactly what he meant. So does anybody else who has ever played Gil's arrangements." And so should anyone who has ever heard his music. These recordings are among the best examples available.

Katz and Jammers

by the Staff

Cellist-pianist-composer-arranger-recording-director Fred Katz (no kin to Dick Katz) was quoted by columnist Jack O'Brian in The New York Journal American *to the effect that no jazz critic had ever been right. Here are reactions to this statement as they* might *have come from some musicians, jazz writers, and entrepreneurs.*

We have added a few identifications for those who are not quite so "inside," but perhaps even these few weren't really necessary.

Stan Kenton: "When the history of our great American art form, and I have been touched to tears by the way those people overseas feel about what we feel so deeply about, it will be seen that the critics lacked the scope, I mean the historical as well as the over-all cosmic and spiritual perspective, to realize where the future was coming from, and that it really was, as I know from traveling with it and on it across and through the length and breadth of our country and beyond and all they were talking about was Count Basie and Duke Ellington, and I certainly admire them and go to see them whenever I can, but they did not have the ears to hear and the blood to absorb what else was happening, the sounds and the volume and the great sweep of that other thing that was happening, that was bursting—What was the question?"

Whitney Balliett (of *The New Yorker*): "I do not believe that jazz critics should discuss music with musicians."

George Wein (founder and first producer of the Newport Jazz Festival): "Since Fred Katz is not yet enough of a draw to

have appeared at either Newport or Storyville as a leader, I have
not had the opportunity to comment on his work in my weekly
column of news and criticism in the *Boston Herald*. Furthermore, it would be poor taste for me to comment on other
critics except to say that, as anyone could see who read what
they said about Newport this year (it may not be a conspiracy,
but it does seem to me that all that lack of taste cannot have
been accidental), they are incompetent, and besides, can any
of them sit down and play piano with Sidney Bechet, or call
Joe Glaser by his first name, or otherwise show that they
really know what's happening?"

Joe Glaser (president of the Associated Booking Corporation): "What the hell do I care about Fred Katz or the critics?
Who do you think owns all this jazz?"

Dom Cerulli (then New York editor of *Down Beat*): "Fred
has a point. It's certainly worth considering anyway. But here
at the *Beat*, we try to give our readers all the latest on the
events in the jazz world and I do think we're doing a good
job."

Leonard Feather (of *Down Beat, et al.*): "I don't think that
Fred Katz (see the *Encyclopedia of Jazz* and the *Encyclopedia
Yearbook of Jazz* [Horizon]) realizes that I knew from the
beginning that Charlie Parker and Dizzy Gillespie were important (see *The Book of Jazz* [Horizon]). Besides, it's your
immediate reaction that counts. Just because a girl comes
from a foreign country, sounds exactly like Billie Holiday, and
sings at Newport doesn't necessarily mean that she *can't* be a
good jazz singer. Fred Katz, by the way, is not featured on
The Weary Blues (MGM) but he might have been. Jelly Roll
Morton couldn't have played good cello if he'd tried."

Duke Ellington: "We love you madly!"

Nat Hentoff: "It is seemingly obvious that Fred Katz's *ex
cathedra* pronouncement has some relevance in the present
context, but what makes him think any critics exist? I mean
functional, mainstream, blues-rooted critics. And anyway,

what about the way they're running Newport? What does Fred have to say about that?"

Bill Cross (then editor of *Metronome*): "None of the critics is conscious enough of the important experimental work being done by Teddy Charles, Teo, and John La Porta. Charlie Mingus has even experimented with a group including *two* cellos."

Don Gold (then Chicago editor of *Down Beat,* and prolific record reviewer): " * * * * Although not one of the jazz greats, Fred does do meaningful work at times, here succeeds in communicating, and may become an important voice."

Norman Granz (of "Jazz at the Philharmonic," Verve records, *et al.*): "I've never met à critic who wasn't looking for free records. This, then, is what they call critics."

Ralph J. Gleason (of *Down Beat* and the nationally syndicated "Rhythm Section"): "Fred Katz doesn't know the business. The critics don't know the business. There's too much pretentiousness around. Do you think Katz or those critics know how much LPs actually sell? Do you think they ever talked to Bunk Johnson? Or went to the Savoy? Or the Onyx? Those were the days, and these could be too if we would just remember that jazz is fun and Erroll Garner."

Martin Williams: "Of course, Fred Katz (what are we to make of the rhythmic mannerisms, bordering on cocktail cello, or of the mystical-post-Zen-cool-jazz pretentiousness, or the lack of genuine thematic development—compare him with Joplin or Morton—that in spite of his musicianship, taste, clarity, and craftsmanship threaten the *jazz* content of Katz's compositions [?]) is attacking a straw man. There are *no* jazz critics."

Morris Levy (then as now—Birdland, Roulette Records, *et al.*): "What the hell do I care about Fred Katz or the critics? Who do you think owns all this jazz?"

Marshall W. Stearns (of *The Story of Jazz*): "I speak as a historian and not as a critic, but I think Fred Katz should read some of the studies of jazz made by trained minds from other allied fields: sociologists, psychologists, anthropologists, and musicologists."

George Frazier (who is careful of his clothes and has written about jazz since the thirties): "I kid you not, there are no jazz critics—certainly none of the younger bearded ones—who go to or know of a decent tailor. And I tell you true, if a man has no taste in collars and cuffs, how can be understand the meaning of the difference between Bobby Short and George Wein? Actually, the best of the younger critics is Joe Glaser although, critic me no critics, none have the Scott Fitzgerald flair of Otis Ferguson, who wrote with the laughter of Tommy Ladnier and the grace of Kid Ory, because he knew that jazz was the Stork Club and Mabel Mercer and that November afternoon at the Plaza when the tawny girls swept by in a pride of Gibsons, and the girl I lived with asked me as she held out her slipper for another drink, 'When are you going to finish your book on *Time?*' "

Joe Newman (then Count Basie's trumpet soloist): "All I want to do is swing."

Bill Russo (who, as a composer, would rather be William Russo): "I have considered the problem of using cellos in jazz, and I am writing a new piece for four cellos, three valve trombones, and Lee Konitz. I won't have anyone improvising. I don't think musicians should be *allowed* to improvise. I hope Fred read from a prepared text. I don't think jazz critics should be *allowed* in their present state of ignorance. I am willing to give a course on the fundamentals of music for critics free of charge; Fred is welcome too."

Father Norman O'Connor (inevitably, known as "the jazz priest"): "In the long run, Katz is right and the critics are right. In the short run, however, I am available to moderate a symposium on the subject."

William Russell (who knows more about Bunk Johnson than anyone): "Who is Fred Katz?"

The State of Dixieland

by Dick Hadlock

Dick Hadlock is a clarinetist who has contributed articles to Down Beat, Metronome, The Record Changer, *and* The Jazz Review.

Eddie Condon: CONDON A LA CARTE, Commodore FL 30,010. Condon, *guitar;* Max Kaminsky or Marty Marsala, *trumpet;* Pee Wee Russell, *clarinet;* George Brunis, Brad Gowans, Benny Morton, or Lou McGarity, *trombone;* Fats Waller, Joe Bushkin, or Gene Schroeder, *piano;* Bob Casey or Artie Shapiro, *bass;* Tony Spargo, Sid Catlett, or George Wettling, *drums.*
It's Right Here for You; Jelly Roll; Save Your Sorrow; Nobody Knows You; Tell 'Em About Me; Strut Miss Lizzie; Ballin' the Jack; Pray for the Lights to Go Out; Georgia Grind; You're Some Pretty Doll; Oh Sister!; Ain't That Hot; Dancin' Fool.

Eddie Condon: JAM SESSIONS AT COMMODORE, Commodore FL 30,006. Condon, *guitar;* Bobby Hackett, Max Kaminsky, or Muggsy Spanier, *trumpets;* Joe Marsala, *alto;* Bud Freeman, *tenor;* Pee Wee Russell, Joe Marsala, *clarinets;* George Brunis, Benny Morton, Brad Gowans, or Miff Mole, *trombone;* Jess Stacy or Joe Bushkin, *piano;* Artie Shapiro or Bob Casey, *bass;* George Wettling or Sid Catlett, *drums.*
Carnegie Drag; Carnegie Jump; Basin Street Blues; Oh, Katherina!; A Good Man Is Hard to Find.

Eddie Condon: CONFIDENTIALLY . . . IT'S CONDON, Design DLP 47. Condon, *guitar;* Bobby Hackett, Billy Butterfield, or Max Kaminsky, *trumpet;* Pee Wee Russell, Ed Hall, possibly Joe Dixon or Johnny Mince, *clarinet;* Lou McGarity, possibly Benny Morton, *trombone;* Ernie Caceres, *baritone;* Gene Schroeder, possibly Dave Bowman or Joe Bushkin, *piano;* Bob Haggart or Bob Casey, *bass;* Joe Grauso, Johnny Blowers, possibly George Wettling or Dave Tough, *drums.*
That's a Plenty; Ballin' the Jack; Cherry; Sweet Georgia Brown; Wherever There's Love; What's New?; Ja Da; It's Been So Long;

Royal Garden Blues; Sugar; Back in Your Own Back Yard; Indiana.

Eddie Condon: DIXIELAND DANCE PARTY, Dot DLP 3141. Condon, *guitar;* Rex Stewart, Billy Butterfield, or Dick Cary, *trumpet;* Herb Hall or Peanuts Hucko, *clarinet;* Bud Freeman, *tenor;* Cutty Cutshall, *trombone;* Gene Schroeder, *piano;* Leonard Gaskin, *bass;* George Wettling, *drums.*
Copenhagen; Riverboat Shuffle; Sugar Foot Stomp; Fidgety Feet; Little White Lies; Louisiana; Dinah; Indiana; Original Dixieland One Step; I've Found a New Baby; China Boy; South Rampart Street Parade; At the Jazz Band Ball; That's a Plenty; Now That You're Gone; Willow Weep for Me; Blue Again; Sugar; Liza; There'll Be Some Changes Made; Nobody's Sweetheart; Clarinet Marmalade; High Society.

Jack Teagarden: BIG "T" 's DIXIELAND BAND, Capitol T 1095. Teagarden, *trombone;* Jerry Fuller, *clarinet;* Dick Oakley, *trumpet;* Don Ewell, *piano;* Stan Puls, *bass;* Ronnie Greb, *drums.*
Wolverine Blues; Weary River; Rippa-Tutti; Tishomingo Blues; Doctor Jazz; Dallas Blues; China Boy; Casanova's Lament; Walleritis; Mobile Blues; Someday You'll Be Sorry.

Pee Wee Erwin: OH, PLAY THAT THING!, United Artists UAL 4010. Erwin, *trumpet;* Kenny Davern, *clarinet;* Lou McGarity, *trombone;* Dick Hyman, *piano;* Tony Gattuso, *banjo* and *guitar;* Jack Lesberg, *bass;* Harvey Phillips, *tuba;* Cliff Leeman, *drums.*
Kansas City Stomps; The Chant; Yaaka Hula Hicky Dula; Temptation Rag; Black Bottom Stomp; Dippermouth Blues; Grandpa's Spells; Dill Pickles; Sensation Rag; Big Pond Rag; Jazz Frappé Rag; Georgia Swing.

Bunk Johnson: Commodore DL 30,007. Johnson, *trumpet;* George Lewis, *clarinet;* Albert Warner, *trombone;* Walter Decou, *piano;* Lawrence Marrero, *banjo;* Chester Zardis, *bass;* Edgar Mosley, *drums.*
The Thriller Rag; When I Leave the World Behind; Weary Blues; Franklin Street Blues; Blue Bells Goodbye; Big Chief Battle Axe; Sobbin' Blues; Dusty Rag; Yaaka Hula Hicky Dula; Shine; Sometimes My Burden Is So Hard to Bear; Sobbin' Blues No. 2.

George Lewis: CONCERT!, Blue Note 1208. Lewis, *clarinet;* Kid Howard, *trumpet;* Jim Robinson, *trombone;* Alton Purnell, *piano;* Lawrence Marrero, *banjo;* Alcide Pavageau, *bass;* Joe Watkins, *drums.*
Ice Cream; Red Wing; Mama Don't Allow It; Burgundy Street Blues; Bill Bailey; Over the Waves; Just A Closer Walk With Thee; Canal Street Blues; Walking with the King; Gettysburg March.

Chris Barber: HERE IS CHRIS BARBER, Atlantic 1292. Varying personnels include: Barber, *trombone*; Pat Halcox, Ben Cohen, *cornets*; Monty Sunshine, *clarinet*; Lonnie Donegan or Eddie Smith, *banjo*; Jim Bray or Micky Ashman, *bass*; Ron Bowden or Graham Burbidge, *drums*.

Hush-a-Bye; Everybody Loves My Baby; Tishomingo Blues; You Don't Understand; Magnolia's Wedding Day; Doin' The Crazy Walk; Diga Diga Doo; Bill Bailey; Willie The Weeper; Trombone Cholly; Papa De-Da-Da; Tuxedo Rag.

Joe Capraro: DIXIELAND DOWN SOUTH, Southland SLP 220. Capraro, *guitar*; Charlie Cardilla or Ray Burke, *clarinet*; Mika Lala, *trumpet*; Bob Havens, *trombone*; Jeff Riddick, *piano*; Sherwood Mangiapane, *bass*; Paul Edwards, *drums*.

Sidewalks of New York; A Good Man Is Hard to Find; The World Is Waiting For the Sunrise; Nobody's Sweetheart Now; Pagan Love Song; The Bucket Has a Hole in It; You Tell Me Your Dreams; Rose Room.

Armand Hug/Eddie Miller, Southland SLP 221. Side 1: Hug, *piano*; Mike Lala, *trumpet*; Harry Shields, *clarinet*; Bob Havens, *trombone*; Ray Burke, *harmonica*; Joe Capraro, *banjo*; Emile Christian, *bass* and *trombone*; Johnny Castaing, *drums*. Side 2: Miller, *tenor*; Armand Hug, *piano*; Joe Capraro, *guitar*; Chink Martin, *bass*; Monk Hazel, *drums*.

Easy Goin' Blues; Mr. Jelly Lord; A Dixie Jam Session; Mad; Buzzard's Parade; Butter and Egg Man; When Irish Eyes Are Smiling; Darkness on the Delta.

Bob Scobey: THE SCOBEY STORY, VOLUME I, Good Time Jazz L 12032. Varying personnels include: Scobey, *trumpet*; Darnell Howard, Albert Nicholas, or George Probert, *clarinet*; Jack Buck, *trombone*; Burt Bales or Wally Rose, *piano*; Clancy Hayes, *banjo*, *guitar*, and *vocals*; Squire Girsback or Dick Lammi, *bass*; Gordon Edwards or Fred Higuera, *drums*.

Pretty Baby; St. Louis Blues; Coney Island Washboard; Some of These Days; Beale Street Mama; Dippermouth Blues; South; Sailing Down Chesapeake Bay; Wolverine Blues; Chicago; Melancholy; That's a Plenty.

Johnny Maddox: DIXIELAND BLUES, Dot DLP 3131. Maddox, *piano*; Matty Matlock, *clarinet*; Mannie Klein, *trumpet*; Moe Schneider, *trombone*; Nappy LaMare, *banjo*; Bobby Hammack, *piano*; Red Callender, *tuba*; Nick Fatool, *drums*.

Bluin' the Blues; Strut Miss Lizzie; Beale Street Blues; Wolverine Blues; Memphis Blues; Royal Garden Blues; St. Louis Blues; Friday Night Blues; Bow Wow Blues; Jelly Roll; Basin Street Blues; Tishomingo Blues; Yellow Dog Blues.

THE THIRTEEN RECENT releases to be discussed—some of
them reissues—represent most of the ground, arid or bounti-
ful, within the province of "Dixieland." Behind this ambiguous label can be found a wide variety of musical attitudes and
aims among scores of musicians, most of them contending
with the built-in limitations of collective improvisation, as
well as more personal problems of self-expression.

The time-honored three- or four-horn "front line," with its
logical delineation of musical roles (trumpet lead, trombone
bass, clarinet embroidering above) is, I believe, more a con-
venient format than an art in itself. It requires little imagination to fashion a passable Dixieland ensemble, although
there are worthwhile challenges for those who care to bother
with them. The opportunities for multilinear collective improvisation are frequently ignored by old-timers and young musicians alike. As Paul Desmond replied when asked recently
if he was tempted to stay with Dixieland for its contrapuntal
possibilities, "Nobody was doing any of it except me." Ob-
serving the ground rules of ensemble playing is not a creative
act, but merely prepares the way for the artist.

The group of musicians who, by historical accident or
commercial design, are associated with Eddie Condon's name
have devoted considerable attention to ensemble playing, as
well as to the development of their individual musical characters as soloists. Nearly all of them worked successfully in
top swing-era bands, but for most the creative fire burned
highest in the climate of relative freedom offered by the small
band and the jam session. Bud Freeman, Pee Wee Russell,
Brad Gowans, Jack Teagarden, Miff Mole, Jess Stacy, and
Bobby Hackett made real contributions to the development
and enrichment of creative thought in jazz. Their restless
search for fresh ways to broaden the jazz language is the chief
characteristic that distinguishes the Commodore reissues from
the routine Dixieland generally offered—even by Condon—
today. These men did not, like early "bop" experimenters, express their disillusionment with the state of musical affairs
before World War II by breaking *away* from tradition (most
of the key men were a little too old to think in those terms

anyway), nor could they condone retrogression of the kind that "revivalists" were advocating. Rather, they attempted to expand within the traditional framework of Dixieland that had served them so well. While many worked out satisfactory solo styles, only a handful were as successful in constructing new ensemble patterns more appropriate to 1938 than to 1918.

Clarinetist Pee Wee Russell is the ensemble musician *par excellence*. Forsaking the undulating lines of more conventional Dixieland clarinetists, Russell adds a cutting edge to the top of the ensemble sound with a powerful but flexible rasping attack. His unusual sensitivity to ensemble harmony is a joy to trumpet players, for it permits them to depart from the melody without fear of crashing head-on into clarinet notes. Russell touches the traditional third above the lead note often enough to construct a "proper" clarinet part, but more importantly he stretches the ensemble fabric with fourths, fifths (this requires an alert trombonist, for the fifth is traditionally his territory), sixths, and ninths, while spinning elastic counterlines that are closer to second trumpet parts than to the arpeggio-dominated filigrees that one is accustomed to hearing in Dixieland and military bands. It is largely his skillful handling of his very personal ensemble role that gives these old Commodore recordings (CONDON À LA CARTE and JAM SESSIONS) an exhilarating vigor undiminished by time.

The most satisfactory ensemble tissues captured on record by Commodore are those involving Russell, Max Kaminsky, and the late Brad Gowans. Kaminsky provides a stocky lead that leaves space for other instruments to editorialize, yet he neither leans on rhythmic drive alone, as Spanier does, nor confuses the proceedings by trying to play Pee Wee's harmonic games, as Hackett seems to do. Gowans achieves with his valve instrument a third part that adds a kind of bass trumpet voice to Russell's and Kaminsky's forthright upper lines. Like Russell, Gowans possessed an extraordinary ear that told him exactly what notes best suited the ensemble texture. Bud Freeman, who contributed a fourth perceptive musical mind to the Russell-Kaminsky-Gowans alliance from time to time, is heard briefly on *Carnegie Jump, Carnegie*

Drag, and *A Good Man Is Hard to Find.* Freeman is unsurpassed as an ensemble tenor man, one who knows how to add fourth harmony to a front line without walking all over clarinet and trombone parts. It is hoped that Commodore will reissue more Freeman sides from their extensive 78 rpm catalog.

For all their concern with creating contemporary ensemble techniques that would work as well as the discarded "Chicago" style, the Condonites remained devoted to the main business of jazz, which is (I believe) individual expression. In this area, the men discussed so far stand considerably above most so-called Dixieland musicians.[1]

The creative rallying point for much of the solo work in and around Commodore's studios was again Pee Wee Russell. In the twenties Russell was working out jazz ideas that were regarded by many observers at the time as too "far out," ideas that probably came largely from Bix Beiderbecke, who was practicing in 1927 what a few early "bop" modernists (Charlie Parker in particular) felt they were discovering some twelve years later. Parker himself claimed to have stumbled onto the idea, in 1939, of "using higher intervals of a chord as a melody line and backing them with appropriately related changes."[2] Which is exactly what Bix Beiderbecke (and, to a lesser extent, Frank Trumbauer) was up to, although most of his cohorts weren't always aware of it and invariably failed to furnish the "appropriately related changes." (This helps us to understand why Bix might have drawn as much inspiration from the harmonically sophisticated scores of Bill Challis *et al* as he did from loose "Dixieland" surroundings.) Here is a classic Beiderbecke solo, recorded in 1929, that illustrates his gift for melodic architecture in the higher

[1] This statement excludes those musicians who were caught in the post-World War II middle ground between "bop" and traditional jazz and turned somewhat reluctantly to Dixieland to make money—men like Joe Thomas, Vic Dickenson, Red Allen, Louis Armstrong, Earl Hines, Roy Eldridge, and others. Obviously, had such artists been truly fascinated by Dixieland, they would have done something along those lines before it became economically prudent to do so.

[2] Orrin Keepnews, "Charlie Parker," *The Jazz Makers,* edited by Nat Shapiro and Nat Hentoff (New York: Grove Press, 1957), p. 209.

intervals of the chord and, in its short sixteen bars, suggests much of what was to come in the next decade or two. Contrast Bix's chorus, with its constant emphasis on sixths and ninths, to the tune as originally written.[3]

Ex. I

[3] Copyright 1922, Leo Feist, Inc. From *Bix Beiderbecke Trumpet Transcriptions*. Edited by Jay Arnold. Robbins Music Corp., 1944.

This was part of the magic of Bix that continued to excite so many jazz musicians, especially Condon and Company, long after his death. His ability to build well-proportioned melodies in the upper harmonic strata of any given tune has seldom been equaled. Before Charlie Parker, Pee Wee Russell was one of a very few jazzmen who comprehended Bix and possessed the necessary musical equipment to explore similar paths. Here is the way Pee Wee got into his solo on *Embraceable You* in 1938.[4] Compare it to Parker's first bar of the same tune[5] almost a decade later:

Ex. 2

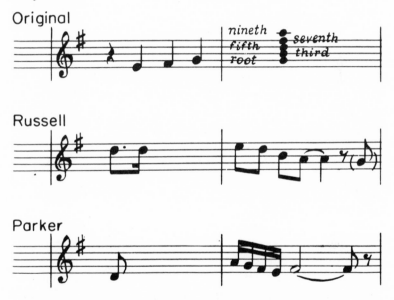

Although Russell moves down from the sixth (suggested by the original melody note) to the ninth whereas Parker descends from the ninth to the sixth, the rhythmic, harmonic, and melodic similarities are obvious.

[4] Transcribed from Commodore FL 20,016, HORN A-PLENTY; Bobby Hackett and his Orchestra.
[5] Transcribed from Dial 203, CHARLIE PARKER; Charlie Parker Sextet. The same opening statement occurs again in *Quasimodo,* which is based on the chord structure of *Embraceable You.*

So we find Gowans, Kaminsky, Hackett, Freeman, and even unadventurous players like George Brunis falling under the Beiderbecke-Russell spell. Other musicians (Red Nichols, Fud Livingston, Adrian Rollini, Jimmy McPartland, etc.) were exploring these avenues in the twenties, but alongside the overwhelming communicative power of Louis Armstrong and Coleman Hawkins, whose direct styles were being widely admired and imitated, the experimental clique must have seemed almost effeminate to many jazzmen. (Hawkins, though, was sensitive to what was going on; listen to *One Hour*,[6] recorded in 1929, as Hawkins, Russell, and Glenn Miller forge a "new" composition in which each solo is part of a sympathetic whole, a rare instance of musical understanding that takes shape as each man opens his solo on the ninth of the initial chord. This effective device is so simple that it is at first unnoticeable, the listener being only vaguely aware that something special has happened to the tune.)

Beiderbecke and Russell are held in esteem because they combined these harmonic devices with personal, persuasive jazz voices in ordered choruses, laced with warm humor, that stand on their own as good music. Except for Lester Young, no one seemed to accomplish as much along these lines until Parker ripened in the forties.

Joe Marsala, who appears briefly on *A Good Man Is Hard to Find*, is a musician who knows his "extensions" (sixths, ninths, elevenths, etc.) but uses them as passing tones or places them on the weak pulse, losing much of the shock value and melodic potential of the device.

Miff Mole, the man who liberated the trombone from the status of jazz clown, is not heard to good advantage on these recordings. He shows but a small sample of his prodigious talent on *A Good Man Is Hard to Find*. *Good Man*, an extended performance originally spread over four twelve-inch 78 rpm sides, suggested rewarding sessions to come with the advent of LP, but unhappily these musicians have been forced to move in the opposite direction instead, toward telescoping

[6] Included on Camden CAL 339.

each performance until only frantic little digests are left. (See below *re* Condon's latest releases on Dot.)

Russell was still in top form in 1943, when *Basin Street Blues* was recorded, but the alliance was broken and the ensemble work is that of any group of good "mainstream" musicians thrown together. Benny Morton, a skilled musician, is sympathetic but lacks the almost mystic ensemble insight of Gowans.

By 1944, individual attitudes had drifted still farther apart. Hackett had been studying his horn and, it seems, Louis Armstrong as well. The results were electric, but much of the old humor and fancy had gone. The new positive Hackett seemed content to play satisfying arpeggios rather than to roam with Russell through uncharted territory. There has always been a place of honor at the Condon table, though, for well-grounded musicians like Hackett with a flair for the elegant. The 1944 transcriptions issued on Design reveal some of the old gang running through ensemble passages almost numbly in order to get to the solos, which they render as convincingly as ever. Only Russell, and sometimes baritonist Caceres, show much concern about who plays what in the collective openings and endings. The tempos are a little too fast, perhaps the first sign that the men who used to get together for fun were now peddling the same product as "concert" music. Facing an audience sitting on its hands in a concert hall, performers are frequently tempted to do something dazzling, or at least to deliver the old goods at a more frenzied pace. Still, there is a cheerful spontaneity about the Design hodgepodge, especially in the solos of Russell and Hackett.

After some fifteen years of methodically converting his friends' music to a commercial formula, Condon, represented by his new Dot release, has turned to mass production methods, stringing tunes together like hot sausages. The musical outcome is about as digestible. His players blow what customers expect them to, flooding the record with "get-hot" mannerisms. Herb Hall sounds like brother Ed. Peanuts Hucko lifts from Goodman, and even Rex Stewart appears to be trying to wear Bill Davison's shoes. Only Bud Freeman, particularly on *China Boy,* remains a firm individual voice struggling to salvage a few musical moments from the blustering carnival around him.

Jack Teagarden's eloquent trombone always seemed to me to be at home with Condon's retinue, as well as with Armstrong, where the soloists were near his level; on his new Capitol LP, Jack has strapped himself to a small band of quietly undistinguished musicians who reduce Dixieland jazz to a spineless recital of ensemble and solo clichés. I don't believe Teagarden has ever been particularly suited to Dixieland, anyway. His work with Pollack, Nichols, Whiteman, Goodman, Freeman, Condon, and his own big band stood out because space was set aside to display Teagarden the soloist.

Like the Condonites, Tea loves to indulge in tunes that have the harmonic and melodic twists of Russell and Beiderbecke built into them. His smoky singing and playing on *Weary River* and *Someday You'll Be Sorry* are warm and delightful. Much of the joy of listening to Jack Teagarden stems from his flawless execution, perfect intonation and his very relaxed manner rather than from unusually imaginative lines or carefully wrought melodic structures. He seems to form ideas flatly in terms of the *trombone,* leaving more gossamer musical realms, unlinked to the mechanics of any one horn, to the likes of Russell and Gowans.

The "revivalists" must have made inroads on some front-rank jazzmen at last, for now we find Teagarden including *Doctor Jazz* and *Tishomingo Blues* in his repertoire. Perhaps former Bunk Johnson pianist Don Ewell had something to do with it. Today Ewell has "progressed" to Fats Waller, but his attempts to find the Waller touch fail because he does not produce the crisp vitality, the buoyant swing, or the musical authority that were prominent in all of Fats's work.

A more decisive tactical victory for the "revivalists" is Pee Wee Erwin's new United Artists release, which offers four Jelly Roll Morton compositions along with miscellaneous vintage rags and stomps. Clarinetist Kenny Davern, who has toyed with every jazz era off and on, jumps casually from imitations of George Lewis and renderings of Morton parts à

la Omer Simeon to busy eclectic counterlines delivered somewhat in the manner of Irving Fazola. Davern's idea of ensemble playing is to punctuate each trumpet phrase with a
soaring glissando that fills the empty space and spills into the
next lead statement. While this procedure conforms roughly
to the bylaws of ensemble counterpoint, repeated use of the
device induces monotony. Worse still, Davern misses several
important harmonic changes, even in the simple *Yaaka Hula
Hicky Dula* and *Big Pond Rag* (actually *Over the Waves*).

Erwin is a good player, but he has seldom advanced anything distinctly his own. Probably his chief claim to jazz fame
is his recorded work with Tommy Dorsey's orchestra, most of
which consists of facile copies of Bunny Berigan's style.

Perhaps Erwin's lack of individuality and Davern's inability
to settle in any one groove are clues to the appeal of anti-
quarianism. Like a professor who escapes the perplexities of
today's world by living in history, the musician who emulates
past performances is on relatively safe and predictable ground.
His musical goals are laid out for him, requiring only hard
work and enthusiasm to reach them. The large burden of individual creative responsibility (which, after all, not *everyone* is
capable of carrying), is gone, for music that may have been
difficult when it was conceived can be reconstructed with comparative ease years later. And the results *can* be lots of fun.

In the hands of these well-schooled musicians, the old Morton arrangements (most of them put together by Mel Stitzel
or Elmer Schoebel) almost come alive—at least more so than
in any post-Morton attempts I have heard. Lou McGarity, incidentally, is Lou McGarity at all times, and a constant delight. He is, in this instance, a man among boys, a man who
knows how he wants to play. Ironically, McGarity's uncom-
promisingly personal amalgam of barrelhouse and "mainstream" is more in context with both the Morton and George
Lewis styles than is Erwin himself!

The Dixieland revival began with the resurrection of Bunk
Johnson, some of whose first records are now re-released on a
Commodore LP. Johnson startled his sponsors by coming out
of retirement to blow with more skill and vitality than they

had expected; so much more, in fact, that critic Gene Williams, one of Bunk's patrons, built a veritable religion around the old man. Perhaps Johnson had kept up with jazz developments more than anyone suspected, for his playing on this 1942 session reflects, in spite of the bothersome din behind him, a sense of melodic development through harmonic alterations that even "younger" men like Keppard and Oliver never revealed on records. In his own way, Bunk was flirting with the use of upper harmonic intervals as melody notes that we have found to be an important element in the work of Beiderbecke and Russell. Here is a typical Bunk Johnson blues phrase:[7]

Ex. 3

This simple melodic statement is enriched in the second measure by an upward movement that touches the sixth, and by a sustained ninth in the fourth bar. Compare it to a characteristic Louis Armstrong blues, which relies more upon bold announcements of durable ideas than upon harmonic subtleties.[8]

Ex. 4

Similar features in the work of the two trumpeters have led many observers to the conclusion that Louis learned much of his style from Bunk. It is more logical, I think, to assume

[7] *Bunk's Blues,* included in *Great Trumpet Styles,* edited by Billy Butterfield. Capitol Songs, Inc., 1945.
[8] *Snag It,* included in *Louis Armstrong 50 Hot Choruses for Cornet.* Melrose Brothers.

that the Johnson we have on records was influenced by Armstrong, for Bunk, after all, was still professionally active when Louis was at his peak. Certainly on *Shine* and on a later recording of *Some of These Days*[9] Bunk shows familiarity with Armstrong's records. *Shine* also presents a more relaxed and free Bunk Johnson than the stodgy re-creations of his distant past. But the blues were not Johnson's forte, for he was a cautious, cool musician, unlike the fiery Armstrong. None of the men on this record, in fact, have much feeling for blues; they cling to a somewhat "legitimate" attitude toward tone control and phrasing. When Lewis' clarinet "sings," it is *song,* not blues. Although severely limited, Lewis' work on this record is brilliant compared to the mechanical two-note grunts of trombonist Albert Warner.

After Johnson's death, Lewis became the darling of that curious segment of the jazz audience that collects "folk" artists. Blue Note, who also recorded Lewis with Johnson, has just issued a 1954 concert that caught Lewis and his New Orleans Stompers in relatively fine form. The almost uncontrolled degree of enthusiasm in the rhythm section seems to ignite Robinson and Lewis, whose contributions, if measured by energy units rather than musical criteria, are exciting indeed. The nondescript vocals by Kid Howard and Joe Watkins add nothing more than playing time to the record, however.

Lewis has gained a bit of poise and harmonic know-how since his first confused dates with Johnson, but he is still a remarkably naïve musician who has learned barely enough of the jazz language to express his modest musical thoughts. Because he seems to have no need for going beyond that—and probably could not if he would—Lewis deserves the respect due an untutored but honest man. He is effective when he pulls all the stops because total involvement does not alter the identity of his music, as it does that of his imitators (Kenny Davern is one), who have to *hold back* their minds and fingers to restrict their melodic, harmonic, and rhythmic tool

---

[9] Included on Columbia GL 520, BUNK JOHNSON.

to the rustic style of Lewis. This artless music, valid for Lewis because there is no suppression of musical knowledge, usually ends in inhibited and self-conscious failure for the imitator.

Kid Howard's playing style is rather like Red Allen's, sometimes even sounding closer to a primitive Roy Eldridge when he uses scale-like runs sprinkled with minor thirds and fourths. Howard is apparently unconcerned about his instrument's role in the ensemble, for he repeatedly smothers Lewis and Robinson in *tutti* passages. The most charitable way to dismiss Robinson is to point out that he is an improvement on Albert Warner.

With the widespread distribution of Lewis' recordings, bands attempting to capture the rough excitement of his New Orleans crew have broken out everywhere, notably in England and Australia.

Chris Barber imported the Lewis pattern into England, using it to interpolate various early jazz styles, mostly gathered from records cut in the twenties. His new Atlantic LP displays a band that is probably superior to any of its American counterparts, and in some ways even better than Lewis' own. Barber is a skilled, if unoriginal, ensemble trombonist; clarinetist Sunshine (that's really his name) catches some of the winsome ingenuousness of his hero without going out of tune (as Lewis frequently does), and all members seem to enjoy what they play immensely. Applying the same basic ensemble formula to each tune, the band stays on safe, though frequently barren, musical ground. In this, as in most revival jazz bands, the *tune* and the *arrangement*, as symbols of other men in other times, are all-important and the performance is the almost mechanical means of preserving them. Most revivalists are, in short, musical curators who hope to keep the properties of early jazz alive for others to enjoy. A harmless pastime, to be sure, but not one that produces much music to be admired, for itself.

Barber's men, incidentally, seem to be more conscious of complementary harmony than were the Lewis or Johnson bands. The New Orleans groups seldom produced three-dimensional ensemble jazz, holding instead to a pattern of simultaneous, occasionally clashing, variations on the original melody; Barber, Sunshine, and trumpeter Halcox attempt to relate to each others' parts vertically as well as linearly. Only Halcox, however, demonstrates any capacity for logical and symmetrical melodies of his own.

Persistent rhythmic emphasis on the first and third pulse, a chronic symptom of revival bands (although oddly, it was Johnson and Lewis who led many traditionalists away from the drop-forge two-beat of Watters and friends), is caused by the inability of Barber's rhythm section to get off the ground. They act as a strait jacket on the horn players, who are forced to place their accents at the most conspicuous points.

Southland's DIXIELAND DOWN SOUTH is a collection of faded trivia featuring some of New Orleans' current store of second-rate jazzmen, most of whom have little to offer other than a limp rehash of stock Dixieland gimmicks. Most interesting performer on the date is trombonist Bob Havens from Illinois, who arrived in New Orleans while playing with Ralph Flanagan's band. He phrases more like Jack Teagarden than any imitator I have heard. Aside from Havens, there is no one on this record with much feeling for blues, ensemble playing, melodic invention, or rhythmic drive. The rhythm section, which is considerably below Lawrence Welk standards, suffers from the most lethargic pianist I have heard since Sunday school days.

Pianist Armand Hug, leading essentially the same group on one side of another Southland release, at least demonstrates that one moderately good pianist can improve a drooping band. The music brightens, but the same limitations preclude our measuring this music by any other than amateur standards. Side 2, though, moves closer to a professional level with the addition of drummer Monk Hazel and tenor man Eddie Miller. Miller is a first-rate jazzman under ideal circumstances, which these are not. He is basically a soloist, but this endeavor to showcase his rollicking solo style is impeded by a clanging rhythm section—most of the trouble seems to come from Hazel's nagging afterbeat—that fails to stimulate

Miller or even to give him fair odds, Still Miller tears into
Butter and Egg Man with gusto and grit. His distinctive use
of sixths and ninths, though less imaginative than Russell's
and generally restricted to passing tones, lends a contemporary
quality to his solos. Only his rhythmic accents (usually placed
on the "strong" beats) keep Miller in an "old-time" category,
and even that seems to be undergoing change. He has discarded many of the clichés that marred his work in the thirties
and has recently adopted a more hard-hitting tone. It is still
a warm sound, though, especially on *Darkness on the Delta*.
(Miller shares the Condon coterie's penchant for unhackneyed
ballads too.) This man deserves a good rhythm section.

Bob Scobey has worked his way from second trumpeter with
Lu Watters to acceptance in Hollywood ex-Bob-Crosby studio
circles as a capable jazzman who wants to, and occasionally
does, swing. However, the records that Good Time Jazz has
just repackaged were recorded in 1950-51 immediately after
the break with Watters, when Scobey was still wielding the
trumpet like a sledge hammer. There are a few peppy tracks
featuring Darnell Howard or Albert Nicholas on clarinet, but
Scobey was still agonizingly muscle-bound at that time.
Howard, an accomplished jazz clarinetist in some respects, is
not a particularly sensitive ensemble player, deliberately
breathing in unison with the trumpet and skittering all over
the horns in the course of each phrase. Al Nicholas, on the
other hand, is a levelheaded musician who seldom blows a
note out of place. His sensuous tone, together with his unhurried respect for order, compensate for his limited imagination
(Nicholas' solos are almost always built on arpeggios that
take in only the most expected intervals), and for the stylized
embellishments that constitute his approach to collective improvisation.

Scobey, according to annotator Ertegun, was seeking simplicity and rhythm in his new musical environment. He found
both, but neglected to refine them with syncopation or dynamics. Listening to the old Watters-dominated Scobey is like
holding one's head under the hood of a Model T at full throt-
tle, but he has improved since these recordings were made.

Clancy Hayes, who sings like a man with sinus trouble, parades his tarnished hokum and gaslight humor in and out of the music with the swaggering audacity of a burlesque headliner.

Going Hayes one better, pianist. Johnny Maddox, on a new Dot release, attempts to drag a band of upstanding musicians with him into the arena of musical dishonor. Neither humorous enough for slapstick nor subtle enough for satire, these caricatures of traditional jazz are what millions of otherwise intelligent people accept as "real" Dixieland—prepared piano, banjo and tuba (Red Callender!), three horns alternating between barnyard effects and staccato jokes. It is embarrassing to read the names of the talented participants: Matty Matlock, Nick Fatool, Moe Schneider. . . .

The thirteen records just examined, all of which will be tossed in retailers' bins marked "Dixieland," cover a range of music broad enough to render the label useless. Behind the parade wagons and striped blazers, beyond the booze and musical backslapping, one may find serious artists, gifted amateurs, buffoons, innovators, imitators, charlatans, hustlers, pioneers, novices, geniuses, has-beens, or craftsmen. I suppose counterparts can be found in any art that must operate as entertainment in order to stay alive.

These records reveal how Eddie Condon took brilliant jazzmen in need of jam-session therapy and turned them into a high-priced act that "creates" on cue. They show us the faltering musicians who were left behind in New Orleans when the money went North. And they demonstrate what became of the undated players—men like Al Nicholas, Jack Teagarden, Benny Morton, Ernie Caceres, Red Callender, Billy Butterfield, Eddie Miller, and Darnell Howard—who were forced by the economics of postwar jazz to become "Dixielanders." Most of all, these records give us some idea of the conceptual diversity and musical latitude encompassed by a single term as meaningless as some of the music it designates—"Dixieland."

Thelonious Monk

by Gunther Schuller

One of the most important events in jazz in the fifties was the re-emergence of Thelonious Monk. Gunther Schuller's survey of his recordings was a part of the first issue of The Jazz Review, *and his later review of Monk followed after about a year and a half.*

HARLEM JAZZ, 1941, Esoteric 548. Charley Christian, *guitar;* Joe Guy, *trumpet;* Thelonious Monk, *piano;* Kenny Clarke, *drums.*
Swing to Bop (Topsy); Stompin' at the Savoy.
Other tracks without Monk.

THELONIOUS MONK: GENIUS OF MODERN MUSIC, Vol. I & II, Blue Note 1510-11. George Taitt, *trumpet;* Sahib Shihab, *alto sax;* Thelonious Monk, *piano;* Robert Paige, *bass;* Art Blakey, *drums.*
'Round About Midnight; In Walked Bud; Monk's Mood; Who Knows.
Thelonious Monk, *piano;* Gene Ramey, *bass;* Art Blakey, *drums:*
Off Minor; Ruby My Dear; April in Paris; Well You Needn't; Introspection; Nice Work.
Milt Jackson, *vibes;* Thelonious Monk, *piano;* John Simmons, *bass;* Shadow Wilson, *drums:*
I Mean You; Epistrophy; Misterioso.
Idrees Sulieman, *trumpet;* Danny Quebec West, *alto sax;* Billy Smith, *tenor sax;* Thelonious Monk, *piano;* Gene Ramey, *bass;* Art Blakey, *drums:*
Thelonious; Humph; Suburban Eyes; Evonce.
Kenny Dorham, *trumpet;* Lou Donaldson, *alto sax;* Lucky Thompson, *tenor sax;* Thelonious Monk, *piano;* Nelson Boyd, *bass;* Max Roach, *drums:*
Carolina Moon; Hornin' In; Skippy; Let's Cool One.
Sahib Shihab, *alto sax;* Milt Jackson, *vibes;* Thelonious Monk, *piano;* Al McKibbon, *bass;* Art Blakey, *drums:*
Straight No Chaser; Four in One; Ask Me Now.

MILT JACKSON (with MJQ and Thelonious Monk), Blue Note 1509.
Milt Jackson, *vibes;* Sahib Shihab, *alto sax;* Thelonious Monk,
piano; Al McKibbon, *bass;* Art Blakey, *drums.*
Willow Weep for Me; Criss Cross; Eronel; Four in One.
Milt Jackson, *vibes;* Thelonious Monk, *piano;* John Simmons, *bass;*
Shadow Wilson, *drums:*
Misterioso; Evidence.
Other tracks without Monk.

THELONIOUS MONK TRIOS, Prestige 7159. Thelonious Monk, *piano;*
Gary Mapp, *bass;* Art Blakey, *drums.*
Little Rootie Tootie; Sweet and Lovely; Bye-Ya; Monk's Dream;
Trinkle Tinkle; These Foolish Things; Bemsha Swing; Reflections.
Thelonious Monk, *piano;* Percy Heath, *bass;* Art Blakey, *drums:*
Blue Monk; Just a Gigolo.

THELONIOUS MONK QUINTETS, Prestige 7053. Thelonious Monk,
piano; Sonny Rollins, *tenor sax;* Julius Watkins, *French horn;*
Percy Heath, *bass;* Willie Jones, *drums.*
Let's Call This; Think of One (take 2); Think of One (take 1).
Thelonious Monk, *piano;* Frank Foster, *tenor sax;* Ray Copeland,
trumpet; Curly Russell, *bass;* Art Blakey, *drums:*
We See; Smoke Gets in Your Eyes; Locomotive; Hackensack.

THELONIOUS MONK, Prestige 7055. Monk, Rollins, Watkins, Heath,
Jones.
Friday the Thirteenth.
Monk, Heath, Blakey:
Work; Nutty.
Monk; Rollins; Tommy Potter, *bass;* Arthur Taylor, *drums:*
The Way You Look Tonight; I Want to Be Happy.

THELONIOUS MONK PLAYS THE MUSIC OF DUKE ELLINGTON, River-
side RLP 12-201. Thelonious Monk, *piano;* Oscar Pettiford, *bass;*
Kenny Clarke, *drums.*
It Don't Mean a Thing If It Ain't Got That Swing; Sophisticated
Lady; I Got It Bad and That Ain't Good; Black and Tan Fantasy;
Mood Indigo; I Let a Song Go out of My Heart; Solitude; Cara-
van.

THE UNIQUE THELONIOUS MONK, Riverside RLP 12-209. Monk; Os-
car Pettiford, *bass;* Blakey.
Liza; Memories of You; Honeysuckle Rose; Darn That Dream;
Tea for Two; You Are Too Beautiful; Just You, Just Me.

THELONIOUS MONK: BRILLIANT CORNERS, Riverside RLP 12-226.
Clark Terry, *trumpet;* Rollins; Monk; Pettiford; Max Roach, *drums.*
Bemsha Swing.
Ernie Henry, *alto;* Rollins; Monk; Pettiford; Roach:
Pannonica; Brilliant Corners; Ba-Lue Bolivar Ba-lues Are; I Surrender, Dear.

THELONIOUS HIMSELF, Riverside RLP 12-235. Thelonious Monk,
piano.
April in Paris; Ghost of a Chance; Functional; I'm Getting Sentimental Over You; I Should Care; 'Round Midnight; All Alone.
Thelonious Monk, *piano;* John Coltrane, *tenor sax;* Wilbur Ware,
bass:
Monk's Mood.

MONK'S MUSIC, Riverside 12-242. Copeland; Gigi Gryce, *alto sax;*
Coleman Hawkins, John Coltrane, *tenors;* Monk; Wilbur Ware,
bass; Blakey.
*Abide with Me; Well, You Needn't; Ruby, My Dear; Off Minor;
Epistrophy; Crepescule with Nellie.*

MULLIGAN MEETS MONK, Riverside RLP 12-247. Gerry Mulligan,
baritone sax; Monk; Ware; Shadow Wilson, *drums.*
*'Round Midnight; Rhythm-a-ning; Sweet and Lovely; Decidedly;
Straight No Chaser; I Mean You.*

SONNY ROLLINS, Vol. 2, Blue Note 1558. J. J. Johnson, *trombone;*
Rollins; Horace Silver; Monk, *piano;* Paul Chambers, *bass;*
Blakey.
Misterioso.
Rollins, Monk, Chambers, Blakey:
Reflections.
Other tracks without Monk.

ART BLAKEY'S JAZZ MESSENGERS WITH THELONIOUS MONK, Atlantic
1278. Monk; Blakey; Johnny Griffin, *tenor sax;* Bill Hardman,
trumpet; Spanky DeBrest, *bass.*
*Evidence; In Walked Bud; Blue Monk; I Mean You; Rhythm-a-
ning; Purple Shades.*

IN RECENT YEARS Thelonious Monk has begun to exert considerable influence on younger musicians, in sharp contrast to earlier years when he was either ignored or misunderstood by all but a few musicians and even fewer critics. It took almost a decade for the legend of the "High Priest of Bop" with all its mystical and cultish fripperies to die down. And today it is much more possible to evaluate Monk purely and squarely on a musical basis, minus all the extramusical bop-hokum. The sober, understanding approach of Riverside Records, the company for whom Monk has been recording since 1955; the significant critical appraisals by men as far apart (geographically) as Martin Williams and André Hodeir; Monk's increasing successfulness in terms of a career; and now even this magazine's first-issue cover picture, sans glasses and cap and for a change not underexposed—all these are indications that the appreciation of Thelonious Monk has reached a stage where a reassessment of his unique contribution to jazz would seem germane.

His recorded work, made over a span of seventeen years, divides itself into three periods: the early formative years, the first break-through of the full original talent (in the late forties to early fifties), and lately a degree of leveling off and matured consolidation. For me the second period is the most exciting because it displays Monk's talent at its freshest and most direct. Compositions like *Criss Cross, Eronel, Evidence* and *Misterioso* are pure, uncluttered musical emanations. They are completely original, remarkably concise,[1] and rather well performed. They are available on Blue Note and Prestige, who have collected the 1947-54 recordings on half a dozen LPs. Many of these recordings still stand up very well on repeated rehearings. Certainly none of them seem dated, largely because Monk never was the bopper so many people thought he was; and he never was "cool" in the bop sense. One searches in vain for the atmosphere and clichés of the bop era (particularly in its late forties stages), and one finds only Monk— original, daring, blunt, occasionally crude, and witty.

Criss Cross (Blue Note 1509) stands out as perhaps *the* Monk masterpiece of this period. It contains all the by now familiar melodic-harmonic characteristics, his innovations in shifting rhythms and accents, but is above all important be-

---

[1] Their conciseness is actually to some extent the indirect result of recording for a ten-inch disc, and today when not all musicians have learned that the greater freedom of the LP also requires greater discipline, the confinement of the three-minute time limit sometimes seems in retrospect like a blessing.

cause it is a *purely instrumental conception.* It is not a "song," a term so many jazz musicians apply to all the music they work with, it is not a "tune"—it is a composition for instruments. In this respect it is in the tradition of such masterpieces as Jelly Roll Morton's *Kansas City Stomps* and Ellington's *Ko-Ko.* But its most radical aspect is that *Criss Cross* is in a sense an abstraction. It does not describe or portray anything specific, it does not attempt to set a "mood" or the like; it simply states and develops certain musical ideas, in much the way that an abstract painter will work with specific nonobjective patterns.

Eronel and *Evidence,* the latter with a stark and tonally oblique introduction, do likewise, but *Evidence* suffers a poor Monk solo. It consists almost entirely of clichés, although admittedly Monk clichés—like the whole-tone scales and *diddledee* repeated triplet figures. Both *Misterioso* and *Four in One* are represented on Blue Note 1509 in alternate masters, the other versions being included in Blue Note 1510 and 1511. Actually all four versions are excellent, but of *Four in One* I prefer the 1509 since it features slightly better solos, some superb Monk accompaniment behind Jackson, and a better balance between Sahib Shihab's excellent alto, Jackson's vibes and Monk's piano. Such a balance is important because, as in so many Monk compositions, the witty answers by the piano need to be at the same level as the "horns" and not in the background.

In the case of *Misterioso* the preference goes definitely to the Monk Vol. 1 (Blue Note 1510) version. (Both incidentally are in a much brighter tempo than the 1957 Rollins-J. J.-Monk performance on Blue Note LP 1558.) *Misterioso* has been one of Monk's most influential recordings, and small wonder. It is a summation of Monk's work up to that time, and, in both composition and solo, a wondrous example of his artistic maturity and his awareness of the challenge of discipline and economy. One chorus of walking parallel sixths sets the mood. Behind Jackson's solo Monk then plays a series of melodic sevenths that in their bluntness are so striking that one can hardly concentrate on the vibes. Monk's own solo sustains this level. It is based on a series of minor second clusters (I will return to these later) and an imperious upward figure. When the "head" returns, instead of mere repetition, Monk enlarges upon it. In an almost Webern-like manner he spreads the pattern of sevenths used earlier over two or three octaves. The resulting dramatic skips, rhythmically oblique to the main theme, are the last link in the chain of heightening intensity that generates this piece.

Incidentally, this idea of varying the exposition when it returns as a final recapitulation was a rather unusual procedure at this time, and is still rare. In thousands of bop and modern jazz performances, opening and ending were identical, and even orchestrating them in harmony rather than unison was thought to be unusual. Monk was a real pioneer in this respect, generally slightly altering his basic thematic material through revoicing, reorchestrating or—as in *Misterioso* and *Evidence*—superimposing upon it previously stated ideas. In both examples these superimpositions are harmonically so unusual that they considerably obliterate the original tonal centers.

Many of the forty-odd titles recorded at that time are only partially successful and some are indeed quite bad. I shall single out only a few. There are (on Blue Note 1510) a very spirited *I Mean You* with good Milt Jackson; *Humph,* one of the many Monk compositions that experiments with parallel chords and tritone (*i.e.,* flatted fifth) melodies, and which features some excellent Idrees Sulieman trumpet; the one-note theme of *Thelonious* with an interesting interpolation of pure stride piano; a fair *Epistrophy* and *In Walked Bud;* an indifferent and out-of-tune *'Round About Midnight* (the later solo version is much more personal); and a whole trio date including *Off Minor* and *Ruby, My Dear,* which seems to have been a hopelessly listless affair, I think, primarily because of the stiff rhythm section. Ramey's plunky bass and Blakey's dull swing-era drumming are like a blanket of fog. (Blakey, of course, has since then been Monk's most constant partner and developed so individually that in the recent Atlantic LP 1278 on some tracks he almost steals Monk's thunder.)

Blue Note 1511 ranges from poor to good. *Suburban Eyes* and *Evonce,* both terribly recorded, are perhaps the closest Monk ever came to bop orthodoxy. The tunes, of course, are not his (the contrast to his own material is a revelation), and in them we hear some fair Danny Quebec and Sulieman, with Monk mostly killing time with clichés. Four other tracks bring Lucky Thompson, Kenny Dorham and Max Roach into the fold with excellent results. *Carolina* in 6/4 time is beautifully orchestrated, has some good Lucky, Dorham, and lively Roach double-timing. *Skippy* is quite unusual: a thirty-two-bar piece in which the first twenty-four bars (piano and rhythm alone) consist almost exclusively of tritones in parallel progressions, while the last eight measures suddenly bring in the three "horns" in a four-bar chromatic scale (voiced in tritones!) and a four-bar fanfare-like phrase (again tritonic). *Let's Cool One* has an interesting moment in the bridge where on an F-chord Monk has trumpet and alto on unison B flat and the tenor on an A, a ninth below. This is one of the first instances of Monk's use of isolated naked ninths (or sevenths). That he really cherished this sound is further substantiated when, during the entire bass solo on the bridge, Monk remains silent except to throw in on the F chord that same bald major ninth. Both *Skippy* and *Let's Cool One* feature fair to good solos by Lucky (listen to how he literally "eats up" the changes), Dorham (very close to the Clifford Brown of a few years later) and a fledgling Lou Donaldson. The haunting *Monk's Mood* is spoiled completely by some inexplicably wobbly out-of-tune (almost hotel-type) Shihab alto. *Straight No Chaser* not only has good Shihab and Milt Jackson but also some driving bass by McKibbon. Both this and *Who Knows,* by the way, are excellent examples of fluent, technically proficient and at times even mellow Monk piano—a good answer to those who say Monk *can't* play that kind of piano.

That kind of piano, it so happens, would be out of place in most of Monk's music. (Imagine his angular and blunt lines played by a Billy Taylor—or even a Tatum or John Lewis.) The tone, the touch, and if you will, even the crudity, are part and parcel of Monk's personality, and in it the components composer-pianist are as inseparable as the elements of an alloy. Incidentally, for those who still tend to doubt Monk's ability to play technically fluent piano, listening to his almost Teddy Wilson-like work on the 1941 Minton's Playhouse LP (Esoteric 548) in *Swing to Bop* and *Stompin' at the Savoy* can be a revelation. Of course there is also the testimony of Mary Lou Williams who says: "While Monk was in Kaycee he jammed every night, really used to blow on piano, employing a lot more technique than he does today. Monk plays the way he does now because he got fed up. I *know* how Monk can play. . . . He told me he was sick of hearing musicians play the same thing the same way all the time."[2]

1952 to 1954 Monk recorded for Prestige (7075, 7027, 7053). The latter two LPs are superior to 7075, but on none of the three is Monk able to add basically to the impression established by *Criss Cross* and other earlier works. On Prestige LP 7027 there are eight tracks, many of which reflect the two influences of Monk's formative years: Harlem stride piano and Kansas City blues-based piano. The latter is especially evident on his famous *Blue Monk*, recorded in 1954. Of special interest are *Little Rootie Tootie*, a latter-day train-song with imitations of a train whistle; *Monk's Dream* with its bridge in minor seconds; *Trinkle Tinkle*, derived from a right-hand embellishment figure quite common among the more florid boogie-woogie pianists and which illustrates the "tinkling" suggested by the title; *These Foolish Things,* sardonically dressed in clashing minor seconds; and *Bemsha Swing* in which, during Max's solo, Monk throws in isolated variants of the main theme—a fascinating touch. (Incidentally Prestige should be ashamed of itself for allowing a record date on such a bad piano; it sounds like a tinny, out-of-tune barroom upright.)

Some of the 1953 and 1954 recordings did not come off too well. I find the ill-fated *Friday the Thirteenth* in terms of performance quite dismal, with so-so solos by Rollins and Watkins and a logy rhythm section. *Work,* recorded a year later, ram-

2 In *Hear Me Talkin' to Ya,* edited by Nat Shapiro and Nat Hentoff.

bles too much, but *Nutty* has a colorful Blakey solo, a distinctive brightly chorded theme, and an over-all optimistic feeling about it.

On Prestige 7053 we fare much better. *Let's Call This* could only be Monk's with its fascinatingly dogged ghost-note melody. *Think of One* (presented in two versions) is another one-note theme with unisons occasionally flaring out into major seconds. The solos by all concerned, especially Julius Watkins, are better on take 1. *We See* is another bright optimistic piece with fair solos. *Locomotive*, a distant cousin of the "train blues," is a superb example of Monk's ability to vary and develop a theme, not just improvising on a chord progression. His entire solo here is based on the opening motive. (Neither Ray Copeland nor Frank Foster seems to have tried to do likewise.) *Hackensack* is another witty piece, interestingly orchestrated. In the last bridge it almost seems as if Monk cruelly imitates Ray Copeland's high-register "clam."

A real revelation for me was Monk's rendition of the Kern tune *Smoke Gets in Your Eyes*. Here Monk deliberately turns it from a tune into a composition by means of instrumentation and chord alteration. He achieves this by splitting up the melody between piano and "horns" and by beautifully altering one chord: A instead of E flat against which he plays a D flat C major seventh in the right hand[3]—one of the most beautiful spots in all of Monk.

We turn now to the six Riverside LPs. Monk's first two albums there were based entirely on music other than his own —Ellington on the first and in THE UNIQUE a variety of standard hits. I cannot agree entirely with Nat Hentoff's position[4] about the first set that Monk's "technique pianistically isn't always adequate for what he wants to express in his own personal language; it is less adequate for this variegated a program." It is also misleading to read the implication that Monk is incapable of "building organic variations on Ellington's initial themes," when Monk is actually one of the few musi-

---

[3] This is as good an example as I can find of the fact that *what* Monk actually plays is not so startling. It is the juxtaposition of notes within a given context that is so highly original.
[4] *Down Beat Jazz Reviews*, 1956, p. 162.

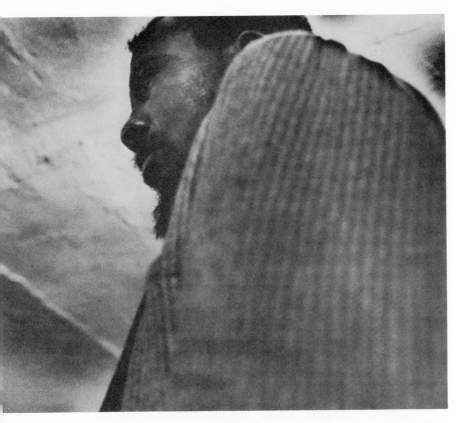

THELONIOUS MONK

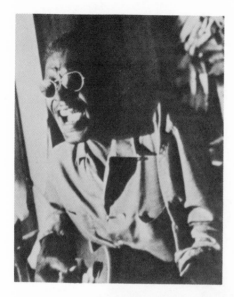

Courtesy of Ed Badeaux

LIGHTNIN' HOPKINS

cians who can do just this, as I've indicated in other parts of this review. But why this Ellington LP did not turn out as fruitful as one might have been led to expect is hard to say. It does suffer—and Nat is certainly right about this—from an over-all dullness. But I suspect that Monk felt somehow psychologically stifled—not technically hampered—by the Ellington *tunes*. This would explain why the one great track, *It Don't Mean a Thing*, and to a lesser extent *Caravan* are the only pieces on which Monk masters the material. Both pieces are more than tunes; they are instrumental compositions, and in *Thing* there was the added challenge for Monk of the one-note theme, something he had already experimented with in his own *Thelonious* and *Think of One*. In Monk's hands *Thing* becomes a harmonic variation on one note (B flat) with ever fresh surprises. Both *Caravan* and *Thing* also contain fascinating bass solos by Oscar Pettiford, especially the three-part chords in *Thing*.

I think it was an illusion on the part of Orrin Keepnews to think that he could get Monk to reach a wider audience through the use of standard tunes. A musician of Monk's individuality and artistic integrity is never easily accepted by a large audience, and it seems fruitless to try to achieve this—at least on the audience's terms. Moreover, it is fallacious to think that people can be lured into accepting Monk if he plays *You Are Too Beautiful* or the like, because such people want to hear those tunes in more orthodox versions. Those who *can* appreciate Monk's concept of these tunes don't need the tunes as a crutch in the first place. (Mr. Keepnews seems to have realized this himself as indicated by his liner notes for a subsequent Monk LP.)

The UNIQUE album flounders on this false premise, and somehow deep within himself Monk may have sensed this. The album seems at times to suffer from overpreparation. In any case, he again seems a prisoner of the tunes with fortunately some exceptions.

Honeysuckle Rose and *Tea For Two* attracted Monk's wry satiric humor. In *Tea,* after a Zez Confrey-type introduction and some rather stiff bowed bass by Pettiford, Monk launches

into purposely stiff old-fashioned piano that lampoons the kind
of piano playing his illusory mass audience probably would
dig. But while Monk makes fun, he does so on a high musical
level, couching his satire in daring bitonal chord distillations.
Likewise in *Honeysuckle,* which is further enhanced by much
use of parallel chords of minor sixths, echoed brilliantly by
Blakey's tomtoms tuned similarly in D flat, C and F. *Liza* is
marred by a seemingly endless stereotype ending, whereas *Just
You, Just Me* is quite superior if only for a long thematic-
melodic variation and a good Blakey solo.

In BRILLIANT CORNERS (Riverside 12-226) the problem
seems to have been primarily that of performance and insuffi-
cient familiarity with the material. While effortless, smooth
playing would probably seem amiss in most any Monk opus,
I find the saxes (Rollins and the late Ernie Henry) needlessly
harsh and out of tune. Monk himself does not play anything
that he had not already done somewhere earlier and much of
it seems routine. As a matter of fact, I found some of this
set emotionally depressing (especially *Pannonica*), which is
understandable perhaps in view of the many rather lean years
Monk has had. The album does come to life again with *Bemsha Swing,* mostly by virtue of a rather light airy rendition,
a fine Pettiford solo and Max Roach's pulsating work on tim-
pani. On *Ba-Lue Bolivar Ba-lues Are,* the disparate elements of
Henry's wailing alto, Monk's stride-ish piano, a strongly Monk-
influenced Rollins solo, some overly busy Roach, and a clean
highly expressive Pettiford solo never quite jell into a unified
performance.

Perhaps, as Martin Williams has said,[5] "one may well despair
of assimilating" all of the "suggestions about future possibilities" contained on this record. It is clear that the *musicians*
who perform with Monk must also be given a chance to assimilate the music they are playing more thoroughly. Orrin Keepnews in his excellent liner notes touches upon the problem,
when, in comparing Monk to other more easily accessible composers, he says: "What he [Monk] offers is not smooth, public-
relations-conscious artifice or surface skills, but merely the

[5] *The American Record Guide,* vol. 24, no. 5, January 1958, p. 231.

music that is in him." He is one of "those non-benders and non-conformers who doesn't happen even to *seem* easy to understand." But precisely because this is so, the performances must be better prepared, or else the obstacles to a broader assimilation are too great. What is left in BRILLIANT CORNERS is a feeling of the potential strength and immediacy of Monk's work but not its realization.

Similarly MONK'S MUSIC (Riverside 12-242) brings into focus the same problem, further aggravated by the inclusion of Coleman Hawkins on the date. One has to say, with great reluctance,[6] that Hawk has considerable trouble finding his way around Monk's music. The record starts with the nineteenth-century hymn tune *Abide with Me*, Monk's (and incidentally Fats Waller's) favorite. It is played in a solemnly intoned, straightforward manner, much like putting a motto at the head of a chapter.

All of Monk's own playing on this record is very, very good; it is strong, lucid, and aggressively leading—a little like Ellington's or Basie's approach with their bands. If all the playing were on Monk's level, this would be a great record. As a matter of fact, Blakey and Wilbur Ware are consistently imaginative, but Coltrane—despite his unquestionable though still experimenting talent—doesn't fare too well on the bridge of *Well, You Needn't* with its difficult-to-be-interesting-on parallel chord changes. (Gryce gets badly hung here, and Copeland manages to skate through with plain up-and-down arpeggios). The odd changes of *Epistrophy* also hamper Coltrane so that his solo emerges in many tiny (and I think unintentionally) disconnected fragments.

Hawkins shows clearly that he is of an earlier generation. Aside from two shaky or false starts—on *Well, You Needn't* and *Epistrophy*, the latter beautifully covered by Blakey, Monk and Ware—Hawk seems often to be thrown by Monk's oblique

---

[6] I say "with great reluctance" because, aside from the obvious fact that Coleman Hawkins is one of the great enduring historical figures of jazz, he was one of the few musicians of his generation who looked with a kindly eye upon the "modern jazz" newcomers, and was in point of fact one of the very few who gave Monk work in the forties. The 1944 engagement on 52nd Street led to Monk's first record date.

accompaniments and sparse angular lines. In *Ruby, My Dear* Monk's insistence on using an E major chord with both an A and a G natural in the right hand confuses and stiffens Hawk every time. He does, however, relax ultimately on this track and brings off some strikingly characteristic phrases. On both *Off Minor* and *Epistrophy* Hawk plays with a dashing, slightly annoyed "ah-the-hell-with-it" attitude, pretty much disregarding Monk's altered harmonies.

The only new composition on this septet record has the whimsical title of *Crepescule with Nellie*, dutifully explained in the liner notes. It is a moody piece, cast in the usual thirty-two-bar AABA format. The second bar of the A-phrase has a typically unorthodox Monk touch: an E flat chord with not only the minor seventh and minor ninth, but also the major sixth and major ninth; thus producing a bitonal combination of E flat and C. Nor does Monk use this dissonance as a passing chord or try to hide it in some way; on the contrary, with his characteristic weighty touch he trumpets it out six times.

THELONIOUS HIMSELF (Riverside 12-235) is a real success. Unhampered by other players and beholden only unto himself, Monk ruminates thoughtfully and caressingly in free tempo on the eight pieces, three of them his own. As Keepnews says, much of the album has a quality of "thinking out loud." Monk makes these tunes completely his own, continually extracting and paring down to the essence of each melody and harmony. They all have a beauty and haunting lyricism, especially *April in Paris, I Should Care,* and *All Alone.* Other adjectives that come to mind are "mournful" and "nostalgic." *'Round Midnight,* Monk's own classic, is intensely personal. The wonderfully delayed upper-register thirds are a kind of delightful torture as one awaits them expectantly. *I Should Care* is worth many rehearings, as Monk toward the end—after a sort of private double-time passage—plays four chords in which, after first striking all the notes hard and sharply, he quickly releases all but one. This kind of chord distillation is one of the most radical aspects of his music, *i.e.,* the idea that one note above all others can most succinctly represent a chord—not a new idea in music, but almost untried in jazz. In the last half of

Care Monk is especially exciting in terms of free tempo playing. His arhythmic, unexpected moves create a tremendous tension.

Monk's Mood, now in free tempo as opposed to the 1947 version on Blue Note, is a fitting finale to the album. Starting as a piano solo, Monk later adds bass and tenor (Ware and Coltrane). Coltrane's poignant, almost altoish tenor exactly fits the plaintive mood of the piece.

My one complaint is that Monk here allows too many of his favorite piano "noodles" (all pianists seem to have them). There were so many and they interrupted the continuity at times so much, that I began to count them. There are fourteen of the five-octave descending whole-tone scales and thirty-four (!) of the cocktail-piano-type ascending figures. Significantly they are absent *completely* in *Functional*, a long blues that despite many modern dissonances and angular lines is as earthy and basic as a Broonzy folk blues. It ends on three notes typical of late Monk (he has also used them on the record with Mulligan and in the *Blue Monk* on the Atlantic LP): a low B flat, and four octaves above a minor ninth B natural and C—another characteristic chord distillation, all other notes being implied.

The MULLIGAN MEETS MONK album is on the surface a good one. Everybody plays well, and the five Monk compositions, one tune by Mulligan, and a standard make good points of departure. But probing more deeply one finds that *basically* Mulligan and Monk don't hear music the same way. It's a little like trying to mix oil and water. There are numerous instances of this difference. Where Gerry, especially in up-tempo pieces, improvises primarily in triadic harmony, adding only sixths and an occasional final flatted fifth, Monk's ear constantly takes him into the furthest reaches of the chords. If I may put it very simply, Gerry always plays the "right" notes, whereas Monk more often than not plays the "wrong" notes that are right! Gerry's rhythm, basically a late swing-era feeling, is also quite far from Monk's wholly original time relationships. With all his musicianly talent, Gerry too often is a man *playing* at playing a solo.

A convincingly clear example of these basic harmonic and psychological differences is the very end of *Sweet and Lovely.* Here Monk plays a highly chromatic odd-patterned ascending figure, partially based on the tune, and Gerry answers in an all-too-familiar regular pattern of descending fourths and fifths— each passage is an exact mirror of its creator's musical ear.

Monk is at his best throughout, especially in his superb accompaniments to Gerry, where he often works with thematic material. Ware turns in beautifully timed and inventive solos, with Shadow Wilson always in firm but discreet support.

The remaining record was made for Atlantic, featuring Monk with Art Blakey's Jazz Messengers. Martin Williams' excellent liner notes are about the best thing so far written on Monk in an analytical vein. Except for one minor error, the notes give an informative, clear-thinking insight into the nature of Monk's work, and I heartily recommend them to all who are puzzled by the phenomenon of Thelonious Monk.

Except for John Griffin's *Purple Shades,* all the compositions are by Monk and all reorchestrated, extended versions of pieces recorded earlier. Throughout the record Blakey's drumming is outstanding, both in his solos and in his support of Hardman and Griffin (especially when he kicks them off in double-time). Blakey adds so many imaginative touches, perfectly executed, that it would be futile to attempt to describe them. Listen especially to *I Mean You.* Some of the highlights of the record are Monk's pointillistic solo (like isolated spurts of sound) on *Evidence,* a solo based on the stark main theme; his theme-derived solos on *In Walked Bud* and *I Mean You;* a very dramatic (mostly low-register) improvisation on *Blue Monk;* and his low barking sounds behind Griffin in *Purple Shades.* Only his solo in *Rhythm-a-ning* is disappointing because it is too derivative of things Monk has done before. Hardman, Griffin and DeBrest are very young and must go some in terms of control and discipline. Nevertheless Griffin's solos on *Rhythm-a-ning* and *Purple Shades* show great promise.

In listening to all these records, several characteristics of Monk begin to stand out. Since some of these are points about which there is often discussion among laymen and musicians alike, I would like to touch upon them briefly in closing.

The first regards the rapid whole-tone scales to which Monk is so addicted. While I would agree that Monk overdoes them, they are nevertheless logical within his harmonic thinking. Whole-tone patterns first make their appearance on the 1944 recordings Monk made with Hawkins. It was in those years that the flatted fifth chords began to be generally used by modern jazz musicians. Now it so happens that the most direct line between the flatted fifth and the tonic is a whole-tone pattern of four notes. Add two more notes and you have a whole-tone scale. Furthermore, when one realizes that a whole-tone scale is, in effect, a straightened-out horizontal version of an ordinary augmented-ninth chord with a flatted fifth (in F for instance: F A C sharp E flat G B natural), one can see how easily one thing led to the other. This whole area of tritones (flatted fifths) and altered-tone chords opened up once musicians discovered the altered bass line. Instead of going directly from E flat to A flat, for instance, they began to interpolate an A natural[7] (tritone from E flat) and soon a whole complex of new key relationships became apparent.[8] And it is in this melodic-harmonic area that Monk has been one of the most imaginative innovators.

Much has been said about Monk's technique or supposed lack of same. Beyond what I've already said (and coming back also to the cluster C and D flat I described earlier in *Misterioso*), I've formed the following opinion or theory. Monk uses his fingers not in the usual arched position pianistic orthodoxy requires but in a flat horizontal way. This determines a number of characteristics in Monk's music. Aside from the tone quality it produces, it makes, for instance, the playing of octaves very hazardous. In playing an octave of two E's, let us say, it would be easy to also hit by accident the D (a tone below the upper E) and the F (a tone above the lower E). I imagine that Monk soon discovered that he could

[7] As in the example from *Smoke Gets in Your Eyes* described earlier.
[8] Since this review is not intended to be a harmony lesson, I must forego further explanation on this score.

exploit his unorthodox finger positions, and began to make use of these "extra" notes which others would have heard as "wrong" and tried to eliminate.[9] The old tradition of approximating blue notes by playing a minor second also fits in here. In this respect Monk went even further. The clash of a minor second became so natural to his ear that on top of one blue note he began to add another right next to it, as in *Misterioso* where the D flat—already a blue note—has another blue note, the C, attached to it, like a satellite.

Also Monk plays more large intervals in his right hand than most pianists. Again this is traceable, physically, to the way he plays. His fingers reach these intervals very naturally; and while this is true of half a dozen other pianists, I think this factor takes on added importance for Monk because of one striking feature of his talent. Where many pianists less original than Monk are exclusively concerned with playing *the* "right" (or acceptable) notes, Monk, at his most inspired, thinks of *over-all* shapes and designs or ideas. His hands to a large extent determine these shapes, and, because he is a man of great talent, or perhaps even genius, he does play the *right* notes, almost as a matter of course. This is to make a fine distinction—a distinction, however, that we need in order to separate the genius from the good musician.

One point remains, the point of Monk's belated influence. First let it be noted that this influence affected almost entirely instrumentalists *other* than pianists. As I've indicated, Monk's music, engendered largely by his unorthodox pianistic approach, resists effective imitation, always the starting point for any overt influence. To play on the piano some of the things Monk does the *way* he does them—even his whole-tone scales, not to mention his more adventurous flights—is virtually impossible for anyone else. Especially in regard to the tone quality Monk gets—a rich, full-bodied, "horn"-like sound, not unlike Ellington's tone.[10] It is therefore natural that he influenced primarily "horn" men (like Rollins and Griffin) who

---

[9] The alternative of relearning piano technique in an orthodox manner would hardly have occurred to a man of Monk's temperament.

[10] It should go without saying, but is often forgotten, that a man's tone on his instrument is inseparably related to the nature of his music.

could absorb his musical ideas without coming to grips with
his technical idiosyncracies—such men could simply transfer
the essence of these ideas to their instrument.

That this occurred years after Monk first set forth these
ideas is not only normal but fitting. His ideas were both advanced and unorthodox. They would have been neither had
they been immediately absorbed by dozens of musicians. Originality is rare and precious and resists easy assimilation. And
in these times of standardization and bland conformism we
should be grateful that there are still talents such as Thelonious Monk who remain slightly enigmatic and wonderful to
some of us.

Thelonious Monk: THELONIOUS ALONE IN SAN FRANCISCO, Riverside
RLP R-312. Thelonious Monk, *piano.*
*Blue Monk; Ruby, My Dear; Round Lights; Everything Happens
to Me; You Took the Words Right Out of My Heart; Bluehawk;
Pannonica; Remember; There's Danger in Your Eyes, Cherie; Re-
flections.*

GIGI GRYCE, Savoy. (Signal S1201). Gryce, *alto;* Thelonious Monk,
piano; Percy Heath, *bass;* Art Blakey, *drums.*
Shuffle Boil; Brake's Sake; Gallop's Gallop; Nica's Tempo.
Gryce, *alto;* Art Farmer, *trumpet;* Jimmy Cleveland, *trombone;*
Danny Bank, *baritone;* Gunther Schuller, *French horn;* Bill Bar-
ber, *tuba;* Horace Silver, *piano;* Oscar Pettiford, *bass;* Kenny
Clarke, *drums:*
Speculation; In a Meditating Mood; Smoke Signal; Kerry Dance.
Eddie Bert, Cecil Payne, Julius Watkins and Art Blakey replace
Cleveland, Bank, Schuller, and Clarke. Ernestine Anderson, *vocals.*
Social Call; The One I Love.

Any new recording by Monk is bound to create considerable
interest. It is significant that, after being active in jazz for
some twenty-odd years, Monk is still one of the most unmis-
takably original and enduring talents on the jazz scene. Even
in today's sated record market, one looks forward to every
new Monk record with the kind of excitement one used to re-
serve for six minutes of new Duke Ellington every few months,
back in the halcyon days of 78's.

Because of Monk's special gifts and his pre-eminence in his
field, we tend to expect great new revelations from him with

each new record. Unlike the average classical audience, the
jazz public wants to hear new things, and its listening appe-
tite is voracious. In a music as young and vital as jazz, this
is perhaps a fitting tribute, but it places a tremendous burden
on the jazz artist. It pressures him into a kind of constant
artistic renewal of himself. Artistic renewal is fine, but it is
not to be pressured; it must arise completely out of the artist's
needs. At the same time the jazz musician dare not outdistance
his audience, because it will certainly desert him at that point.
To hoe this fine line between artistic regeneration and commercial marketability is not easy. It is not even desirable, since the
two goals are basically incompatible. And yet many a musician
finds himself in this spiral-shaped trap.

Such thoughts come to mind while listening to this new
Monk LP, and account for my somewhat ambivalent feelings
toward it. These thoughts come to mind because Monk—with
characteristic independence—will not be pressured into either
position. Certainly MONK ALONE IN SAN FRANCISCO is in no
way commercially compromising; however, it also fails to tell
us anything new about Monk and his music. It thus raises the
issue of whether a man of great talent must create striking
new images at every turn, or whether he can sometimes be
allowed to coast along on previous achievements. The answer
depends, I suppose, in part on *how long* he coasts.

But there is more to it than that. In essence, the question
this record raises is of a philosophical (artistic-moral) nature,
rather than a musical one. For certainly Monk's musicianship
is, as usual, beyond cavil. On this or any other record Monk
creates an original self-contained musical world. Within it
there may be degrees of greater or lesser inspiration, but
Monk's world could never be mistaken for another's. Still the
question remains: is stylistic originality enough?

I think the answer depends on the criteria one wants to assume. Taken as a single event, as a moment in a man's life,
as the record of a man's feelings and thoughts on a given afternoon in San Francisco, as a single record issued by a record
company, it is enough. But in an ultimate sense, as an event
within the comparative totality of a man's life and his creative

output, it is *not* enough. To put it another way: in view of such inspired earlier pieces as *Criss Cross* or *Misterioso,* would we want to remember Monk solely by this San Francisco record? I doubt it. For myself, my *feelings* tell me that I expected more of Monk, while my *mind* and *reason* tell me that an artist has a right *not* to say something new once in a while.

Curiously enough, Monk does his most imaginative playing on this record *not* on his own tunes, but on the Tin Pan Alley ballads. Perhaps the reason for this is that three of the Monk originals are based on the blues changes; and even the non-blues originals are—as is Monk's habit—treated very much like blues. Within a man's own style and over a period of some twenty years, how many new ideas can he be expected to have on a series of changes as elemental as the blues? The harmonic, melodic and rhythmic discoveries Monk made in the blues form all go back ten to fifteen years, and have, by now, infiltrated the styles of dozens of other jazzmen, becoming almost a common language. I think for Monk the challenge has (perhaps only momentarily) gone out of the blues.

A challenge of sorts still seems to exist in the four tunes by Berlin, Dennis and others, where Monk in characteristic fashion transforms these songs into striking vignette-size "compositions." In all four instances, Monk's unsentimental, forthright approach is in itself a devastating comment on the tunes. With typical forcefulness, he uses the material as a means to an end. Out of the flabby originals, Monk miraculously draws forth musical thoughts of rocklike implacability—especially in the rather massive, dissonance-tinged chordal treatment of something called *You Took the Words Right out of My Heart.* (Here Monk applies one of his favorite devices, that of keeping both the tonic and its leading tone present in virtually *all* chord formulations—almost like a pedal point.)

Whether in his own compositions or those of other writers, the over-all mood of the record is a darkly introspective one. The album title—with emphasis on the word "alone"—seems very appropriate. A sad and lonely mood pervades these performances, in direct contrast to so much contemporary jazz, which is either happily (and superficially) funky or acrid and

bitter. But over the whole record, the sameness of mood begins to sap at one's powers of concentration, especially since
mood and atmosphere are not the only elements which are
somewhat lacking in variety. On a purely musical level, the
performances show the same unconcern for contrast. As one
listens to the entire LP in continuity, one has the definite feeling that Monk's fingers seem to be going always to the same
places on the keyboard, and finding the same patterns and
figurations. A favorite Monk ending, found already on many
earlier recordings, occurs
no less than three times, on
Blue Monk, Bluehawk and
Round Lights — the three
blues! Likewise the endings
of *Pannonica* and *Reflections* are almost identical.
And many other patterns,
used on records in the last
ten years, recur with de-
bilitating regularity. This is
borne out by comparative
listening to those Monk

pieces recorded previously. Some are better here, others better
there. Some indeed seem to be attempts to recapture the sound
and over-all shape of earlier versions—which is certainly a
composer's privilege. *Ruby, My Dear* is a case in point. Here
Monk emulates the whole coda of the earlier recording except
for one striking difference in the final cadence. Where the

earlier record had a none-too-unusual
A flat chord resolving to D flat, the
new version—whether by accident or
predetermination would be hard to say
—alters *one* note, but with a fascinating aural difference: the A flat resolving to D flat changed to a B flat,
still resolving to D flat. I gather that
for many jazz enthusiasts, any remote-
ly analytical thinking about notes,

pitches and chords is simply odious.
Nonetheless, musicians deal with
sounds, chords and notes; and it is
precisely what they do with these basic
ingredients, how they "select" them,
that we are able to differentiate one
from another. The choice of a B flat
rather than an A flat may be a matter
of complete indifference to some (although a tryout on the piano might

convince a few). But "choice of notes" is still one of the basic
means by which a musician can reveal himself artistically. And
—as in the above example—Monk's choice was an unexpected
one, and therefore of interest—at least to me as a fellow musician.

A recent reissue of a three- or four-year-old record, half of
which features Monk's piano within a quartet led by Gigi
Gryce, affords us an opportunity to compare with the San
Francisco set. The four pieces recorded on the earlier date
included one by leader Gryce and three by "sideman" Monk,
among the latter one of his most original lines, *Gallop's Gallop*.

Monk's solos on these sides are among his very finest, and
are much more outward going and fluent than on the more
recent date. In fact, I think they are among the best of Monk's
playing on records. The fluency of feeling is further aided and
abetted by the tight rhythm ensemble of Blakey and Heath.
Blakey especially, despite a feathery light touch, gets a pun-
gent beat and infectious sound, that together with Percy's
springy bass lines are a joy to hear. Blakey's and Monk's exchanges of fours on *Gallop* are also worth a number of listen-
ings. By comparison Gryce seems much the least effective of
the four. Some of Monk's "changes" give him real trouble,
and in general, he doesn't quite connect up with the music
as well as he should. This is especially true of *Gallop's
Gallop*.

Gryce's own *Nica's Tempo* rounds out the side. In the context of the record, it reminds one rather forcefully that Gryce's

piece—unlike Monk's—has no *real* melody, but rather a line consisting vaguely of the top notes of a chord progression.

Hearing the new Riverside and Savoy records side by side, one is led to the hope that Blakey and Monk will someday work and record together again.

Sonny Rollins and Thematic Improvising

by Gunther Schuller

Also a part of the first issue of The Jazz Review *was Gunther Schuller's analysis of Sonny Rollins'* Blue 7. *The piece had a widespread effect including an apparently strong effect on Rollins himself, who later told one interviewer that he never intended to read his notices again.*

SINCE THE DAYS when pure collective improvisation gave way to the improvised solo, jazz improvisation has traveled a long road of development. The forward strides that characterized each particular link in this evolution were instigated by the titans of jazz history of the last forty-odd years: Louis Armstrong; Coleman Hawkins; Lester Young; Charlie Parker and Dizzy Gillespie; Miles Davis; collectively the MJQ under John Lewis' aegis; and some others in varying but lesser degrees. Today we have reached another juncture in the constantly unfolding evolution of improvisation, and the central figure of this present renewal is Sonny Rollins.

Each of the above jazz greats brought to improvisation a particular ingredient it did not possess before, and with Rollins thematic and structural unity have at last achieved the importance in *pure* improvisation that elements such as swing, melodic conception and originality of expression have already enjoyed for many years.

Improvisatory procedures can be divided roughly into two broad and sometimes overlapping categories which have been called *paraphrase* and *chorus* improvisation. The former consists mostly of an embellishment or ornamentation technique, while the latter suggests that the soloist has departed completely from a given theme or melody and is improvising freely on nothing but a chord structure. (It is interesting to note that this separation in improvisational techniques existed also in classical music in the sixteenth to eighteenth centuries, when composers and performers differentiated between ornamentation [*elaboratio*] and free vibration [*inventio*].) Most improvisation in the modern jazz era belongs to this second category, and it is with developments in this area that this article shall concern itself.

In short, jazz improvisation became through the years a more or less unfettered, melodic-rhythmic extemporaneous composing process in which the sole organizing determinant was the underlying chord pattern. In this respect it is important to note that what we all at times loosely call "variation" is in the strictest sense no variation at all, since it does not proceed from the basis of varying a given thematic material but simply reflects a player's ruminations on an *unvarying* chord progression. As André Hodèir put it in his book *Jazz: Its Evolution and Essence,* "Freed from all melodic and structural obligation, the chorus improvisation is a simple emanation inspired by a given harmonic sequence."

Simple or not, this kind of extemporization has led to a critical situation: to a very great extent, improvised solos— even those that are in all other respects very imaginative— have suffered from a general lack of over-all cohesiveness and direction—the lack of a unifying force. There are exceptions to this, of course. Some of the great solos of the past (Armstrong's *Muggles,* Hawkins' *Body and Soul* [second chorus], Parker's *Ko-Ko,* etc.) have held together as perfect compositions by virtue of the improviser's genial intuitive talents. (Genius does not *necessarily* need organization, especially in a strict academic sense, since it makes its own laws and sets its own standards, thereby creating its own kind of organization.) But such successful exceptions have only served to emphasize the relative failure of less inspired improvisations. These have been the victims of one or perhaps all of the following symptoms: (1) The average improvisation is mostly a stringing together of unrelated ideas; (2) Because of the *in-*

dependently spontaneous character of most improvisation, a series of solos by different players within a single piece have very little chance of bearing any relationship to each other (as a matter of fact, the stronger the individual personality of each player, the less uniformity the total piece is likely to achieve); (3) In those cases where composing (or arranging) is involved, the body of interspersed solos generally has no relation to these nonimprovised sections; (4) Otherwise interesting solos are often marred by a sudden quotation from some completely irrelevant material.

I have already said that this is not altogether deplorable (I wish to emphasize this), and we have seen that it is possible to create pure improvisations which are meaningful realizations of a well-sustained over-all feeling. Indeed, the majority of players are perhaps not temperamentally or intellectually suited to do more than that. In any case, there is now a tendency among a number of jazz musicians to bring thematic (or motivic) and structural unity into improvisation. Some do this by combining composition and improvisation, for instance the Modern Jazz Quartet and the Giuffre Three; others, like Sonny Rollins, prefer to work solely by means of extemporization.

Several of the latter's recordings offer remarkable instances of this approach. The most important and perhaps most accessible of these is his *Blue 7* (Prestige LP 7079). It is at the same time a striking example of how *two* great soloists (Sonny and Max Roach) can integrate their improvisations into a unified entity.

I realize fully that music is meant to be listened to, and that words are not adequate in describing a piece of music. However, since laymen, and even many musicians, are perhaps more interested in knowing exactly how such structural solos are achieved than in blindly accepting at face value remarks such as those above, I shall try to go into some detail and with the help of short musical examples give an account of the ideational thread running through Rollins' improvisation that makes this particular recording so distinguished and satisfying.

Doug Watkins starts with a restrained walking bass-line and

is soon joined by Max Roach quietly and simply keeping time. The noncommital character of this introductory setting gives no hint of the striking theme with which Rollins is about to enter. It is made up of three primary notes: D, A flat and E.[1] The chord progression underlying the entire piece is that of the blues in the key of B flat. The primary notes of the theme (D, A flat, E) which, taken by themselves, make up the essential notes of an E seventh chord thus reveal themselves as performing a double function: the D is the third of B flat and at the same time the seventh of E; the A flat is the seventh of B flat and also (enharmonically as G sharp) the third of E; the E is the flatted fifth of B flat and the tonic of E. The result is that the three tones create a bitonal[2] complex of notes in which the blue notes predominate.

At the same time, speaking strictly melodically, the intervals D to A flat (tritone) and A flat to E (major third) are about the most beautiful and most potent intervals in the western musical scale. (That Rollins, whose music I find both beautiful and potent, chose these intervals could be interpreted as an unconscious expression of affinity for these attributes, but this brings us into the realm of the psychological and subconscious nature of inspiration and thus quite beyond the intent of this article.)[3]

This theme then—with its bitonal implications (purposely kept pure and free by the omission of the piano), with its melodic line in which the number and choice of notes is kept

[1] The notes C, D flat and A in bar 5 are simply a transposition of motive A to accommodate the change to E flat in that measure, and all other notes are nonessential alterations and passing tones.

[2] Bitonality implies the simultaneous presence of two tonal centers or keys. This particular combination of keys (E and B flat—a tritone relationship), although used occasionally by earlier composers, notably Franz Liszt in his *Malediction Concerto,* did not become prominent as a distinct musical device until Stravinsky's famous *"Petrushka—Chord"* (F sharp and C) in 1911.

[3] It should also be pointed out in passing that *Blue 7* does not represent Rollins' first encounter with these particular harmonic-melodic tendencies. He tackled them almost a year earlier in *Vierd Blues* (Prestige LP 7044, MILES DAVIS COLLECTOR'S ITEMS). As a matter of fact, the numerous similarities between Rollins' solos on *Blue 7* and *Vierd Blues* are so striking that the earlier one must be considered a study or forerunner of the other. Both, however, are strongly influenced, I believe, by Thelonious Monk's explorations in this area in the late forties, especially such pieces as *Misterioso* (Blue Note LP 1511, THELONIOUS MONK, VOL. 1).

at an almost rock-bottom minimum, with its rhythmic simplicity and segmentation—is the fountainhead from which issues most of what is to follow. Rollins simply extends and develops all that the theme implies.

As an adjunct to this twelve-bar theme, Rollins adds three bars which in the course of the improvisation undergo considerable treatment. This phrase is made up of two motives. It appears in the twelfth to fourteenth bars of Rollins' solo, and at first seems gratuitous. But when eight choruses later (eight counting only Rollins' solos) it suddenly reappears transposed, and still further on in Rollins' eleventh and thirteenth choruses (the latter about ten minutes after the original statement of the phrase) Rollins gives it further vigorous treatment, it becomes apparent that it was not at all gratuitous or a mere chance result, but part of an over-all plan.

A close analysis of Rollins' three solos on *Blue 7* reveals many subtle relationships to the main theme and its three-bar sequel. The original segmentation is preserved throughout. Rollins' phrases are mostly short, and extended rests (generally from three to five beats) separate all the phrases—an ex-

Ex. I   x = *primary notes*

Ex. 2

cellent example of how well-timed silence can become a part
of a musical phrase. There are intermittent allusions to the
motive fragments of his opening statement. At one point he
introduces new material, which, however, is also varied and
developed in the ensuing improvisation. This occurs four bars
before Max Roach's extended solo. A partial repetition of
these bars *after* Max has finished serves to build a kind of
frame around the drum solo.

In this, Rollins' second full solo, thematic variation becomes
more continuous than in his first time around. After a brief

Ex. 3

restatement of part of the original theme, Rollins gradually evolves a short sixteenth-note run which is based on our Ex. 1, part a. He reworks this motive at half the rhythmic value, a musical device called diminution. It also provides a good example of how a phrase upon repetition can be shifted to different beats of the measure thus showing the phrase always in a new light. In this case Rollins plays the run six times; as is shown in Ex. 3 the phrase starts once on the third beat, once on the second, once on the fourth, and three times on the first beat.[4]

Another device Rollins uses is the combining and overlapping of two motives. In his eighth chorus, Rollins, after reiterating Ex. 2, part a, continues with part b, but without notice suddenly converts it into another short motive (Ex. 4) orig-

Ex.4

inally stated in the second chorus. (In Ex. 5 the small notes indicate where Rollins would have gone had he been satisfied with an exact transposition of the phrase; the large notes show what he did play.)

Ex.5

But the crowning achievement of Rollins' solo is his eleventh, twelfth and thirteenth choruses in which out of twenty-eight measures all but six are directly derived from the opening and two further measures are related to the four-bar section intro-

---

[4] It is also apparent that Rollins had some fingering problems with the passage, and his original impulse in repeating it seems to have been to iron these out. However, after six attempts to clean up the phrase, Rollins capitulates and goes on to the next idea. Incidentally, he has experimented with this particular phrase in a number of pieces and it threatens to become a cliché with him.

Ex. 6

ducing Max's drum solo. Such structural cohesiveness—without sacrificing expressiveness and rhythmic drive or swing—one has come to expect from the composer who spends days or weeks writing a given passage. It is another matter to achieve this in an on-the-spur-of-the-moment extemporization (Ex. 6).

The final Rollins touch occurs in the last twelve bars in which the theme, already reduced to an almost rock-bottom minimum, is drained of all excess notes, and the rests in the original are filled out by long held notes. The result is pure melodic essence (Ex. 7). What more perfect way to end and sum up all that came before!

Ex.7

a is derived from our Ex. 2, part a; b from Ex. 2, part b; c from Ex. 1; d from Ex. 4; f from Ex. 1, motive a; and g comes from the same, using only the last two notes of motive a; e is derived from the new material used in the "frame" passage around Max's solo.

Measures written in small notes use nonrelated material.

Bar 26 in this example is an approximation; Rollins delays each repetition by a fraction of a beat in such a way that it cannot be notated exactly.

This then is an example of a real variation technique. The improvisation is based not only on a harmonic sequence but on a melodic idea as well.[5] It should also be pointed out that Rollins differs from lesser soloists who are theme-conscious to a certain extent but who in practice do not rise above the level of exact repetition when the chords permit, and when they don't, mere sequential treatment. Sequences are often an easy way out for the improviser, but easily become boring to the listener. (In fact, in baroque music, one of the prime functions of embellishment techniques was to camouflage harmonically sequential progressions.) In this respect Rollins is a master since in such cases he almost always avoids the obvious and finds some imaginative way out, a quality he has in common with other great soloists of the past, e.g., Prez, Parker, etc.

On an equally high level of structural cohesiveness is Max Roach's aforementioned solo. It is built entirely on two clearly discernible ideas: (1) a triplet figure which goes through a number of permutations in both fast and slow triplets, and (2) a roll on the snare drum. The ingenuity with which he alternates between these two ideas gives not only an indication of the capacity of Max Roach as a thinking musician, but also shows again that exciting drum solos need not be just an *un*-thinking burst of energy—they can be interesting and meaningful compositions. Behind Rollins Max is a fine accompanist, occasionally brilliantly complementing Sonny's work, for example eleven bars after his drum solo, when he returns with a three-bar run of triplets followed a second later by a roll on the snare drum—the basic material of his solo used in an accompanimental capacity.[6]

Such methods of musical procedure as employed here by Sonny and Max are symptomatic of the growing concern by an increasing number of jazz musicians for a certain degree of intellectuality. Needless to say, intellectualism here does

[5] In this Rollins has only a handful of predecessors, notably Jelly Roll Morton, Earl Hines, Fats Waller and Thelonious Monk, aside from the already mentioned Lewis and Giuffre.
[6] A similarly captivating instance of solo thematic material being used for accompanimental purposes occurs in the first four bars of John Lewis' background to Milt Jackson's solo in *Django* (Prestige LP 7057).

not mean a cold mathematical or unemotional approach. It does mean, as by definition, the power of reason and comprehension as distinguished from *purely* intuitive emotional outpouring. Of course, purists or anti-intellectualists (by no means do I wish to *equate* purists with anti-intellectuals, however) deplore the inroads made into jazz by intellectual processes. Even the rather reasonable requisite of technical proficiency is found to be suspect in some quarters. Yet the entire history of the arts shows that intellectual enlightenment goes more or less hand in hand with emotional enrichment, or vice versa. Indeed the great masterpieces of art—any art—are those in which emotional *and* intellectual qualities are well balanced and completely integrated—in Mozart, Shakespeare, Rembrandt. . . .

Jazz too, evolving from humble beginnings that were sometimes hardly more than sociological manifestations of a particular American milieu, has developed as an art form that not only possesses a unique capacity for individual and collective expression, but in the process of maturing has gradually acquired certain intellectual properties. Its strength has been such that it has attracted interest in all strata of intellectual and creative activity. It is natural and inevitable that, in this ever broadening process, jazz will attract the hearts and minds of all manner of people with all manner of predilections and temperaments—even those who will want to bring to jazz a roughly five-hundred-year-old musical idea, the notion of thematic and structural unity.

And indeed I can think of no better and more irrefutable proof of the fact that discipline and thought do not necessarily result in cold or unswinging music than a typical Rollins performance. No one swings more (hard or gentle) and is more passionate in his musical expression than Sonny Rollins. It ultimately boils down to how much talent an artist has; the greater the demands of his art—both emotionally and intellectually—the greater the talent necessary.

A close look at a Rollins solo also reveals other unusual facets of his style: his harmonic language for instance. Considering the astounding richness of his musical thinking, it comes as a surprise to realize that his chord-repertoire does not exceed the normal eleventh or thirteenth chord and the flatted fifth chords. He does not seem to require more and one never feels any harmonic paucity, because within this limited language Rollins is apt to use only the choicest notes, both harmonically and melodically, as witness the theme of *Blue 7*. Another characteristic of Rollins' style is a penchant for anticipating the harmony of a next measure by one or two beats. This is a dangerous practice, since in the hands of a lesser artist it can lead to lots of wrong notes. Rollins' ear in this respect is remarkably dependable.

Dynamically, too, Rollins is a master of contrast and coloring. Listening to *Blue 7* from this point of view is very interesting. There is a natural connection between the character of a given phrase and its dynamic level (in contrast to all too many well-known players who seem not to realize that to play seven or eight choruses played resolutely at the same dynamic level is the best way to put an audience to sleep). Rollins' consummate instrumental control allows him a range of dynamics from the explosive outbursts with which he slashes about, for instance, after Max's solo (or later when he initiates the fours) to the low B natural three bars from the end, a low note which Sonny floats out with a breathy smoky tone that should make the average saxophonist envious. Rollins can honk, blurt, cajole, scoop, shrill—whatever the phrase demands without succumbing to the vulgar or obnoxious. And this is due largely to the fact that Sonny Rollins is one of those rather rare individuals who has both taste and a sense of humor, the latter with a slight turn toward the sardonic.

Rhythmically, Rollins is as imaginative and strong as in his melodic concepts. And why not? The two are really inseparable, or at least should be. In his recordings as well as during several evenings at Birdland recently Rollins indicated that he can probably take any rhythmic formation and make it swing. This ability enables him to run the gamut of extremes—from almost a whole chorus of nonsyncopated quarter notes (which in other hands might be just naïve and square but through Rollins' sense of humor and superb timing are transformed into a swinging line) to asymmetrical groupings of fives and sevens or between-the-beat rhythms that defy notation.

As for his imagination, it is (as already indicated) prodigiously fertile. It can evidently cope with all manner of material, ranging from Kurt Weill's *Moritat* and the cowboy material of his WAY OUT WEST LP (Contemporary 3530) to the more familiar area of ballads and blues. This accounts no doubt for the fact that to date his most successful and structurally unified efforts have been based on the blues. (*Sumphin'*, for instance, made with Dizzy Gillespie [Verve 8260] is almost on the level of *Blue 7;* it falls short, comparatively, only in terms of originality, but is also notable for a beautifully organized Gillespie solo.) This is not to say that Rollins is incapable of achieving thematic variations in non-blues material. Pieces such as *St. Thomas* or *Way Out West* indicate more than a casual concern with this problem; and in a recent in-the-flesh rendition of *Yesterdays,* a lengthy solo cadenza dealt almost exclusively with the melodic line of this tune. His vivid imagination not only permits him the luxury of seemingly endless variants and permutations of a given motive, but even enables him to emulate ideas not indigenous to his instrument, as for instance in *Way Out West* when Rollins, returning for his second solo, imitates Shelly Manne's closing snare drum roll on the saxophone!

Lest I seem to be overstating the case for Rollins, let me add that both his live and recorded performances do include average and less coherent achievements—even an occasional wrong note, as in *You Don't Know What Love Is* (Prestige LP 7079)—which only proves that (fortunately) Rollins is human and fallible. Such minor blemishes are dwarfed into insignificance by the enormity of his talent and the positive values of his great performances. In these and especially *Blue 7,* what Sonny Rollins has added conclusively to the scope of jazz improvisation is the idea of developing and varying a *main* theme, and not just a secondary motive or phrase which the player happens to hit upon in the course of his improvisation and which in itself is unrelated to the "head" of the composition. This is not to say that a thematically related improvisation is *necessarily* better than a free harmonically based one. Obviously any generalization to this effect would be unsound: only the quality of a specific musician in a specific performance can be the ultimate basis for judgment. The point is not—as some may think I am implying—that, since Rollins does a true thematic variation, he therefore is superior to Parker or Young in a nonthematic improvisation. I am emphasizing primarily a *difference* of approach, even though, speaking quite subjectively, I may feel the Rollins position to be ultimately the more important one. Certainly it is an approach that inherently has a potential future.

The history of classical music provides us with a telling historical precedent for such a prognosis: after largely nonthematic beginnings (in the early Middle Ages), music over a period of centuries developed to a stage where (with great classical masters) thematic relationships, either in a sonata or various variational forms, became the prime building element of music, later to be carried even further to the level of continuous and complete variation as implied by Schoenberg's twelve-tone technique. In short, an over-all lineage from free almost anarchical beginnings to a relatively confined and therefore more challenging state. The history of jazz gives every indication of following a parallel course, although in an extraordinarily condensed form. In any case, the essential point is not that, with thematically related solos, jazz improvisation can now discard the great tradition established by the Youngs and Parkers, but rather that by building *on* this tradition and enriching it with the new element of thematic relationships, jazz is simply adding a new dimension. And I think we might all agree that renewal through tradition is the best assurance of a flourishing musical future.

Sonny Rollins

by Larry Gushee

Schuller's analysis also got comment in a later issue in a review by Larry Gushee.

SONNY ROLLINS AND THE BIG BRASS, Metrojazz E1002. Sonny Rollins, *tenor;* Nat Adderley, Clark Terry, Reunald Jones, Ernie Royal, *trumpets;* Billy Byers, Jimmy Cleveland, Frank Rehak, *trombones;* Dick Katz, *piano;* Rene Thomas, *guitar;* Henry Grimes, *bass;* Don Butterfield, *tuba;* Roy Haines, *drums;* Ernie Wilkins, *arranger.*
Grand Street; Far Out East; Who Cares; Love Is a Simple Thing.
Rollins; Grimes; Charles Wright, *drums:*
What's My Name; If You Were the Only Girl in the World; Manhattan; Body and Soul.

GUNTHER SCHULLER CONTENDS that Sonny Rollins has added a new dimension to jazz improvisation chiefly by using techniques of thematic variation. Schuller does not denigrate other approaches: ". . . we have seen that it is possible to create pure improvisations which are meaningful realizations of a well-sustained over-all feeling. Indeed, the majority of players are perhaps not temperamentally or intellectually suited to do more than that." I am not convinced that we can ask more of music than that in the long run. Of course, the point is not just that Rollins analyzes a tune in his playing, re-uses, extends, develops, varies the tune or figures in it, but that in so doing he gives to a piece a superior coherence of his own, and not just the result of repetitive chord structures.

The unified structure thus achieved would, presumably, make Sonny Rollins' work aesthetically pleasing at least from an analytical point of view. But need musical coherence follow if it were *not* a "meaningful realization of feeling"? I assume that a musical style is significant more for its power to capture the imagination, than for the specific techniques it uses. Though analysis reveals Rollins' right to be regarded as a serious artist, it ignores (or glosses over or attempts to explain away) many disparate elements in his musical thinking. For I believe Rollins really a romantic who has a sense of the "glory of the imperfect."

Many of these disparate elements may be heard on this LP. In the intro of *Grand Street* Ernie Wilkins caught the spirit of Sonny's unconventional phrasing, but in other respects the accompaniments are unsympathetic. Particularly if one has listened to the trio side first, the piano seems quite gratuitous. This is especially evident in two instances on this tune and *Far Out East,* where Dick Katz almost mechanically echoes the stuttering repeated-note motive Sonny is partial to. But I suspect that the fault is not in the accompaniment per se, but in the way Sonny reacts to it, and the way he chooses to play in its context. *Grand Street* has the advantage of an attractive tune. *Far Out East,* a Wilkins original of the *Jeepers Creepers* family, is humdrum and poorly performed: the trumpet figures are sloppily executed and the rhythm never establishes a firm pulse. Midway through his chorus, Sonny plays a phrase from the *Irish Washerwoman,* as if to dissociate himself from the proceedings. Unfortunately the interpolation also detracts from the coherence of his solo. In a proper context it might be musical humor (although that is usually pretty dreary), but Sonny is neither musical wit nor buffoon, and his quotations, and belches, come across with fatal earnestness as a kind of self-destructive irony.

Who Cares juxtaposes guitar, bass, and piano interludes which sound like excerpts from three different tunes, and something seems to have gone wrong with the recording balance too. But there are coruscating phrases from Rollins toward the end that redeem this band.

Love Is a Simple Thing opens with tenor and tuba couple, a neat bit of orchestration also used effectively on *Grand Street.* In his solo, Sonny takes one tack after another and develops none. Rene Thomas, the voice of reason on this entire side, shows how a solo can be constructed within the confines of one chorus of a standard tune.

Three tunes on the B side are Sonny with bass and drums, and one is wholly unaccompanied—although one of the trio performances, with sparse accompaniment, is virtually *a capella*. *What's My Name* begins with a facet of Rollins' talent which I much appreciate: his ability to state a melody with absolute directness and simplicity, but at the same time to introduce just enough variation in pitch and rhythm to give the line a high degree of internal tension. Structurally, the arrangement is curious; the same eight-bar passage is used for prelude and postlude. While it works in terms of doing *something* (anything) in order to get started, it has no obvious relationship to anything else in the tune. And since it isn't a significant chunk of music in itself, its use as a coda struck me as highly arbitrary and formalistic. This device is also used on the unaccompanied *Body and Soul* and works no better. Calling any formal structural procedure arbitrary is, of course, no condemnation. The trouble here, I think, is that an introduction using material strikingly different from that heard in the tune arouses some expectation of hearing it again, but what follows after is so long that the edge of expectation is dulled—it no longer matters whether we hear the intro again. (Imagine, for instance, if Joe Oliver had used the intro to *Dippermouth* at the end of the record as well. On the other hand, the intro to *Salt Peanuts* works as a postlude, because it is part and parcel of the principal theme.)

The absence of any competing voice on this side lends relief to Rollins' procedure in improvisation. He re-uses phrases of the original theme all right, but with a great deal of figuration between them, in such a way that individual phrases of the original no longer have the position in the chord structure of the tune they originally had. Rollins is, so to speak, out of phase with the chord progression and, since the chord progression in jazz is so much a part of the metrical pattern, with the rhythmic structure of the tune as well.

While it is true that Rollins plays "off the chord," it is not that he doesn't know any better. Rather he is trying to remove

himself from the environment of the tune, as usually conceived, just as, in choosing tunes like *If You Were the Only
Girl in the World,* he tries to remove himself from the jazz
repertory.

Rollins' phase-shift is not the almost automatic procedure
employed by many jazzmen of the past, by Louis Armstrong
for one. It works both ways, since phrases are also compressed
and seem to come too soon. Certain jazz improvisations suffer
by being too consistent in texture, too insistent on the same
kind of rhythmic motion. Rollins exaggerates in the other direction, and his solos are a mosaic of figures, sharply differentiated. Some are reminiscences of the tune, some vulgar noises,
explosive low tones, choked clucking, false fingerings, and
some are filigrees borrowed from Charlie Parker. Among the
most striking tiles in the mosaic are the awkward, perhaps deliberately naïve (some say "corny") rhythmic motives that
seem arcana from some locked book to which only Rollins has
the key.

It must be hard to play for a man like this. Henry Grimes
has a great deal of trouble presenting a coherent bass line.
Manhattan is particularly disturbing in this respect. Grimes
plays so many non-chord tones on accented beats that no sensation of effective chord change is possible. Perhaps this is
the way Sonny wants it, for, presumably, he thereby has more
room to move around. In that case, the whole function of the
bass needs to be reconsidered, especially its metrical role.

On the last band Sonny and his horn stand alone, and I
think that is where he wants to be. Here he is free to swing
or not, extend the chord or not. *Body and Soul* is an obvious
choice as Leonard Feather points out in the liner notes: the
listener would be aware of the structure of Sonny's improvisation in terms of chorus, bridge, etc. But, equally obviously, it
can be seen as a challenge to Hawk, and the kind of jazz he
represents. The effort to enlarge the horizons of jazz will, I
think, eventually do away with jazz as such. There are too
many cultured and sophisticated musicians with great gifts for
improvising for jazz to remain something you can tap your
foot to. It will be a good thing for our musical culture in

general to regain some of the vitality and unity of the past when improvisation and composition went hand in hand. And it will be good for jazz to be faced with the necessity of dealing with problems of form and content. But that is in the future. Meanwhile, Sonny Rollins is suffering from the growing pains as are others—to name only two, Charlie Mingus and Gil Evans. Although there are many passages in his playing where he blows freely and with vigor, Rollins leaves the impression that he is dissatisfied: with his horn, with the limitations of jazz tunes, with the playing of other musicians. In wanting to be himself he gives us too much, and too much that is obscure from an emotional and a musical point of view.

Preoccupation with form and formal procedure is no guarantee of coherence, as I think the history of nineteenth-century music demonstrates. At the same time, such a preoccupation often overshadows other drives, which perhaps go deeper or are perhaps opposed to it. The majority of nineteenth-century composers found their artistic salvation in the external stimulus provided by a musical text or program. Whether this provides a specific lesson for jazz, I don't know; but I think Sonny would do well to force his lyric gifts to the limits, even at the expense of other considerations.

What Rollins gives us, on this LP as elsewhere, is a running record of his unformed and vigorous artistic urge. There is too much there for us to regard it merely as skillful, charming, clever improvising. Still, it is not as though Sonny had succeeded in abstracting himself from the context of jazz, not as though there were no large element of tradition, of powerful and ingenuous blowing that steadies the vessel in the roughest waters. But I think more confidence in the effectiveness of his own playing and a less aggressive approach to the (perhaps illusory) problem of communication would leave him free to develop a personal style on whatever ground he wishes; but one that creates its own context, as it were, rather than annihilates it.

Paying Dues: The Education of
A Combo Leader

by Julian "Cannonball" Adderley

*Among our most faithful musician contributors were Art
Farmer and Julian "Cannonball" Adderley. The piece which
follows reveals an aspect of the life of a musician that has
seldom found its way into print. It was written as Cannonball
was on the verge of success with his own quintet.*

I HAD BEEN in Florida after my first trip to New York to
finish my teaching assignments. I formed my first band toward
the end of 1955. Having worked in New York, I was—naïvely
—sure that the best Florida musicians could meet the challenge of the major club circuit. I also had Junior Mance, an
old army buddy with the group. We had a few warm-ups in
Florida, and then my manager, John Levy, booked us in
Philadelphia. We had rehearsed two and a half weeks. We
spent a couple of days in New York before hitting Philadelphia, and during that time my Florida men heard the New
York musicians. Then, in Philadelphia, they also had to cope
with the fact that Philadelphians like John Coltrane and Red
Garland, home for the weekend, were standing around listening.

It was soon clear that being competent in Florida had nothing to do with New York competition. (In my own case, for
example, guys who seemed to me to swing when I was in
Florida no longer do.) By the second day in Philadelphia,
John Levy decided to fire everyone. (This was January, 1956.)
Jack Fields, an ex-musician and then owner of the Blue Note,
was also somewhat upset. I had gotten great response in that

room on the way to Florida with Kenny Clarke, bassist Jimmy
Mobley and pianist Hen Gates, but on the way back, I found
out that you can't fool anybody in Philadelphia. Jack lent me
some money, and I hired Specs Wright as drummer, but I
had to keep the bass player for a while or give him two weeks'
pay. He couldn't keep an even tempo on fast numbers so we
had to stop playing fast things for a while.

We went on to Detroit and Cleveland for two weeks each,
and when we got to New York, I eventually hired Sam Jones.
We kept going for the rest of the year with a book based in
large part on what my brother Nat and I wrote and some of
the usual jazz standards. We began to record, but there were
problems at Mercury. The man then in charge of jazz there
pretty largely decided what we recorded, who the arrangers
would be, and who would publish any originals we brought in.
I tell you frankly that I didn't know at that time that I could
protest and I didn't at first go to John Levy with the problem. I had signed a five-year contract with the company and
the options were entirely at their discretion. (I later found
out the union wouldn't allow more than three-year contracts.)
At first, being unknown, I didn't even get any advances for
my dates. Then there was a publicity splash of sorts, and they
started that business about "the new Bird" which has plagued
me ever since.

We were able to keep working fairly steadily through 1956.
There was one stretch with two weeks off and various periods
with a week layoff. We had come to New York with a little
money, and Nat and I both had cars, so that transportation
was no problem. The sidemen were paid only when we worked;
there was no one on retainer, so to speak.

I learned that year how important it is to keep the books
accurately and to keep accounts separate. We were getting
about $1,000 a week for five men. Out of that came $150
commission for my manager and booking office, $75 in union
taxes, a third of which we eventually got back, about $125
in federal withholding taxes, and maybe another $15 in social
security taxes. Now we should have deposited the money due
the government in a separate account every week. But after a

while, we began spending that money because we also had gasoline bills, hotel bills (for ourselves, etc.). We were paying the sidemen $125 out of which they had to pay their hotel bills.

By September of the next year, 1957, although we had been working steadily, we were about $9,000 in debt. We had had no royalties from our recordings and had only made scale for making them. Besides, a lot of recording costs were charged against us which shouldn't have been. The band had not been particularly successful in that we had done about the same amount of business all the time. Very few clubs lost money on us, but they didn't make a hell of a lot either. That's another thing I've learned. A combo's price should be geared so that everybody can make money. If a leader can't make it except for a bigger figure than is wise for the club, he just shouldn't play that club. Some guys, once they become successful, double their price, but although we draw better now than we've ever done, I prefer to gear my price—in specific cases—to the room. I mean to men like Charlie Graziano at the Cork 'n Bib who took chances on me when I wasn't especially a draw. Some of the other musicians forget too quickly. A leader, by the way, doesn't have to depend on an owner's figures to tell how much business is going on. He can tell by the activity of the waiters and by seeing whether the people are drinking. A place can be packed, but if the waiters aren't busy, nothing's happening. It's very simple.

For example, there was a time when Miles drew a lot of one-beer drinkers. Chico Hamilton would come in, not draw as much, but an owner would make as much money—then, not now—with Chico as with Miles because Chico drew more drinkers, and he cost $1,000 less.

Anyway, we finally broke up that first band. After twenty months, we still couldn't get more than $1,000 a week. At that time, Horace Silver was also scuffling; so were the Jazz Messengers (the group Blakey had with Bill Hardman) and Les Jazz Modes. Nobody was really making it except for Miles, Chico and Brubeck. I had gotten an offer from Dizzy to go with his small band. I was opposite Miles at the Bohemia, told him I was going to join Dizzy, and Miles asked me why I didn't join him. I told him he'd never asked me.

Miles had helped me when I first came to New York. He told me whom to avoid among the record companies, but unfortunately I didn't take his advice. Al Lion of Blue Note was one man he recommended, and Miles also told me about John Levy. Miles began telling me something musically about chords, but I sort of ignored him. I was a little arrogant in those days. Then, about three months later, I saw an interview in which Miles had said I could swing but I didn't know much about chords. But by that time I'd begun to listen to Sonny Rollins and others, and I had realized I knew very little about chords. You can play all the right changes and still not necessarily say anything. Finally, I learned how to use substitute chords to get the sound I wanted.

Well, Miles kept talking to me for two or three months to come with him, and when I finally decided to cut loose in October, 1957, I joined Miles. I figured I could learn more than with Dizzy. Not that Dizzy isn't a good teacher, but he played more commercially than Miles. Thank goodness I made the move I did.

I was with Miles from October, 1957, to September, 1959. Musically, I learned a lot while with him. About spacing, for one thing, when playing solos. Also, he's a master of understatement. And he taught me more about the chords, as Coltrane did too. Coltrane knows more about chords than anyone. John knows exactly what he's doing; he's gone into the melodic aspects of chords. He may go "out of the chord," so-called, but not out of the pattern he's got in his mind. From a leader's viewpoint, I learned, by watching Miles, how to bring new material into a band without changing the style of the band. And when it was necessary at times to change the style somewhat, Miles did it subtly so that no one knew it.

In a way, I suppose, I was a kind of stabilizing influence on the band. Two of the men he had—fine musicians—weren't always exactly on time or dependable. As in most groups, not all the sidemen made the same amount of money. When he heard I was going to leave, Miles did offer to guarantee me an annual salary of $20,000, which was more than I was making.

Especially when he started to use Bill Evans, Miles changed his style from very hard to a softer approach. Bill was brilliant in other areas, but he couldn't make the real hard things come off. Then Miles started writing new things and doing some of Ahmad's tunes. When Philly Joe left the band, Miles at first thought Jimmy Cobb wasn't as exciting on fast tempos, and so we did less of those. And although he loves Bill's work, Miles felt Bill didn't swing enough on things that weren't subdued. When Bill left, Miles hired Red again and got used to swinging so much that he later found Wynton Kelly, who does both the subdued things and the swingers very well. Wynton is also the world's greatest accompanist for a soloist. Bill is a fine pianist, and his imagination is a little more vivid so that he tries more daring things. But Wynton plays with the soloist all the time, with the chords *you* choose. He even anticipates your direction. Most accompanists try to lead you. Red is another excellent accompanist. He fits well with the drummer always and doesn't leave you anything to do but go where you want to.

As for rehearsals, we had maybe five in the two years I was there, two of them when I first joined the band. And the rehearsals were quite direct, like, "Coltrane, show Cannonball how you do this. All right, now let's do it." Occasionally, Miles would tell us something on the stand. "Cannonball, you don't have to play *all* those notes. Just stay close to the sound of the melody. Those substitute chords sound funny."

I certainly picked up much advantage as a potential leader from the exposure of being with Miles. We differed somewhat about acknowledging applause, but he let us do what we wanted to do. He really does care what the audience thinks, but he just doesn't believe in bowing, etc. I feel it's O.K., so I smile or something. He *would* tell us to leave the stand if we had nothing to do up there.

As for polls and critics, from what I gathered while with Miles and as a leader, the polls as such have little effect on a musician, but they do have an effect on potential customers who don't know much about jazz. That's why the *Playboy* poll is probably the most important of them all, which is why I get disgusted with some of the results.

Economically, the reviews of critics in *The New Yorker, Saturday Review* or *Hi-Fi/Stereo Review* mean more than those in *Down Beat* or *The Jazz Review*. The musicians, however, respect the trade paper writers, by and large, more than the others. A review in *Playboy* means nothing in contrast to a vote for me in the Critics' Poll but it may mean more money eventually.

Getting back to the problems of being a leader, I had planned when I joined him to stay with Miles about a year. But I stayed longer. Miles was getting more successful and there was the business recession. I was functioning meanwhile as a kind of road manager—paying off the guys, collecting money. Meanwhile I'd been getting inquiries from club owners about when I'd start my own band again because they kept noticing the response when my name was announced. I told John Levy I'd try it again if he could get the group a minimum of $1500 a week. Nat helped me in the recruiting. I gave him the list of the guys I'd contacted. John got about two months for us at $1500 a week. We broke in at Peps in Philadelphia, then went on to the Jazz Workshop in San Francisco. To start with, we had about twelve to fourteen things in the book. It just happened to work out that we had several gospel-type numbers. Nat and I had some originals in the book, and we got more material from Duke Pearson of Atlanta, now in New York, and Randy Weston. The album we made for Riverside at the Jazz Workshop is the biggest seller I've ever had, and one big factor is Bobby Timmons' *This Here* in it. Bobby wrote the tune in San Francisco although he'd been working on it before. The tune sort of gave us a sendoff, and everything else seemed to fall in. The album went into five figures within five weeks. It has already sold more than all my Mercury albums combined—except for the string album.

Now we're booked into the summer, plan to go to Europe then and play the Cannes Festival, and come back for several of the American festivals. We haven't got it made yet though. I'm still looking for real security, but I haven't been able to figure out yet how to get it—not in this business.

Tony Scott

by Julian "Cannonball" Adderley

Cannonball Adderley's comments on the jazz trombone and clarinet styles, a part of his review of a Tony Scott record, were an earlier contribution.

TONY SCOTT: THE MODERN ART OF JAZZ, Seeco CELP 425. Tony Scott, *clarinet;* Jimmy Knepper, *trombone;* Clark Terry, *trumpet;* Sahib Shihab, *baritone saxophone* on three and four; Bill Evans, *piano;* Milt Hinton, *bass;* Henry Grimes, *bass* on one and five; Paul Motian, *drums.*
Five; She's Different; The Lady Is a Tramp; Tenderly; Blues for 3 Horns; I Remember You; Lullaby of the Leaves.

THIS IS NOT a revolutionary record, but I think it has some of the best Tony Scott I've heard since he was at Minton's, because he doesn't include the kind of things he did on some of the Victor albums, the pretentious things. He's got all good men—I'm surprised. Bill Evans is one of my favorite piano players. I don't think any young modern treats a ballad like he does. He has a way of playing simple rhythmically and complex harmonically, but everything flows so. He has such a thorough knowledge of harmony that everything seems simple.

I love Clark Terry. I don't know exactly why. He's not that exceptional although he is very competent. He's imaginative, soulful, has an original sound and he uses tonguing technique better than any jazz trumpet player I know. It doesn't sound like technique when he does it; it just seems to fit. My brother Nat was strongly influenced by Clark, and Clark has told me time and again that he's been influenced by Nat, and I'm beginning to believe it. I don't think that much of Clark stuck with Miles, although Clark was an idol of Miles's when Miles was a boy. I also don't think Miles influenced Clark in recent years. I think Rex Stewart was Clark's strongest influence.

I don't like the way Tony Scott plays ballads too well; he uses his technique too much on them. He's best at a slow medium tempo, like on *Blues for 3 Horns,* because he has a tendency to build. As for Ben Webster's influence on him, I don't think it shows except for sound. Tony has a big, fat sound. I still think Tony is more influenced by Bird than by Ben on ballads.

I like to hear Sahib play blues. He's what I call traditionally funky. He's able to create the mood—that's the thing that's important.

Knepper is a very good trombonist. But J. J. has spoiled me with regard to a trombone sounding like a trombone. I mean that Knepper, though he's very good, is too tied to the instrument. J. J., on the other hand, is a soloist who happens to use the trombone. Therefore, if you call Knepper an "original" trombonist, you may be right. If you mean an "original" soloist, in the sense in which I'd use the term for J. J., that's something else. Similarly, I think Jimmy Cleveland is an original trombonist but not the original jazz soloist J. J. is. J. J. has a style and it's the kind of style that allows men on other instruments beside the trombone to emulate it, and they wind up sounding in part like J. J. I'd say Knepper is like a modern Jack Teagarden. A man like Curtis Fuller emulates J. J. from a trombone point of view, and a player like Kai Winding was originally a J. J. emulator (not in content but from the viewpoint of the trombone). Knepper's influences, however, sound more traditional—Teagarden, Urbie Green. Even his sound sounds similar to Teagarden's in some spots.

The rhythm section on this record is beautiful. Paul Motian is one of the steadiest drummers around. Paul and Bill Evans work very well on this. The rhythm section plays better when Grimes rather than Hinton is the bassist because Milt's beat is so dominant. Henry has a tendency to sit down on the beat so that it's there when the soloist arrives.

Back to Tony. His strong points are his sound, technique

and genuine feeling for the blues. His weak points: for one
thing, he does something that some people say they find in
my playing, but I don't think it's there so often. He starts
something and doesn't finish the statement, but instead goes
into something else. He tries to play too much; sometimes
he'll triple up for no apparent reason. And there are times
when I would question his taste.

Tony is one of the easiest guys to play with. He has a vast
repertoire and seems to know how to play tunes in the right
tempo. And he certainly plays a lot more warmly than De
Franco.

The clarinetists I most dig, however, are the real traditional ones—Barney Bigard, Russell Procope, Artie Shaw.
Shaw was so lyrical and the thing that helped him was that
Benny Goodman was just the opposite. Goodman was a real
craftsman while Shaw was real lyrical. Some of Shaw's solos
would be classics today regardless of instrument. His record
of *Stardust*—with Butterfield—is one of the greatest I've ever
heard. Shaw has been too much overlooked. He also, by the
way, had one of the original cool bands. I mean the one that
was contemporary with Goodman during the heyday of
swing. They showed restraint and a little more taste from the
content point of view. The Goodman band was more on the
surface and let's say was more the "hard bop" of the swing
era as opposed to the Shaw band which was cool and restrained. I think Gil Evans is an admirer of those Shaw bands.

One thing I want to give Goodman credit for. He was one
jazz musician who got rich playing jazz. He did get a couple
of breaks, but he deserved everything he got. I don't know
how he did it; I'd like to find the secret.

One reason there seem to be few modern jazz clarinetists
is that the instrument is difficult to begin with. It's not the kind
of horn you pick up and start honking. Nobody today is
really exceptional on the instrument. The Giuffre thing is not
so much a clarinet thing as the fact that he uses it to solo
on as he would use any of his multiple instruments. He doesn't
pretend to be a virtuoso.

Another reason is that it's hard for a clarinetist to get a

sideman's job in present-day combos. All clarinet players, it seems, have to be leaders to stay on the instrument. Rolf Kuhn is an exception, but that's because he hasn't been here long enough. Same is true of the French horn. If Julius Watkins doesn't get a job in a big band, he has to be a leader of a small combo. Same problem with a man who wants to emphasize flute, and it's even becoming true of trombone. You have to be a lead to get a job.

To summarize this record: on it Tony is back to where I think he should be—a blowing and free-swinging type thing instead of all that paper.

Introducing Steve Lacy

In our "Introductions" to young jazzmen, we have tried to set down some of the attitudes that promising musicians were bringing to the music in the late fifties and early sixties. The series began with this essay on Steve Lacy, which is actually (and anonymously) the work of his wife, Bobbie.

STEVE LACY, TWENTY-FIVE, is a native New Yorker. He has a wife, two children, two cats, and lives in a loft just off the Bowery, over a cellophane bag factory. Being in a manufacturing district enables him to play his soprano saxophone any hour of the day or night.

Steve began playing jazz about eight years ago. His first gig was at the Stuyvesant Casino (not far from his present neighborhood), and he was billed as the "Bechet of Today." His work in Dixieland continued for the next couple of years with men like Rex Stewart, Max Kaminsky, Buck Clayton, Pee Wee Russell and Lips Page. He spent six months in Boston at the Schillinger School of Music (described by him as a fiasco during school hours, but at least making possible sessions at the Savoy that proved enlightening). At the school he was a curiosity as the only Dixieland musician and the only soprano saxophonist. It was during this period, through records, that he started to absorb Lester Young and more modern jazz. Back in New York, a mutual interest in Ellington brought him together with Cecil Taylor, who was to influence his life profoundly. Cecil broadened his interests considerably and for three years they worked gigs together. With Cecil, he recorded one album for Transition and a second record resulted from the appearance of a Taylor group at the Newport Festival of 1957.

During this period Steve also led various short-lived groups (cocktail, society, Dixieland, swing) and made recordings with Dick Sutton, Tom Stewart and Whitey Mitchell. He studied for short periods with Cecil Scott, Harold Freeman, Joe Allard, Lee Konitz and Cecil Taylor, gaining experience in a variety of directions.

Leaving Cecil's group in order to mature on his own, Steve began to study by himself. Gil Evans asked him to participate in an album for Prestige called GIL EVANS PLUS TEN. (Gil had heard Steve on the Arthur Godfrey Show with his Dixieland group several years before.) As a result of this recording with Gil, he obtained a contract with Prestige and recorded STEVE LACY, SOPRANO SAX, and, a year later, his recently released STEVE LACY PLAYS THE MUSIC OF THELONIOUS MONK.

Steve says of his Monk album, "When I heard Monk's record of *Skippy*, I was determined to learn it if it took me a year. It took me a week to learn and six months to be able to play it. I had such a ball learning it that I started to look into his other tunes. I had previously recorded *Work*. Each song of Monk's that I learned left me with something invaluable and permanent, and the more I learned, the more I began to get with his system. Soon I realized I had enough material for ten albums.

"Monk's tunes are the ones that I most enjoy playing. I like his use of melody, harmony and especially his rhythm. Monk's music has profound humanity, disciplined economy, balanced virility, dramatic nobility and innocently exuberant wit. Monk, by the way, like Louis Armstrong, is a master of rhyme. For me, other masters of rhyme are Bird, Duke, Miles, Art Blakey and Cecil Taylor.

"I feel that music can be comprehended from many different levels. It can be regarded as excited speech, imitation of the sounds of nature, an abstract set of symbols, a baring of emotions, an illustration of interpersonal relationships, an intellectual game, a device for inducing reverie, a mating call, a series of dramatic events, an articulation of time and/or

270

space, an athletic contest, or all of these things at once. A jazz
musician is a combination orator, dialectician, mathematician,
athlete, entertainer, poet, singer, dancer, diplomat, educator,
student, comedian, artist, seducer, public masturbator and
general all-around good fellow. As this diversity indicates, no
matter what you do, some people are going to like it, and
other people not. Therefore, all you can do is to try to satisfy
yourself, by trusting the man inside. Braque said, 'With age,
art and life become one.' I am only twenty-five, and I trust
that I will one day really be able to satisfy myself and at the
same time express my love for the world by putting so much
of myself into my playing that others will be able to see themselves too. Jazz is a very young art and not too much is
known about it as yet. You have to trust yourself and go your
own way.

"Since there are no soprano saxophone players, I take my
inspiration from soprano singers, as well as other jazz instrumentalists, painters, authors, entertainers and that thing that
grows wildly in New York, people. I like to observe people on
the subways, what they express just by sitting there. I had a
ball during the newspaper strike this past year, because people
couldn't hide as they usually do. I would like to be able to
portray what I feel for my fellow creatures. My horn has a
texture, range and flexibility which is ideal for myself and my
purposes. I have been grappling with the difficulties of it for
some time now and can very well understand why no one else
has attempted to play anything on it more complex than the
stylings of the thirties. The instrument is treacherous on several levels: intonation, dynamics, and you can't get gigs on it.
At this point, I am beyond the point of no return and my
wife and children have agreed to go with me all the way.

"The most gratifying and enlightening musical experience
for me in the past few months was playing with Gil Evans'
fourteen-piece band for two weeks at Birdland opposite Miles
Davis and his marvelous group. It was the first time that I
had ever played with such a large ensemble and it was the
start of my investigations into the possibilities of blending my
sound with others. I was the only saxophone in the band and

sometimes played lead, sometimes harmony parts or contrapuntal lines, other times obbligato, and quite often I was given a chance to blow with the whole band behind me—perhaps the greatest thrill of my life thus far. Gil is a splendid orchestrator, a brilliant musician and a wonderful friend. Sometimes when things jelled, I felt true moments of ecstasy; and recently, when a friend of mine who worked with the Claude Thornhill band in the forties, when Gil was the principal writer, said that some nights the sound of the band around him moved him to tears, I knew exactly what he meant. So does anybody else who has ever played Gil's arrangements.

"The contemporary saxophonists whose work most interests me are John Coltrane, Sonny Rollins, Ben Webster, Ornette Coleman, Jackie McLean, and Johnny Hodges. Being a saxophone player, when I listen to these men I not only can feel what they are doing artistically but also follow their playing as a series of decisions. While working at Birdland those two weeks with Gil, I naturally had a chance to dig Coltrane and appreciate his, at times, almost maniacal creativity. He has a fantastic knowledge of harmony and, like the other members of Miles's group, including, of course, Miles himself, seems to be really searching out the vast resources of scales."

"Sonny Rollins, on the other hand, rather than concentrating on scales, has devoted a large portion of his mind to plastic values and the effects of various shapes on each other. Sonny's playing, it can be clearly seen, derives largely from extremely intensive research into all facets of saxophone playing per se. Ben Webster is the master of sound. His use of dynamics indicates the great dramatic sensitivity of this most mature of all saxophone players. His masculinity and authority can only be matched in jazz by that of Thelonious Monk.

"Ornette Coleman is the only young saxophone player who seems to be trying for a conversational style of playing and is the only· one I have heard who is exploring the potentialities of real human expression, something which has a tremendous impact on me. I have yet to hear him in person, but his playing (not his writing) on the album I did hear moved me. Jackie McLean has the most rhythmic vitality and, so far, the least discipline of all these saxophonists. He expresses his own personality with his sound and has tremendous swing and energy. Hearing his blues sounds has always been for me a haunting and, at the same time, exhilarating experience. I have always loved Johnny Hodges. He is a true aristocrat.

"The difference in the personalities of all of these men, who manage to indelibly express their uniqueness in their music, is to me the most profound demonstration of the validity of jazz, because I feel that the communication of human values is the main purpose of any art.

"Besides jazz, I enjoy the works of Stravinsky and Webern and certain works of Schoenberg, Berg, Bartok and Prokofieff; also African and Indian music. When I get dragged with everything, I try Bach. I find they all help my ear enormously. As far as the way these musics influence my own playing, all I can say is that *everything* is an influence. When I say everything, I mean just that, from the rhythm of children's speech to the patterns of the stars. I believe that the only way for me to develop myself is the way thoroughly proven by the men who have made jazz what it is—that is, to play as often and as publicly as possible, with as good musicians as will tolerate me."

Introducing Wilbur Ware

by Bill Crow

The one exception to our rule that "Introductions" should be done in the form of interviews was bassist Bill Crow's analysis of Wilbur Ware's style as a strikingly original use of basic and traditional materials.

SOMEONE TOLD ME about Wilbur Ware around 1955 when he was still in Chicago . . . that he was "something else" and shouldn't be missed. When he finally came to New York, I was pleased to discover that he was not just another good bass player, but an unusually original artist. After hearing Wilbur several times with Monk, and with his own group at the Bohemia, and upon listening to some of his records, I am convinced that he is one of our truly great jazz musicians. I don't mean that he has invented anything new in the way of lines, forms, or sound, but he has chosen an approach to these elements that does not follow the general evolution of bass style from Blanton through Pettiford, Brown, Heath, Chambers, Mingus, etc. Wilbur uses the same tools that other bassists use, but his concentration is more on percussion, syncopation and bare harmonic roots than on the achievement of a wind-instrument quality in phrasing and melodic invention. His solos are extremely melodic in their own way, logically developed and well balanced, but they are permutations of the primary triad or reshuffling of the root line rather than melodies built from higher notes in the chord. Musical Ex. 1 (from his own Riverside album THE CHICAGO SOUND [Riverside RLP 12-252] the first of two bass choruses on *31st and State*) illustrates his approach well. His entrance to the first

Because most people who read music are not familiar with the jazz player's habit of mentally re-evaluating notations that do not fit his conception of phrasing, I have written Ex. 1 in 12/8 though the musicians are undoubtedly thinking in terms of four beats to the measure. The usual ways of writing the first measure of Ex. 2 are inaccurate but often written for musicians who understand the liberties that must be taken with phrasing; the more accurate 4/4 rendition using eighth-note triplets (Ex. 3) becomes cluttered with triplet signs, and incorrectly indicates the phrasing to musicians bar establishes the tonality in no uncertain terms, and his return to the figure in the second bar sets up the pattern of alternating strong, simple melodic phrases with light, broken figures that indicate the chords and excite the rhythm—a sort of self-accompaniment.

In measures 5, 6, 7, 9 and 11 (don't count the first pickup as a measure), Wilbur often deliberately uses what bass players refer to as a "short sound," that is, he uses rests between consecutive notes of a phrase rather than trying for the legato, "long sound" preferred by most jazz bassists. He uses the long sound when it will enhance his line, but isn't at all one-way about it.

Since the bass is tuned in fourths, this interval and the neighboring fifth are the easiest to finger anywhere on the instrument, and Wilbur makes use of them more frequently than any others. He does it, however, with such imagination that he has developed it into a formal style within which he functions beautifully. He often uses these intervals as double-stops, moving them however the harmony will allow parallel movement, but never allowing himself to be backed into a corner where the continuation of an idea in double-stops would require an impossible fingering. It's also interesting to notice his use of octaves and open string harmonics, as easily fingered ways to extend the basic chord into different registers of the instrument without running chords and scales.

On *Decidedly* from the MULLIGAN MEETS MONK album (Riverside RLP 12-247) there are a number of good illustrations of Wilbur's approach to the bass line. During the opening choruses he builds them principally of roots, fifths and octaves with very little scale walking. After Gerry's breaks he has the harmonic control, since Monk lays out, but rather than immediately walking chords he plays a counterrhythm on a G harmonic through the first three changes, where G is

---

who lay way back on triplets. The disadvantage to 12/8 is the strangeness of using dotted-quarter rests, but it can be read strictly as written and will produce quite an accurate rendition of the original.

the fifth of the first chord, the ninth of the second chord and an anticipation of the root that the third chord resolves toward (D_7 to G_7). Here the pedal device sets off Gerry's melodic idea beautifully and kicks off the chorus with great strength.

On Monk's first chorus of the same tune Wilbur starts with alternating beats of root and fifth that firmly establish the bottom of the chord. At the beginning of the second piano chorus he uses alternating roots and major sevenths (a half step below the root) for the same purpose, then double-stopped roots and fifths. His own chorus is walked, first into a rather insecure section of his high register, then abruptly to low open strings and a few double-stopped chromatic fifths. In one spot he shifts from walking on the beat to walking on the upbeat for four bars, and then back again. At the end of his chorus he uses a cycle of fourths for a turn around into the next chorus. As you see, he manages to develop this solo melodically, rhythmically and harmonically without venturing away from the basic form of four quarter-notes to the measure.

On Monk's *Straight No Chaser* in the same album, his two choruses of blues include rhythmic figures on one note, double stops, syncopated downbeats, melodic quotes and normal trochaic phrases without losing any of the simplicity, space and clearness of line that mark his work. He was an ideal bassist for Monk, since he seems to share Monk's conception of the value of open space, repeated figures, cycles of intervals, rhythmic tension and relaxation . . . and at the same time he tends to the business of providing strong roots that give Monk's harmonic conception an added richness.

Besides the variety and color that Wilbur creates in his lines there is the most obvious feature of his playing, a tremendous 4/4 swing that has the same loose, imprecise but very alive feeling of carefree forward motion that you hear in Kenny Clarke's drumming. I can't describe it accurately, but the best image I can think of to suggest it is Cannonball Adderley doing the Lindy. There is flowing movement all through the measure, and not just where the notes are.

On albums released so far, Wilbur is teamed with a number of musicians who represent many styles. The role of the bassist is a little different in each case, depending on how much or how little ground the drummers and piano players like to cover. Without altering his basic approach Wilbur manages to adjust perfectly to each situation, relating as well to Dick Johnson on Riverside RLP 12-252 and Zoot Sims on RLP 12-228 as he does to Ernie Henry on RLP 12-248 and Johnny Griffin on RLP 12-264. He is combined with some excellent pianists (Kenny Drew, Monk, Wynton Kelly, Dave McKenna, Junior Mance) and drummers (Philly Joe, Wilbur Campbell, Shadow Wilson, Osie Johnson). In the main these albums are good examples of vigorous, swinging rhythm sections, and accurate representation of Wilbur's playing both as accompanist and soloist.

Wilbur is, for me, a reaffirmation of the idea that deep expression can be reached through simplification of form—each new discovery need not always be a more complex one. The difference between the extremely sophisticated simplicity of Wilbur Ware and the primitive simplicity of a beginner is as wide as that between simple drawings of Klee or Miró and those of a child. Artistic curiosity will constantly experiment with mechanical complexity, but it is the resolution of such constructions into simple universal terms that is ultimately satisfying. Wilbur's terms are simple, and his artistic expression most profound.

Introducing Scott La Faro

by Martin Williams

About a year after this article was written, Scott La Faro was killed in an automobile accident near his family's home in up-state New York during the Fourth of July weekend. In him jazz lost one of its most technically proficient and harmonically imaginative bassists; to call him "promising" would be to ig-nore the real achievements that were already a part of his brief career. (Incidentally, only a few weeks after this inter-view, La Faro did become a member of the Ornette Coleman quartet for several engagements.)

"IT'S QUITE A wonderful thing to work with the Bill Evans trio," said bassist Scott La Faro. "We are really just beginning to find our way. You won't hear much of that on our first rec-ord together, except a little on *Blue in Green* where no one was playing time as such. Bill was improvising lines, I was playing musical phrases behind him, and Paul Motian played in free rhythmic drum phrases."

La Faro is dissatisfied with a great deal of what he hears in jazz, but what he says about it isn't mere carping. He thinks he knows what to do about it, at least in his own playing. "My ideas are so different from what is generally acceptable nowa-days that I sometimes wonder if I am a jazz musician. I re-member that Bill and I used to reassure each other some nights kiddingly that we really were jazz musicians. I have such re-spect for so many modern classical composers, and I learn so much from them. Things are so contrived nowadays in jazz, and harmonically it has been so saccharine since Bird."

Charlie Parker was already dead before Scott La Faro was

aware of him, even on records. In fact Scott La Faro was not really much aware of jazz at all until 1955.

He was born in 1936 in Newark, New Jersey, but his family moved to Geneva, New York, when he was five. "There was always the countryside. I miss it now. I am not a city man. Maybe that is why Miles Davis touches me so deeply. He grew up near the countryside too, I believe. I hear that in his playing anyway. I've never been through that 'blues' thing either."

La Faro started on clarinet at fourteen and studied music in high school. He took up bass on a kind of dare. "My father played violin with a small 'society' trio in town. I didn't know what I wanted to do when I had finished school, and my father said—half-joking, I think—that if I learned bass, I could play with them. When I did, I knew that I wanted to be a musician. It's strange: playing clarinet and sax didn't do it, but when I started on bass, I knew it was music." He went to Ithaca Conservatory and then to Syracuse; it was there, through fellow students, that he began to listen to jazz. He got a job in Syracuse at a place called the Embassy Club. "The leader was a drummer who played sort of like Sidney Catlett and Kenny Clarke. He formed my ideas of what jazz was about. He, and the juke box in the place—it had Miles Davis records. And I first heard Percy Heath and Paul Chambers on that juke box. They taught me my first jazz bass lessons. There was also a Lee Konitz record with Stan Kenton called *Prologue*."

In late 1955, La Faro joined Buddy Morrow's band. "We toured all over the country until I left the band in Los Angeles in September, 1956. I didn't hear any jazz or improve at all during that whole time." But a few weeks after he left Morrow, he joined a Chet Baker group that included Bobby Timmons and Lawrence Marable. "I found out so much from Lawrence, a lot of it just from playing with him. I have trouble with getting *with* people rhythmically and I learned a lot about it from him. I learned more about rhythm when I played with Monk last fall; a great experience. With Monk, rhythmically, it's just there, always."

La Faro remembers two other important experiences in California. The first was hearing Ray Brown, whose swing and

perfection in his style impressed him. The other came when he
lived for almost a year in the mountaintop house of Herb Gel-
ler and his late wife, Lorraine. "I practiced and listened to
records. I had—I still have—a feeling that if I don't practice
I will never be able to play. And Herb had all the jazz records; I heard a lot of music, many people for the first time,
on his records."

In September, 1958, La Faro played with Sonny Rollins in
San Francisco, and later he worked with the same rhythm section behind Harold Land. "I think horn players and pianists
have probably influenced me the most, Miles Davis, Coltrane,
Bill Evans, and Sonny perhaps deepest of all. Sonny is technically good, harmonically imaginative, and really creative. He
uses all he knows to make finished music when he improvises.

"I found out playing with Bill that I have a deep respect for
harmony, melodic patterns, and form. I think a lot more imaginative work could be done within them than most people
are doing, but I can't abandon them. That's why I don't think
I could play with Ornette Coleman. I used to in California;
and we would go looking all over town for someplace to play.
I respect the way he overrides forms. It's all right for him, but
I don't think I could do it myself.

"Bill gives the bass harmonic freedom because of the way
he voices, and he is practically the only pianist who does. It's
because of his classical studies. Many drummers know too
little rhythmically, and many pianists know too little harmonically. In the trio we were each contributing something and
really improvising *together*, each playing melodic and rhythmic
phrases. The harmony would be improvised; we would often
begin only with something thematic and not a chord sequence.

"I don't like to look back, because the whole point in jazz
is doing it *now*. (I don't even like any of my records except
maybe the first one I did with Pat Moran on Audio Fidelity.)
There are too many things to learn and too many things you
can do, to keep doing the same things over and over. My main
problem now is to get that instrument under my fingers so I
can play more music."

Introducing Eric Dolphy

by *Martin Williams*

Since his appearance with the Charlie Mingus group spoken of in this interview, Eric Dolphy has become one of the most active participants in what musicians are calling (for lack of a better name) "the new thing." Besides recordings and engagements on his own, he has become a member of the George Russell sextet and participated in a remarkable recording of Ornette Coleman's, a continuous free improvisation of thirty-eight minutes called Free Jazz, *involving trumpeters Don Cherry and Freddy Hubbard, bassists Scott La Faro and Charlie Hayden, and drummers Billy Higgins and Ed Blackwell, besides Dolphy and Coleman, in a "double quartet."*

HEARING ERIC DOLPHY play with the Charlie Mingus quartet at the Showplace, it was hard for some of us to realize we had heard him before. But it was he who took over Buddy Colette's book with Chico Hamilton in 1957. And Dolphy was for many years a part of that Los Angeles jazz underground about which a great deal more should be known; that city is full of talented musicians only a few of whom make the recording studios or are able to earn their livings by playing their horns.

When I asked Eric Dolphy whom he listened to, the first two names that came to him were Art Tatum and John Coltrane. It is not surprising to one who has heard Dolphy that he should name them, for both of them have very special harmonic senses. But Tatum's imagination was almost exclusively harmonic; and Coltrane is, like Coleman Hawkins, frequently an arpeggio player. Dolphy's talent seems to be melodic, and as he develops we should hear him more and more using his very flexible harmonic ear to select the notes for the creation of original melodic lines. He is already a nearly virtuoso alto saxophonist as well as an exciting soloist.

Eric Dolphy was born in Los Angeles thirty-one years ago. He started playing clarinet at eight and saxophone at fifteen. The first jazz musician he remembers having heard was Fats Waller, and when he began to hear Duke Ellington and Coleman Hawkins, his ears were opening. "I used to ask myself, 'what is that?' at the things they played. I wanted to know how they did all of them." He heard everyone he could hear, he says: Ellington, Hawkins, Benny Carter, Benny Goodman, the Basie band. Then Charlie Parker.

"Then Bird was it," he says. "I went to school with Hampton Hawes, and he was the first to tell me about Bird. I didn't believe him at first. I couldn't believe anybody could be *faster* than Hawkins, for one thing."

The first professional job Dolphy had was at a dance, and Charlie Mingus was on bass. "He played the style he does now in high school," interrupts Mingus. "A lot of guys out there did including Buddy Colette—I don't know what happened to him. We used to play that way with Lloyd Reece."

One of the most important men in Los Angeles to many a young jazz musician is trumpeter-leader Gerald Wilson. "He's very encouraging and helpful to all young musicians," Dolphy says, "no matter how well he may be doing himself. He keeps everybody aroused and interested in music. It's so important because otherwise so many people would have nothing to look forward to and no hope of being able to earn their way in music. I have recorded an arrangement he wrote eighteen years ago—it hasn't been released yet—and it sounded so fresh. He was 'modern' when I was very, very young. There are other people I should thank too, but if I name Chico, Harold Land, Buddy, Walter Benton, Lester Robinson, Ernest Crawford— that's just a beginning." On Gerald Wilson, Addison Farmer adds, "Just about everyone out there has learned from Gerald. It is such a pleasure to play his music. And he always keeps learning too."

When he joined Hamilton, Dolphy learned all the reeds, and he traveled, "hearing everyone in the country." He says, "I listen and try to play everywhere I go. In Kansas City I heard John Jackson and lots of good saxophonists. I played with a pianist called Sleepy that they say Bird used to play with all the time. So many wonderful players."

Dolphy stayed a year with Hamilton, contributed some pieces to the book (*Miss Movement* is his) but left in 1958 in New York. His chief jobs since then have been with George Tucker at Minton's and with Mingus.

"In my own playing, I am trying to incorporate what I hear; I hear other resolutions on the basic harmonic patterns, and I try to use them. And I try to get the instrument to more or less speak—everybody does. I learned harmony from Lloyd Reece; he really opened my ears to it, and I also studied it in school."

Comparisons between Dolphy's work and Ornette Coleman's are probably inevitable and will just as probably plague both of them from now on. "Ornette was playing that way in 1954. I heard about him, and when I heard him play, he asked me if I liked his pieces and I said I thought they sounded good. When he said that if someone played a chord, he heard another chord on that one, I knew what he was talking about because I had been thinking of the same things." Mingus adds: "He doesn't sound a thing like Ornette Coleman. He phrases more like Bird. And he has absorbed Bird rhythmically."

"Yes, I think of my playing as tonal," Dolphy said in answer to a question. "I play notes that would not ordinarily be said to be in a given key, but I hear them as proper. I don't think I 'leave the changes,' as the expression goes; every note I play has some reference to the chords of the piece.

"I feel very happy to be a part of music," he added modestly. "It is really wonderful to feel I can make my living as a musician now because I never wanted to do anything else."

Ornette Coleman

by Quincy Jones, Martin Williams, Hsio Wen Shih

The relationship of The Jazz Review *to Ornette Coleman's work has a rather special history. Nat Hentoff first heard his playing when he vistied Los Angeles to work on notes for several of producer Les ·Koenig's Contemporary LPs, including Coleman's. Hentoff subsequently solicited reviews of Coleman's records for* The Jazz Review *from several musicians, hence the comments below of composer-arranger, band leader Quincy Jones on his first exposure to Coleman's music.*

Coleman later attended the 1959 session of the School of Jazz at Lenox, Massachusetts; earlier the school's director John Lewis, had told Francis Thorne in an interview we had published: "I can tell you this . . . there are two young people I met in California—an alto player named Ornette Coleman and a trumpet player named Don Cherry. I've never heard anything like them before. Ornette is the driving force of the two. They're almost like twins; they play together like I've never heard anybody play together. It's not like any ensemble that I have ever heard, and I can't figure out what it's all about yet. Ornette is, in a sense, an extension of Charlie Parker and the first I've heard. This is the real need that I think has to take place, to extend the basic ideas of Bird until they are not playing an imitation but actually something new. I think that they may have come up with something, not perfect yet, and still in the early stages but nevertheless very fresh and interesting."

In "A Letter from Lenox" in our October 1959 issue Martin Williams wrote of Coleman that he seems to be opening up "the way for jazz to grow," that he makes "a new sensibility for one's ears, heart, and mind."

Ornette Coleman: SOMETHING ELSE! ! ! !, Contemporary C3551.
Ornette Coleman, *alto;* Don Cherry, *trumpet;* Walter Norris, *piano;*
Don Payne, *bass;* Billy Higgins, *drums.*
*Invisible; The Blessing; Jayne; Chippie; The Disguise; Angel
Voice; Alpha; When Will the Blues Leave?; The Sphinx.*

FIRST OF ALL, that's a fine bass player—good sound *and* time.
He and Don Cherry, the trumpet player, have tremendous
authority.

These cats sound very sincere. They have that thing that
makes for real jazz, that makes it really breathe and live on its
own. Usually, the jazz that kills you the most is the jazz that's
helping to strengthen our language. And we need all the vowels
we can get.

You can tell these guys are young. Their emotions are not
matured but that might be to the good, because they might
be a little more daring because they're not set.

I must say I'm a little puzzled at some of the statements
Coleman makes in the notes as contrasted with this record.
He speaks of letting the melodic lines form the harmonic patterns. You can't do that with the pianist playing fixed changes
and the bass player playing a set line. He also says he'd like
to have the changes different each time. To do that, you'd
have to eliminate the pianist and the bass player or else have
done extensive research in mental telepathy.

I still dig what he's doing though. It's a matter of growing
pains. Age should give him more taste melodically. He'll settle
down and get more of a message over. He seems to be searching in a manner similar to Monk. He hasn't gone past Monk
by any means. *Invisible* seems to me to have the same basic
feeling, the same basic attitude as *Epistrophy.*

But the seasoning isn't there yet. I also don't think he has
enough tone control. Maybe it's a plastic reed. It's a young
voice—a voice before the voice changes. He does get his voice
into his horn, but the intonation is questionable sometimes.

He speaks in the notes about his concern for getting a
human sound in his playing by getting the right pitch. Well,
he may be stretching that analogy too far. A lot of the things

he's doing only an exceptional human voice could do, and
then not naturally. If he means talking through the horn, it all
depends on the type of speech he means. Inarticulateness isn't
pleasant to listen to. At the moment, he talks the way a teen-
ager might.

Same thing with his written lines. They have a lot of richness, but they're not developed yet. A teen-ager talks with not
too much authority because he's not really sure what he's talking about. When Coleman does get authority, he'll be able to
say more and say it more deeply with less.

His work is a combination of a lot of elements—Bird,
Monk, etc. His *combination* of these elements may well be
original, but I don't think there are as yet any original contributions of his own. There is something there that can be
original and that will develop. His present occasional incoher-
ence is probably the price he's paid for seeking originality,
but he hasn't found anything really original yet.

Everybody in the album has a good conception of time, and
everybody understands the role of improvisation in relation
to the rhythm section. Unlike many young players, they don't
try to swing *for* the rhythm section. It takes good understanding of jazz rhythm to play *with* rather than *for* a rhythm section. A lot of young guys don't have faith in the rhythm
section, and try to swing it. They don't leave enough of the
proceedings to what will naturally come out of the human
element in jazz, the rapport between the players. The mature
jazz musician always has enough confidence to know what to
leave to the human element, whereas the young horn player
tries to swing every beat of every bar and tries to fill up all
the holes. The authoritative jazz players, however, know how
much a half-note rest swings. Coleman, in summary, has something to build on and I think he believes in what he's doing.

QUINCY JONES

Ornette Coleman: TOMORROW IS THE QUESTION, Contemporary M
3569. Ornette Coleman, *alto;* Don Cherry, *trumpet;* Percy Heath,
bass; Shelly Manne, *drums.*

Tears Inside; Mind and Time; Compassion; Giggin'; Rejoicing.
Red Mitchell, *bass;* replaces Heath:
Lorraine; Turnaround; Endless.

THIS RECORD WAS made before the formation of the Ornette
Coleman quartet with Charlie Haden and Billy Higgins (now
La Faro and Ed Blackwell) and before all the things that have
been happening in their music since, but it should certainly
not be overlooked. It contains a superior composition, for one
thing, in *Lorraine* and an exceptional blues line, for which
Tears Inside is a superb title. (The ideas in the lines of things
like *Compassion* and *Rejoicing* seem the ones with the greater
possibilities, however.) The record also has a cohesion, which
the first Contemporary, with its apparently inhibiting and certainly clashing piano, did not have, and which the first Atlantic
record, though made in the first excitement that now *four*
players were grasping the nature of this music, did not have
either. The cohesion here is conservative compared either to
the possibilities the Atlantic suggests or the developments and
order that have come since, but it is here. Perhaps it is because of Manne, Heath and Mitchell. Whatever their understanding of the music, they are more than sympathetic and
enthusiastic.

Manne seems to me to understand least in that he speaks in
the notes of being "free" in this music, but plays, at least in
his solo on *Lorraine* and behind Cherry on *Turnaround,* almost carelessly. Both bassists *think* tonally, of course. Heath
carries a heavy rhythmic and emotional burden beautifully;
one can feel his enthusiasm in every note. He seems to grab
onto a tonal area but when he does stray from it, he does it
almost boldly. That is in contrast to Mitchell who is, as one
would expect, more interested in lyric melody per se. He is
more conservative about leaving tonality, as if he had to work
his way *through* intervals before leaving them.

Don Cherry's problems as an improviser so far are ideas
themselves; certainly not stating them. I think his solo on *Tears*
would have its logic for any ears, and his use of the theme
melody itself on his *Giggin'* solo might be an excellent introduction to how this music goes.

Ornette seems to be just the opposite. It is curious to hear even musicians say that he "plays anything that pops into his head; it doesn't matter." Of course what pops into his head includes a lot, and he may try out most of it, as he certainly should. But again, of course, it does, or it will, matter. (But don't forget that what pops into *most* people's heads is old Louis Armstrong, Lester Young or Charlie Parker phrases.) He solos last on *Turnaround;* perhaps it is the relative conservatism of all that has preceded him, but he starts with an interpolation of *Do I Love You* (he seldom interpolates I am glad to say) and is quite abrupt and startling in the way that he breaks down that conservative atmosphere. But soon there is an area of rhythm and melody that he has outlined and is exploring.

It seems to me that every valid innovation in jazz (by which I chiefly mean Armstrong and Parker) has had a rhythmic basis. (And every attempt at innovation that failed did not.) A couple of years ago there seemed two possibilities. There was Coltrane's way of accenting and phrasing his short notes which seemed to want to subdivide Parker's eighth-note rhythm into sixteenths. The other was the very free reorganization of rhythm and meter of Monk, most strikingly used in that *Bags' Groove* solo. (It was in Rollins too and, as Dick Katz once said, something very like it seemed to be in Lester Young's later work.) Rhythmic subdivision seems possible in Ornette's work, but free meters seem far more likely. They certainly put fewer inhibitions on melody. Of course this is not a "finished" music, nor is what one can hear now from the Coleman quartet "finished" improvising, nor has anyone suggested that it is. Hearing this music now is like hearing Armstrong *before* Chicago or hearing Parker *in* Kansas City—perhaps not even like that, since what Coleman is working on represents in a sense an even more radical departure from established convention.

Coleman's group is bound to attract that curious fringe that automatically wants whatever is "new" and those to whom any outpourings of the intuition or the unconscious are automatically "art." For the rest of us it is a question of hearing a group passionately, receptively and effectively working out something very, very important and, even now, very beautiful. One may regret that these men take jazz beyond tonality before jazz had completely absorbed those resourceful and enriching inversions that are standard equipment to the classical musician. Perhaps jazz has refused to accept these inversions and has rushed through European harmony in only sixty years because, as George Russell says, it never really was a tonal-harmonic music in the first place.

But who will play Ellington to this Armstrong?

It is absurd to ask at this point, of course. And I would not ask if I did not wonder if George Russell might be the man to make such a contribution.

MARTIN WILLIAMS

Ornette Coleman: CHANGE OF THE CENTURY, Atlantic 1327. Ornette Coleman, *alto;* Don Cherry, *trumpet;* Charlie Haden, *bass;* Billy Higgins, *drums.*
Ramblin'; Free; Face of the Bass; Forerunner; Bird Food; Una Muy Bonita; Change of the Century.

FEW JAZZMEN HAVE the fertility of invention to write seven originals for a single LP, and even fewer have the sense of musical direction to record an LP entirely made up of their own originals. Duke, Monk, Mingus; how many more?

At least three of the seven tunes (compositions?) here are highly accomplished and intriguing. *Ramblin'* is a good hillbilly-flavored jazz tune, an interesting study in contrasting meters, and an effective display piece for a virtuoso bass player. *Free* is almost no more than a boogie-woogie bass line, but who would have expected those quarter notes on the beat, mostly broken chords, to be played to give that effortless soaring quality? It's certainly a horn player's conception, rather than that of a pianist or a manuscript paper writer. *Una Muy Bonita* may be the most melodic and accessible of Coleman's tunes so far, and the contrast between the charming folkish melody and the bass figure is typical of Coleman's ability to get a great variety of texture from this quartet.

Ramblin' is probably the only unqualified success on the

record, theme, ensembles, solos and all. Coleman's solo, which emerges so smoothly from the head, may not be on changes, but it is a model of logical construction and a fine example of how his solos work. Listen to the way he works with fragments of the theme, pokes them, nudges them, extends them into a run or a single, long, sustained note, rephrases the notes on the beat like Pete Brown, and then shifts his time conception to give his playing relief and variety. Cherry opens his solo with the same motif which also closes Ornette's solo; here, and elsewhere, he uses a lot of material in his solo that Ornette has already worked over, which may help continuity, but also may be a sign of an overdependence on Ornette's vision that does not necessarily speak well for the future of this young man's playing. Haden's bass solo, mostly in double stops, shows us that he is technically a masterful bassist, and also suggests how much wider and more rewarding his sources are than those of most jazz bass players; he may be the first bassist since Wilbur Ware to move away from the Blanton-Pettiford-Brown axis. And Billy Higgins' very original cymbal accompaniment to the bass solo is a delight for energy, steadiness, and variety.

Most of the other tunes are rather badly played, especially the ensemble parts. *Bird Food* is an exception, but it's just one of those synthetic Charlie Parker tunes concocted out of some of Bird's favorite intervals and rhythmic figures, and routined like his quintet recordings with Miles, improvised bridge and all. Cherry's fine solo, after the first chorus, seems to show the kind of music in which he still feels most at ease.

The head to *Change of the Century* is played especially badly—ragged enough to sound full of unintended dissonances and the kind of clashes of overtones that Coleman has used deliberately and well elsewhere. Even Ornette's solo sounds a little ill at ease with the tempo, and Cherry's is practically chaotic. But most of Ornette's solo work, especially on *Ramblin'* and *Free*, should remind us that he is a highly traditional player; that he loves some of the strong and simple rhythmic ideas of the thirties as much as he does the more complex and subtle conceptions that Parker introduced. I cannot imagine most players of his generation using some of those patterns that are so far from the hip and the modern. His solo on *Forerunner*, with its extreme dynamic contrasts, and that ascending phrase, sharply increasing in volume, that almost explodes at the listener, shows a love of contrast that runs through all his music.

Next to Ornette, the date is Haden's. On *Ramblin'*, *Bonita*, and the rather commonplace tune called *Face of the Bass*, he shows a vivid and dramatic talent in his solo work, and his accompaniments are always simple, always fitting, always uncluttered. Higgins swings throughout, and in several places responds to the other players in a way that one does not always find in drummers, especially young drummers.

This is Coleman's fourth LP in less than two years, and the ragged ensemble work suggests that several of the tunes were recorded too soon. Of course the compositions (tunes?) should have been recorded, and of course the session did take place last October before the group began working regularly, but is Ornette falling into the easy trap of becoming bored with the tunes himself before the group has really gotten comfortable playing them? And is he in the danger, since his solos are free of the normal disciplines of repetitive chord structure, of making all his solos too much in the same pattern? There seems to be evidence in this recording for both suspicions. I hope I'm wrong, for this musician, and his collaborators, have a completeness in their approach to all the aspects of their music which is both rare and promising.

Incidentally, Ornette has said (in a recent issue of *Metronome*) that none of his recordings have been doctored by splicing in the studio. This is not entirely accurate, for one of the trumpet solos on this LP was spliced in from another take. I was there.

HSIO WEN SHIH

The Symposium

by Joe Goldberg

Joe Goldberg may have had Ornette Coleman in mind in "The Symposium." We have suspected as much.

WHEN THE TRUE jazz innovator comes along, every six weeks or so, fearful obstacles lie in his path; too much publicity combined with what Jon Hendricks so tellingly called "lack of acceptance," and the like. This magazine would like to spare the true creative artist such indignities, since too often they represent mere opportunism on the part of the jazz press and other elements in the jazz business. Therefore, when we first heard about Ansel Jones, we made an unprecedented move. All the important jazz writers were contacted, a plane was chartered (at this time we should like to acknowledge with deep appreciation the assistance of the Fjord Foundation), and a picnic lunch was packed by the ladies auxiliary, directed by the Baroness Nica. We all set forth for Beaumont, Texas, where the Ansel Jones Duo was playing.

After that junket, copies of his new LP YESTERDAY IS NOT THE ANSWER were distributed. And the reflections and opinions of all of the country's most important critics on Ansel Jones were recorded. In this way, the reader can compare all the conflicting opinions on Ansel Jones, side by side, handy for reference. And the jazz writers save themselves quite a bit of trouble, for they all discovered Ansel Jones at the same time, and therefore have no axes to grind.

But first, a word about Ansel Jones. He is a shy man, and one is instantly impressed by his deep sincerity, his need to make music, and his love of jazz. As Ansel himself said to us

—we were seated around a long table at the Texas Dog Bar and Grill, where Ansel's group was playing, and Ansel, warmed by the presence of so many men who believe in what he is trying to say, relaxed his ordinarily Spartan rule against verbalization—"I am deeply sincere. I love jazz, and I need to make music."

Much of Ansel's life in music is explained by his instrument, a strange, ungainly copper trumpet that he carries with him affectionately at all times. All his life, Ansel had wanted to become a serious composer, and had saved his pennies so that someday he might attend the Julliard School of Music. The day after his application to Julliard had been refused, Ansel walked calmly into the metal working shop at the high school, carrying the pennies he had been saving. Without a word, he tossed them into one of the huge cauldrons there. By night he had melted them down and had forged from the molten copper a trumpet.

He and pianist Porter Smith form the entire group, Naturally, their exclusion of the conventional rhythm section raised several questions, and for the answer to those, we turned to Porter Smith, who can be much more articulate about his music than can Ansel. "We don't need no rhythm," he said.

There you have it; the background of the Jones-Smith Duo. What follows is a cross-section of opinion from some of the finest jazz commentators in the world. It's all fiction, of course, but then so is most criticism.

Ralph Gleason (of *Down Beat* and the nationally syndicated "Lively Arts"): I like this group, and anybody who doesn't had just better not ever talk to me again, that's all. Their music has been analyzed in too much detail elsewhere for me to repeat the obvious here, but just let me say one thing. The act of melting down pennies to make a trumpet, in defiance of the federal law against defacing currency, is a nose-thumbing gesture of the artist against authority that shows a kind of courage I have only found in the poetry of Jon Hendricks and the humor of Lenny Bruce. And if you don't hear that parallel in the music, as well as overtones of Allen Ginsberg, Dylan

Thomas and Paul Klee, then your ears are stopped up by prejudice, and I don't want to have anything to do with you.

Whitney Balliett (of *The New Yorker*): Ansel Jones, a thin, diffident young man who resembles a twelve-stringed lute placed on its end at an angle of seventy-three degrees, is getting music from his self-smelted horn that may radically change the shape of jazz. In a typical solo, he will start with a sort of agonized laziness, as if he were awakening from a dream caused by having eaten too much welsh rarebit the night before, and then, in about the third chorus, he will, in a series of short, splatting notes that give the effect of a catsup bottle hit once too often on its end, abruptly switch into a fast tempo that belies the furry bumbling that preceded it. All this time, his pianist, Porter Smith, a torpid ellipse of a man, lays down a firm, inky foundation that anticipates the leader's meanderings with the precision of a Seeing Eye Dog weaving its way through a Coney Island beach crowd on the Fourth of July. In one composition, *Duplicity*, the two men hit the same note simultaneously midway through the second bridge, and it had the shattering emotional impact of two old friends meeting by chance after years of aimless wandering.

Gene Lees (then editor of *Down Beat*): I'm not as friendly with Ansel Jones as I am with Quincy and some of the other guys, but some of the things they play remind me of tunes I've heard in my extensive collection of Hindemith and Stravinsky records. I suppose the critics will say they use counterpoint, because critics like that word, but they don't. They use fragmentation of theme.

Martin Williams: It is impossible to write about the music of Ansel Jones without using the word "artist." His compositions are five-strain rondos with the fourth strain omitted (ABACAE), and, in using this approach, he might seem to incorporate the sense of form that had previously been notable in only the work of, say, a Jelly Roll Morton, a Duke Ellington, a John Lewis, a Thelonious Monk. But Jones has, in the most natural way in the world, gone one step beyond the work of these masters. He has omitted the fourth strain. (A strain, it should be explained at this point, is an identifying feature of the work of Morton, roughly corresponding to a riff in the Ellington band of the forties, an episode in the work of John Lewis, or a theme in the compositions of Thelonious Monk.) Omitting the fourth strain now seems an amazingly simple step to have made, but it takes an Ansel Jones to make that step. A man might deserve the title of artist for having done much less. But there is still more to this man's achievement. In the improvised passages, the strains—all four of them—are abandoned in favor of blues or *I Got Rhythm*. Perhaps a word of explanation is in order here. If I abandon my strain, I am then not playing the song I wrote, which gives me enormous freedom, although it plays hell with my discipline.

John S. Wilson (of *The New York Times* and *High Fidelity*): I do not understand the music of Ansel Jones, but he definitely shares a place with those men who have left us an identifiable body of music—Morton, Ellington, Lewis and Monk. In his execution, he gets a tweedy sound that is aptly suited to the cordovan tones produced by his pianist, Porter Smith. It will be interesting to see what their next album produces. I have not mentioned the other members of the group because there are no other members. This suggests a similarity to other duos —Don Shirley and Mitchell-Ruff—that can be misleading.

Ira Gitler (of *Down Beat*): I like half of this record, the Porter Smith half. Porter Smith is playing jazz. He has that old Horace thing going. But Ansel Jones, who sounds like Miles Davis (major influence), with slight overtones of Don Jacoby and the merest hint of Rafael Mendez, is not playing jazz. He is playing a copper trumpet. Nobody ever played jazz on a copper trumpet before. I don't think I trust it.

Bill Coss (then editor of *Metronome*): This review is not appearing in the new *Metronome*, which contains many interesting features and departments, such as record reviews, notes on where the bands are playing, and a crossword puzzle page, because we are all getting together, in the interest of jazz, and telling you, straight out and no holds barred, what we think of Ansel Jones. That, I think, is the true spirit of jazz. We stand right up there and tell you what we think, regardless of the pain, agony, torment and soul-tearing frustration of our inner selves. We are laying it on the line. And that is what jazz is. It is more than just music. It is freedom, irrepressible good spirits, a bottle of Scotch and your girl on Saturday night, and, yes, it is those here-it-is-Sunday-morning-and-where-did-the-night-go-blues, too; it is all of that, and more, too; it is the jeering laugh at the policeman's swinging club because you know you're clean, buddy, so what the hell?

Because of space limitations, my review of Ansel Jones will not appear in this column, but it will be in next month's issue of the new *Metronome,* along with a piercing analysis of Charles Mingus and a term paper on the role of the coffee house in jazz.

Symphony Sid (jazz disc jockey): Ansel Jones is another of the great gentlemen of jazz who has been so swinging over the years. We like his music because it is Progressive and American, and he is appearing on our great swinging show at the Coliseum along with many of the other great gentlemen of jazz who have been so swinging over the years.

Leonard Feather (of *Down Beat, et al.*): Although Ansel Jones has not yet done many of the things that we have come to know are equated with jazz greatness—he has not taken a blindfold test (*Down Beat*), been mentioned in the *Encyclopedia of Jazz* (Horizon Press) or been recorded on the Metrojazz label—he shows a certain amount of talent. However, *is* talent truly a criterion?

Nat Hentoff: It is important that the world become aware of what is going on in Beaumont, Texas. As the plane crossed the Mason-Dixon line, I noticed that certain of the passengers had been given containers with a large black "N" stenciled on them. Is this the America of Dwight MacDonald? That night, at the Texas Dog, I could hear little of the music over the clacking of my typewriter (I was writing a profile on Phil Foster for the *Daily Forward*), but I did hear one shattering fragment of *belles-lettres* that moved me deeply.

After the above comments were turned in, there was a round-table discussion on the work of Ansel Jones. Highlights are reproduced below.

Feather: What do you think about this fellow, Ed?

George Crater (of *Down Beat's* pseudonymous humor column): Don't call me by my right name.

Williams: It certainly is a relief from all the blues-based-pseudo-funk we've been used to.

Jon Hendricks (of Lambert, Hendricks, & Ross): Well, man like, that's soul, y'know?

Gleason: You tell 'em, Jon, baby.

Lees: I think anything that extends the area of jazz is welcome. At *Down Beat,* we're going to sponsor a jazz booth at the next Conference of Christians and Jews, and get a delegation from Lexington to come and swear they never played jazz.

Wilson: I'd like to get back to what Martin was saying. Martin, how do you distinguish between funk and pseudo-funk? They employ the same harmonies, don't they?

Hendricks: One's got soul, baby, and one hasn't.

Gleason: You tell 'em Jon, baby. Isn't this a wonderful kid? The Sammy Davis, Jr. of jazz.

Gitler: That sounds like something Lenny Bruce might have said.

Gleason: Where do you think I got it?

Hentoff: Lenny Bruce is a devastating commentator on our contemporary social scene.

Coss: That's what jazz is. A devastating comment on our social scene.

Balliett: Lenny Bruce reminds me of an overturned milk truck.

Wilson: What do you mean by that?

Balliett: If you can't see how Lenny Bruce is like an overturned milk truck, I don't see how I can explain it to you.

Williams: I thought we were talking about Ansel Jones. It is very important that we all decide what position we are going to take on this man.

All: Let's ask Cannonball for an opinion. He's a musician. He'll know.

Two Reviews of "Third Stream" Music

by Martin Williams

By now the term "third stream" has been so thoroughly abused that it needs clarification. It has nothing to do with the use of occasional effects—a blue note here, a rhythm there —that we know in the work of Stravinsky, Ravel, Milhaud, etc. It also has nothing to do with a jazz musician's effort to incorporate classical form into jazz. "Third stream" pieces try to combine authentic jazz improvisation with written classical forms. The term itself was coined by Gunther Schuller, and he has said that certain pieces by John Lewis, William Russo, Werner Heider, and others also belong to the "third stream."

I Nice Distinctions at Town Hall (1959)

THE JOINT Town Hall concert by the Modern Jazz Quartet and the Beaux Arts, one of the country's best string quartets, involved a new work each by John Lewis and Gunther Schuller written for both groups and developments by the MJQ of themes from the new movie score for *Odds Against Tomorrow*. It also involved one's early apprehension about just what kind of music that was going to be.

The best way to begin is on the more familiar ground of what each group did separately.

A lovely performance of Haydn's Opus 74, No. 1 by the Beaux Arts Quartet could teach us a lot. We do a lot of talking about group integration and responsiveness; these men live it, musically and visually. We also talk about jazz as the "living" music; this music is as alive to these men as anything the MJQ plays is to its members. There has been a lot of talk since the twenties about classicists having cut themselves off from the dance. Not only in the minuet but throughout this piece, these men were more directly in touch with dancing than half of the jazzmen, including "mainstreamers," now playing in New York. And the complexity of texture that four instruments achieve in their idiom should be a challenge to everybody.

The MJQ finished the evening with a program that somehow seemed overlong. To put second things first, I do not think that the group should play *It Don't Mean a Thing* and *Fontessa* (now the third section of a three-part *The Comedy,* which is not sustained) on the same program; their similarity is apt to make the latter seem a merely trapped-up version of the former, which it is not. A new piece, *Pyramid* (a gospel-like blues composed by Ray Brown in tribute after a Mahalia Jackson concert), seemed more interesting as performed, however imperfectly, at Music Inn a month earlier. This time the tempo was constant, but the rhythm shifted from parade (impeccable press-rolls from Connie Kay) to church (Connie beautifully suggesting triplet hand clapping). The earlier rhythmic structure involved twice doubling the tempo, then twice halving it again (hence the title) but with no consequent disunity in the structure or emotional flow of the piece. The two themes from *Odds Against Tomorrow* were called *The Caper* and *Cut No. 9.* I had better first repeat my conviction that, although jazz film scoring may give needed work to good musicians, it cannot sustain really creative people nor rally any art, because film scoring by its nature must be a self-effacing craft. It is not my purpose to review the Harry Belafonte film, but I will remark that it seemed to me a very skillful, very entertaining, essentially trashy thriller, with an either naïve or corrupt moral which I can only interpret to say that race prejudice prevents bank robberies. John Lewis wrote what is in context a frequently superior, ingeniously unified film score; he did not, as in *No Sun in Venice,* merely accompany scenes with fragments of Quartet performances.

In concert, the Quartet simply takes the melodies heard in

the movie as point-of-departure. As such, they do not seem to me among the best things in the Quartet's book. But at least two of the members of the MJQ are surpassing themselves. Connie Kay is becoming (as everyone should know by now) one of the most resourceful and skillful drummers in jazz. And Percy Heath played with a deep personal involvement and imagination.

All of which brings us to the center of the program: the two works for both groups. Everyone said that John Lewis' *Sketch* was well titled; actually it was barely a sketch and just a bit more than a trifle. But a very successful trifle and one based on the same kind of eloquently simple melody that his best pieces have. It demonstrated something perhaps learned in that unfortunate encounter with the Stuttgart Orchestra last year, as if Lewis had said, "Very well, these men phrase differently. Can I write a piece in which I do *not* try to make them accent our way, but let them use their idiom while we use ours, and still maintain unity?" The answer seems to be that he could, at least with a sketch.

Schuller's piece carried the same principal further. The first consideration with Gunther Schuller's *Conversation* seems to me not facile talk about "hybrids," because for the very first time in such efforts one knew that one had heard a real composition, not an attempt but a musical work. I think the secret of its success lies in his having faced frankly and squarely the differences in quality and implicit emotional attitude between the two idioms and made those differences the basis of his piece. Of course, Schuller did not (as have so many composers of pompous "symphonic jazz" nonsense from the twenties on) try to recast the most obvious and banal concert hall devices and structures in jazzy phrases sprinkled with blue notes—nor would he. He is not Morton Gould—nor Graas or Macero. But neither did he (as in his *Transformation*) try to integrate or gradually ally the idioms. He seems to have said, "These musics are different in several ways: they sound different, and emotionally they look at things differently; let's meet that difference." To outline this work briefly and with simplifications, he introduced strings (with some exceptionally skillful percussive and harmonic complements from the MJQ) in his own atonal idiom to build gradually to one of the most melodic yet believable pitches of tension I have heard outside of Bartok, to relieve it abruptly by some fairly free and relaxed improvising by the Quartet. Soon, as the MJQ builds its own creative emotions, the strings re-enter to reintroduce the tension beneath them, and gradually an interplay brings about a rather John-Lewis-like resolution to finish the piece.

Faced with a piece of music like this one, I wonder if it is not best to lay aside, at least for the moment, the question of whether or not such things—such "third stream" performances —*should* be done. They are obviously going to be done. And that night in Town Hall I had the feeling that for the first time they were being done well. I knew, at least, that the jazz was there honestly and unashamedly as what it is, and its implicit nature was being used creatively. I wanted to know what kind of music such a success would lead to.

II Full Face (1960)

ACCORDING TO THE program notes, the final concert in Charles Schwartz's wholly commendable series of "Jazz Profiles" at the Circle in the Square was to present the "Jazz Compositions" of Gunther Schuller. To quote Schuller's introduction, the music would "show the various possible ways of combining jazz and classical music." Neither statement is a really accurate description of what one heard that evening, and the second turned out to be nearly nonsense.

The participating musicians were Ornette Coleman (alto); Bill Evans (piano); Scott La Faro and Buell Neidlinger (bass); Sticks Evans and Paul Cohen (drums); Eric Dolphy (alto, flute, bass clarinet); Barry Galbraith (guitar); Eddie Costa (vibraphone); Robert DiDomenica (flute); and the Contemporary String Quartet: Charles Tregar and Joseph Schor (violins); John Garvey (viola); and Joseph Tekula (cello).

The evening was decidedly a credit to everyone involved: the composer, the jazz musicians, and the string quartet. It was, from beginning to end, an evening of music and (let's be frank about this) not like many a jazz concert where something really interesting might happen one minute in ten. If the strings did have some trouble with jazz phrasing at times, it is less a discredit to them than it is a reflection of a situation in American music—a situation which, to their credit, they have undertaken to change.

An evening of music, a constantly enjoyable and enlightening one and, I believe, a very important one.

Abstraction No. 1, with Ornette Coleman and the string quartet as major participants, was the most "classical" piece: a jazz musician improvising as part of a mirror, serial composition in the contemporary idiom; a building of textures and rhythms to a climax, then an exact reversal. *Abstraction* was performed twice, once before the intermission, once after. Coleman's grasp of the piece was so thorough that he was able to find his way in it not only with two different improvisations but in two different ways. On the first performance he improvised *within* the textures (an early Mozart concerto would be a good analogy); on the second against and in a parallel foil to them (as in a Beethoven concerto, to continue the analogy).

Almost opposite was *Little Blue Devil* a section of Schuller's concert work of last year programmed on pictures by Paul Klee—a written "classical" composition using jazz form and phrasing.

Transformation, the earliest work heard, and *Conversation,* from last year's concert by the Modern Jazz and Beaux Arts quartets, take opposite approaches. The former gradually transforms classical writing into jazz improvising, and back. Despite another excellent solo by Bill Evans, the approach still seems to me to deny the force and uniqueness of each idiom and the alliance seems an almost sentimental one. *Conversation,* as I have said before, *uses* the conflict and tension between the two idioms, their ways of phrasing, and their separate virtues, as its basis. It seems to me a success—and perhaps the beginning of wisdom. Bill Evans achieved the very difficult task of both preceding and following a good solo by Eddie Costa and still giving the whole improvisational section continuity and wholeness. He did it, chiefly by using the same musical ideas in both his solos, but on his return he incorporates all the tension that Costa had built in the meanwhile.

In a rather different way, *Progression in Tempo* seems to me also a failure. Perhaps I am judging a performance and not a composition, but a good deal of the writing somehow seemed Ravel or Gershwinesque in effect, rather like those fay, bluesy pieces of the twenties. Costa and Evans were a contrast, of course. Also, it is true that jazz groups do increase tempos and that, although they do not always do it intentionally, it can be exciting. However, jazz musicians do it as a response to what is happening in the .music. To impose it from without is a different matter. (But does Schuller know Will Ezell's *Barrell House Woman?*)

The two other pieces on the program were the most important. The four *Variants on a Theme of John Lewis* used *Django*. Barry Galbraith's statement of the theme was lovely, but for the first time in the evening there was a marring sluggishness in the string quartet's playing, and I doubt that Schuller wanted the second section played with that slight schmaltz that John Garvey gave it. I also suspect that Eric Dolphy could have used more space for his solo; players his age just aren't used to pacing brief solos. Schuller's various handlings of that wonderful bass figure were a marvel, and its simple effectiveness is the strongest temptation to put it to banal use, as other versions of *Django* have shown.

Variants on a Theme of Thelonious Monk was four variations of *Criss Cross*. It is my chief reason for using the word "nonsense" above, for Schuller's "arrangement" of Monk's theme seems to me in no sense a classical work. It is a jazz work and, I think, a splendid one. Whatever the work may owe in form to Schuller's other life is quite assimilated; it certainly has no air of the "experiment" or the practice room.

In the first section, Ornette Coleman improvised first and he used Monk's melody as his basis in a way I wish Monk could have heard. Bill Evans entered behind him to prepare for the second soloist, Dolphy (on bass clarinet); then Costa. Each soloist began for several bars under the previous improviser in a kind of overlapping, free polyphony—and hearing Ornette Coleman and Eric Dolphy improvising simultaneously on a Monk theme was, in itself, more than most jazz concerts have to offer. The second variant was slow and got a somber mood from Monk's patterns I would never have thought appropriate or even possible. Coleman embellished written parts. The third went largely to Dolphy and Scott La Faro, and their excellent improvising included a wonderful spontaneous cadenza. The final section began with a Monkish rebuilding of the theme by the strings and included solos by Galbraith (who seems to me a better player than improviser), Dolphy on flute, and Coleman. Again they reflected the creative enthusiasm with which every musician participated in the evening. What I have said here about this *Variants* on *Criss Cross* is merely a few notes based on hearing one performance. It is, I believe, a major work (based on Monk's already major piece!) not only within the jazz idiom, but legitimately extending it. If I have any reservations, it would be that the writing for the strings in the first section seemed a bit thick for so rhythmically provocative a theme, but, again, that may have been a (quite forgivable) matter of performance.

As I began by saying, it was an evening of music, and one did not have to wait out nine minutes for the one when something really happened. Of course, except for the work of a handful of the really brilliant improvisers, the only protection jazz has ever found against the possibility of failure in those other nine minutes is the one Don Redman gave it so well: get something good down on paper. It has been ten years since something this important for a group of this size was to go down on paper. And thanks particularly to Coleman, Dolphy, La Faro, and to Schuller—and to Monk—it has as important a relevance to the next ten years as to the past.

Ray Charles

by Henry Woodfin

Ray Charles became famous as a rock-and-roll singer, and it has readily been acknowledged that his first efforts were imitations of the old King Cole Trio. Jazz musicians of almost every school and style not only loved and respected his music but have also heard in its forceful spontaneity a part of their own heritage which some felt had been neglected.

Ray Charles: WHAT'D I SAY, Atlantic 8029. Ray Charles, *vocals* and *piano;* David Newman, *tenor;* on *What Kind of Man Are You* the vocalist is Mary Ann Fisher; other personnel unidentified.
What'd I Say; Jumpin' in the Mornin'; You Be My Baby; Tell Me How Do You Feel; What Kind of Man Are You; Rockhouse; Roll with My Baby; Tell All the World About You; My Bonnie; That's Enough.

Ray Charles: THE GENIUS OF RAY CHARLES, Atlantic 1312. On tracks 1, 3, & 6: Ray Charles, *vocals* and *piano;* Clark Terry, Ernie Royal, Joe Newmann, Snookie Young, Marcus Belgrave, John Hunt, *trumpets;* Melba Liston, Quentin Jackson, Thomas Mitchell, Al Gray, *trombones;* Frank Wess, *flute, alto saxophone, tenor saxophone;* Marshall Royal, *alto saxophone;* Paul Gonsalves, Zoot Sims, David Newman, *tenor saxophones;* Charlie Fowlkes, Bennie Crawford, *baritone saxophones;* Freddie Greene, *guitar;* Eddie Jones, Edgar Willis, *basses;* Charlie Persip, Teagle Fleming, *drums.*
On tracks 2, 4, & 5: Billy Mitchell replaces Zoot Sims.
On tracks 7-12: Ray Charles, *vocals* and *piano;* Allen Hanlon, *guitar;* Wendell Marshall, *bass;* Ted Sommer, *drums;* orchestra conducted by Harry Lookofsky.
On track 12 only: Bob Brookmeyer, *trombone.*
Let the Good Times Roll; It Had to Be You; Alexander's Ragtime Band; Two Years of Torture; When Your Lover Has Gone; 'Deed I Do; Just for a Thrill; You Won't Let Me Go; Tell Me You'll Wait for Me; Don't Let the Sun Catch You Cryin'; Am I Blue; Come Rain or Come Shine.

ONE OF THE most interesting recent events in jazz has been the rise of Ray Charles from comparative obscurity in the world of rhythm-and-blues to a position on the jazz scene. Charles has been acclaimed as singer, instrumentalist, and band leader in favorable terms indeed. The major part of this attention has been paid to Charles as a singer. Charles's vocals are of about four kinds. There are the "gospel blues" which, artistically at least, make up the most important part of his repertoire. But Charles is also a juke box success, and we find him working with a more popular blues form which uses the same gospel elements but in which the material is handled as rather sophomoric love songs which apparently appeal to a teen-age audience. Charles also works occasionally with purely comic songs which he develops without gospel fervor. Finally, he has recently begun to use popular songs and ballads, using only slight gospel overtones.

Of course, gospel music uses many of the stylistic devices common to both jazz proper and to the blues (blue notes, syncopation, antiphonal patterns, etc.). But gospel music is devotional and exhortatory; it is both an act of devotion and a call to devotion by the faithful or saved to those not so fortunate. It celebrates the joy and exaltation of the singer in salvation or the promise of salvation. Despite all they have in common gospel music differs profoundly from the blues and jazz. Ray Charles's blues singing combines the religiously exalted fervor of the gospel singer with the strictly secular concerns of the blues singer. A Ray Charles blues performance is completely different in meaning from a gospel performance, yet it is filled with similar emotional overtones. In many of his most startling works Charles virtually makes an incantation of the song and simulates the spiritual possession which is a part of gospel. But the quality of the possession invoked by Charles is sexual and even a part of his concern with the worldly side of sexual relations. Little wonder that Big Bill Broonzy should express shock over Charles's work.

Many of Charles's gospel blues songs (*Tell All the World About You* here and *I Got a Woman* and *Talkin' About You* from his earlier LPs, Atlantic 8006 & 8025) are virtually parodies of gospel songs. This element plus the jubilant hotness of the performances at their best make a startling, appealing, and moving combination.

The quintessence of Charles's gospel blues comes on his Newport recording of *A Fool for You* (Atlantic 1289). Here he steadily works into a vocal frenzy and then a vocal incantation with a series of howls and cries which, in the context of the song, present an exacerbated eroticism. I know of no more startling blues performance on record than this. Many of his other gospel blues recordings tend in this direction, but only the Newport recording arrives at this limit beyond which such an art cannot go; his desperately reiterated monosyllables act out the exaltation and despair of total erotic possession. It is the zenith of this side of Charles's art.

In his more popular material such as *Ain't That Love, Drown in My Own Tears,* and *Funny (But I Still Love You)* on the earlier LPs there is a similar procedure; the only difference is that these songs are more sentimental in presentation and pedestrian in content, and Charles's hints at the style of his more notable efforts do not break the cloying sentiments.

Of all the gospel blues LPs by Charles the current one is the least impressive. Only *Tell All the World About You* and *That's Enough* are comparable to his previous successes. The other numbers range from the banality of *You Be My Baby* to the attempt in *My Bonnie* to blue *My Bonnie Lies Over the Ocean.* Surprisingly enough, *Jumpin' in the Mornin'* attempts to emulate Joe Turner, but the results seem glib and unconvincing.

A minor part of Charles's work is represented by *Roll with My Baby* which is like his earlier *Greenbacks* and *Blackjack.* While the material of all these songs is rather slight, they are deftly developed and extremely amusing. *Roll with My Baby* is much less successful than *Greenbacks* which is surely one of the funniest things in the idiom.

The new LP devoted to Charles as a singer of pop songs represents a considerable achievement. Although he strikes me as somewhat unsteady on the first six tracks, where he is backed by a large band, I think he acquits himself well on *Let the Good Times Roll, Two Years of Torture,* and *When Your Lover Has Gone.* The rather perfunctory arrangements by Quincy Jones, Ernie Wilkins, and Al Cohn frame Charles adequately but little more, and the solo work of Paul Gonsalves and David Newman is indifferent. On the remaining six tracks he is backed by—of all things—a string and woodwind section, a choir, and some sentimental arrangements by Ralph Burns. He takes control amazingly and produces work that is nearly continuously interesting. *Don't Let the Sun Catch You Cryin'* in particular is a minor masterpiece which both surprises and gratifies. Of course, it would seem that the blues-tinged material here is well suited to Charles, but he does not really handle it in his gospel manner; he sings in a deceptively simple and straightforward manner which results in a wry, ironic sadness touched with humor. He deftly plays off his interpretation against a schmalzy background which would have overcome a lesser artist. Each of the other numbers has good moments with *You Won't Let Me Go* probably outstanding. As a jazz singer Charles is certainly taking chances working with this sort of material and accompaniment, but an achievement like *Don't Let the Sun Catch You Cryin'* is well worth the risk.

Charles's recorded performances on piano and alto sax range from the funky blues which he produced with Milt Jackson (Atlantic 1279) to the jazz that he plays with his own group on his instrumental LP (Atlantic 1259). Charles is not a remarkable instrumentalist. The LP with Jackson has enough deliberate funkiness so that the listener may doubt its sincerity. I doubt that Charles on piano and alto would have enjoyed the attention he has had were it not for the success of Charles the singer.

The obvious question about Charles is why he should be granted such wide recognition by modern jazzmen. I think the answer can be found in problems that have faced modern jazz since the early fifties and solutions that have been propounded. Charles came to prominence when hard bop did. Hard bop was and is an attempt to fill the gap left by the waning of both bop and cool. The solution, a temporary one

I think, was found in a return to the gospel and blues traditions. With groups such as Horace Silver's and Art Blakey's this school soon became the dominant one. This is not the place for a full examination of the successes and failures of this school, but such a trend does go a long way toward explaining Charles's reputation. In Charles the jazzmen found a singer who was doing in the rhythm-and-blues vein just what they were attempting to do in jazz.

Charles at his best is a remarkable singer. Sometimes the excitement of his gospel blues seems somewhat overworked, nor is his art as emotionally deep and moving as that of a Muddy Waters or a Lightnin' Hopkins. Nevertheless, his best work is direct and thoroughly convincing emotionally. If Charles has decided to work in the popular song medium, it may be only too easy to follow the course of a Nat Cole. However, a number like *Don't Let the Sun Catch You Cryin'* shows the really interesting possibilities; he may be just beginning.

Lightnin' Hopkins: Blues

by Mack McCormack

Mack McCormack is a Houston writer whose knowledge of Lightnin' Hopkins is long-standing and first hand. His essay succinctly exposes the function of modern communal bard that Hopkins and so many other blues singers fulfill.

THERE'S A TINSMITH on Houston's narrow, throbbing West Dallas Street who's watched the shuffling crowds pass his window for more than forty years. He's seen all the great Texas blues minstrels begging up and down the sidewalk.

When the shop first opened, it was the hulking figure of Blind Lemon Jefferson who came with a guitar in one hand, a folding chair in the other, to sit at the corner and moan his songs in a voice like a gasping trombone.

O-o-o-oh! Black snake crawlin' in my room . . .

Between brawls and prison terms Leadbelly spent his time dodging from one bar to another with his twelve-string guitar, singing the ballads and chain gang songs that had just won him a pardon from the Texas Prison System.

Lawd, I been down yonder where the lights burn all night long . . .

Blind Willie Johnson wandered by dangling a tin cup and shouting his blues-patterned spirituals.

When I get to heaven gonna sit and tell,
Tell them angels ring dem bells.

Texas Alexander worked the street with youthful Lonnie Johnson providing the guitar accompaniment.

> *White man born with a veil over his face,*
> *Could see the trouble before it taken place.*

In recent years the undisputed monarch of the street has been a lanky, animated man whose songs are a mixture of the traditional motifs and his own casually made improvisations.

> *If I miss the train, I got a big black horse to ride.*

Like the minstrels before him who've come bubbling out of the East Texas "Piney Woods," his songs speak the esoteric language of the blistering cotton lands and river bottom prisons. The guitar sets the mood, underscores the sharply drawn tales of poverty, gambling, bad men, hard work, and escape. A flow of implike gestures and mocking asides to the circle of listeners makes the songs as personal as an intimate conversation.

> *Well, I come down here with my guitar in my hand,*
> *I'm lookin' for a woman who's lookin' for a man.*

Sam Lightnin' Hopkins is unaware of contemporary jazz-and-poetry; yet he is one of its finest exponents. He lopes through Houston's Negro wards singing about a bus strike, about a fight with his wife, about the evil-doing of the mythical Jack-stropper. He meets a friend out of a job and a moment later a lightly rocking boogie figure sets the background for a broken verse line of patter about the pains of job hunting. After a moment of whispering in some girl's ear, his guitar chops out bitter, ringing crys as he half-talks, half-sings the ironies of being a man in a world full of fickle women. A line can have the blunt stab of T. S. Eliot:

> *You ever see a one-eyed woman cry?*

In another moment Lightnin' can become a playwright,
staging, acting and ad-libbing the dialogue of some spon-
taneously conceived drama. It may be about a vagrant farm
boy coming home from prison, pausing to ask worried questions of a neighbor, and wryly capsuling his own experience:

*Bad on me . . . and you know it was a shame on
everyone else.*

For the greater part of his forty-seven years this has been
Lightnin's contribution to his oddly private society—the dependent but isolated Negro wards of a southern city. He is a
fascinatingly complete man: even the least of his routine
actions seem in tune with the earthy cynicism that characterizes his songs. A man with a tribal sense of belonging to his
culture, he is outside the modern dilemma. Lightnin' the man
is the same as Lightnin' the artist. Rising from a tangle of bed-
clothes in a cheap rented room to breakfast on two bottles of
beer, he's fully attuned to the tragic sense of life. *"Now* is the
time," he's liable to mutter, "any other time and I may be
dead and gone. So I can't help but get up and sing the
blues. . . ."

The essence of Lightnin's art is a special form of autobiography. His songs all have their basis in actual experience
which he recaptures with dramatic gravity and a gift for
succinct detail. At times he generalizes, just as often he simply
reminisces. One such is of a ritual soup prepared for birth-
day parties at his home. ". . . every time the ground cracked,
ole Pa gets a 'tater. Ma says 'Look around here' and there she
stands with a 'mater. . . . They used to call it Bunion Stew."

In both song and conversation Lightnin' often looks back
to his family and life in the Piney Woods: "All my daddy
could do was shoot people and call set—you know, call set
for square dancing and all that? He wasn't nothing, my daddy.
My momma is Frances Hopkins—she's seventy-six years old
now and she always say, 'Sam, I depend on you,' and I always say, 'Momma, you know I'm here.'

"Used to pick cotton, make forty cents a hundred. Times

was kinda hard then. Make fourteen dollars and give my momma seven. There's my sister and two brothers living but I take care of her, go back all the time just to see her. Sundays I'd sing for the church just to make her happy. It was in the church they let me fool with the organ and the piano, and I learned to play them too. I'd sing them sanctified songs but not so much 'cause mostly I'm with the blues.

"When I was eight, nine years old, there wasn't no flour in the barrel and I walked away from there with a guitar slung across my shoulder and a-singin' 'I'm gonna trip this town, and I ain't gonna trip no more.' I'm from up at Leon County —that's about halfway between Houston and Dallas. Fact of the matter, town where I was born is called Centerville because of that. And I was born March 15—you know the government made that day into income tax day—March 15, 1912.

"All them blues-singing people come from up there. Right next to where I'm from it's Limestone County where Blind Lemon is from. Across the Trinity River, it's Houston County and that's where Texas Alexander came from—he was my first cousin. When I was just a little boy I went to hanging around Buffalo, Texas, where all them preachers came together for them association meetings. Blind Lemon, he'd come too and do his kind of preaching and I'd just get up alongside and start playing with him. He never run me off like he did them others who'd try. So I complimented ole Blind Lemon on *I Walk from Dallas, I Walk to Wichita Falls* and *You Ain't Got No Mama Now (Black Snake Moan)*. Just a little kid I was.

"At that time I was working for a white family and they treat me just the same as their own boys. They treat me so good I thought I *was* just as good. They taken me in because I was hungry. I did work around the house and they sent me to school and all. Then I didn't know about things; it was later I found out I wasn't supposed to be as good as white people. Yeah, I was half grown before I found out about how some people'd call you 'son of a bitch' or 'nigger' and it didn't mean nothing. Other people'd say the same words and it'd mean you something lower'n animals. So I took to living off gambling and my singing—never had nothing to do with people that call me 'boy' and then wait for me to say 'yessuh.'

"I stay with my own people. I have all my fun, and I have all my trouble with them. Trouble, yeah. One time I had to cut a man that kept foolin' with me and that put me in the county farm up at Houston County. Several times I had them chains around my legs for stuff I'd got into. Another time—it was the night before I was supposed to go into the army—I was in a gambling game and I took an old boy's money. That fool waited outside for me and when I came out he slipped a grizzly knife right in close to my heart. That took care of the army. I laid up in that Jeff Davis hospital and made a song about all the men going across the water, all the women staying home with me.

"I been married nine times and every one of them gals I stayed with has a song I made up about her . . . Katie Mae, Ida, Glory Bee. I ran a little policy around town, had me a secret gambling place, maybe even had a few money women on the line, but I gave up all that when I started recording. Recorded here in Houston, out in California, once in New York. Don't you know that's a lot of records? But mostly I got cheated out of my royalties. One time I got $5,100 royalties but most of the time I didn't get nothing. Once it was $2,500 I was supposed to get and didn't. I was gonna get a lawyer on it, but he was here, and he couldn't do nothing out there. Plenty people cheated me, singing my songs. All them songs, I made 'em up. Make up a song about everything that happens. The time I was in Los Angeles I sang them *My California* and the time they called me to New York I sang 'I come a long way from Texas to shake · glad hands with you. . . .' "

Lightnin's recording career is dotted with songs reflecting his highly private moods. A hang-over turned into *Lightnin' Don't Feel Well* and a personal phobia became *Airplane Blues*. He refuses to sing one song of protest, *Tim Moore's Farm*, because after its release on the now defunct Gold Star label

Mr. Moore's brothers paid Lightnin' a visit. His most famous composition is a narrative of a woman's costly attempts to have her hair straightened. *Short-Haired Woman* typifies Lightnin's orphic-mannered handling of subjects and problems close to the heart of his environment.

I went to make a swing out with my woman
And a "rat" fell from her head like one from a burning barn.

Lacking the guile and aggressive ambition of others who have been led far afield by rock and roll, Lightnin' has never been a success in the terms understood by the music industry. Despite his nearly two hundred recordings (scattered on Aladdin, Gold Star, Modern, Score, Jax, Sittin' In, Herald, RPM, Decca, TNT, Harlem, Chart, Ace, and Mercury) only glimpses of his personality are to be found in these sides. Recording directors have consistently forced tasteless material, amplified guitars, and heavy-handed drummers on these sessions.

He first came to the attention of the music business just after World War II when a virtual pipeline to the West fed Texas artists to Los Angeles record companies, shaping the experimental models of what is now rock and roll: a form of the blues designed by sound engineers for the thump and screech acoustics of a juke box. Aladdin records asked a Houston businesswoman to locate an authentic country blues artist (Capitol Records had recently recorded Leadbelly and the other labels were suspecting a trend). She found Texas Alexander and Lightnin' on Houston's Dowling Street. Alexander had just been released from prison and was eager to resume his recording career (sixty-four sides on the early Okeh and Vocalion labels) which had been cut short by his conviction. Making a good story out of a sordid incident and trying to ease the woman's fear of Alexander, Lightnin' told her the man had been sent to prison for one of his records about "she got box-back nitties and great noble thighs, she works under cover with a boar hog's eye." But the lady refused to have anything to do with the aging blues singer (Alexander died about 1955, forgotten and never again recorded). A trip to Los Angeles was arranged that included Lightnin' and two boogie-style pianists, Amos Milburn and Thunder Smith. A recording session was held at the RKO studios with several movie stars standing around, delighted by Lightnin's raw, traditional art. Song writers who had prepared material in keeping with the current trends despaired as Lightnin' used it merely as a basis for his own impromptu verse. Engineers cursed as two takes of the same title were found to be utterly different songs. While in Los Angeles, he was outfitted with an amplified guitar and a small combo and booked into dance halls. He was saddled with the name Lightnin' because "when I did *Rocky Mountain* where I'm fast with my fingers they said 'we'll call you Lightnin'.' " Refusing to accept the mold into which he was being pressed, and disgusted with the process, Lightnin' returned to Houston's sidewalks.

He has continued to record but refused any other dealings with music industry. His fear of alien territory (the world outside Texas) and his unpredictable streaks of self-assertion have put off subsequent offers of bookings on the rock-and-roll circuit. Lately there have been offers from the concert-hall field which, since the death of Big Bill Broonzy, lacks any comparable artist in the blues idiom. With the urging of friends his qualms have gradually abated and he recently appeared on the Houston Folklore Group's "Hootenanny-in-the-Round" held on the Alley Theater's arena stage. It was his first appearance before a large gathering of white people as well as his first formal concert. "Things that's different always make me hold back," Lightnin' said, explaining his caution, "but they seemed to like me and that makes me like to sing."

In the same leery fashion he's mused the possibilities of traveling to Europe. "I get to thinking about all the women over there—and then I get to thinking all that water to cross."

Lightnin' does not understand the outside world and is only slightly tempted by what it offers. Fame does not appeal to him—as a man adulated throughout Houston's Third, Fourth, Fifth, and Sixth Wards, he regards wider fame as unimportant. Lightnin' seldom mentions his birthplace because his friends are busy claiming him from their own home town; walking half a block along Dowling Street he'll stop to exchange mystic comments and promissory kisses with half a dozen young ladies. The possibility of money always interests him. But he knows it will disappear in a flurry of handouts, gambling, and spending.

This year, however, brought one marked change in his career. For the first time he was recorded singing, talking, and playing according to the bent of his own personality. In these documentary recordings filled with extemporaneous comment and verse—eight selections released on a Folkways LP and fifteen selections on a Tradition LP—he sings his own unique blues, about a twister howling across Texas, about a chain gang in the Trinity River bottom, about the women he likes to exhort with the cry, "Okay, now . . . twist it!"